Creating Your Professional Path
Lessons From My Journey

Gerald Corey
Professor Emeritus of
Human Services and Counseling
California State University, Fullerton

American Counseling Association
2461 Eisenhower Avenue
Alexandria, VA 22331
www.counseling.org

Creating Your Professional Path
Lessons From My Journey

American Counseling Association
2461 Eisenhower Avenue, Alexandria, VA 22331

Director of Publications Carolyn C. Baker

Production Manager Bonny E. Gaston

Copy Editor Kay Mikel

Editorial Assistant Catherine A. Brumley

Text and cover design by Bonny E. Gaston

Library of Congress Cataloging-in-Publication Data
Corey, Gerald.
Creating your professional path: lessons from my journey/Gerald Corey.
      p. cm.
   Includes bibliographical references.
   ISBN 978-1-55620-309-1 (alk. paper)
      1. Counseling—Vocational guidance.   2. Career development.
   3. Vocational guidance.   I. Title.
   BF637.C6C5727 2010
   158'.3023—dc22   2009043765

Dedication

To all those who have enriched my life,
both personally and professionally;
and to those whom I have had the privilege of mentoring,
who are now mentoring others.

≈

Contents

Preface

The idea for this book, *Creating Your Professional Path: Lessons From My Journey,* has been on my mind for more than 5 years. A major part of my professional work has involved mentoring students in various ways. In this book, I want to act as a mentor to you by sharing some of what I have learned from my personal and professional experiences.

In many ways, this book is autobiographical. I describe the evolution of my professional path, focusing on teaching, writing, and consulting, and show how my personal and professional paths have intersected. My professional journey has included a number of different positions: high school teacher, community college psychology instructor, teacher educator, practitioner of individual and group counseling, consultant, psychologist, and counselor educator. My passion is being an educator, and you will learn about some of the courses I often teach, what I get from teaching, and lessons I have learned through my experiences as a teacher. Your path may be different from my own, but I hope you will be able to apply many of the lessons I share from my journey as you create your own personal and professional path.

In writing this book, I want to talk directly and personally to you, my readers, who include students currently enrolled in graduate counseling programs, recent graduates, new professionals, and those who are or will be mentoring others. As I share the lessons I have learned and am still learning from my journey, I encourage you to reflect on your own professional path. In addition to my lessons, 18 students in graduate programs or new counseling professionals have contributed stories about their own professsional journeys. These contributors share their vision, describe the challenges and roadblocks they faced, emphasize what was helpful to them in pursuing their career path, and provide recommendations for getting the most from your school experiences. Although their personal stories are diverse, they share a common thread. All of these contributors faced both internal and external barriers when pursuing their goals and struggled in various ways, yet they did not let these obstacles stop them from continuing on their professional path.

This is a book about mentoring. When I speak of mentoring, I do so in a broad way, and some phrases that come to mind are teacher, coach, adviser, sponsor, facilitator of personal and professional development, source of encouragement, colleague, confidant, friend, counselor, role model, and resource person. Mentoring is a cyclical process: Many of those whom I have mentored are now mentoring others themselves, and the cycle of life continues. Most of us have at least some vague idea about what we would like to do professionally, yet moving that vision toward reality is not an easy journey. We may face both internal and external obstacles that must be overcome before we can achieve our goals. In this book, I focus on some of the individuals who inspired me when I had little faith in myself. Many of us recall significant mentors who helped us create our unique path, and many of us have a desire to give back to others. My view of the mentoring process includes both how we were mentored by others, and now, how we take steps to pass on to others what we have learned. For me, a meaningful life includes giving back and striving to make a difference. I hope to stimulate your thinking about the kind of personal and professional journey you want to create for yourself. This is not a skills-oriented book, a regular textbook, or a "how-to" book, yet if this book achieves its purpose, you will find it to be both practical and personal.

Most chapters include some reading resources that provide an in-depth discussion of many of the topics introduced here. By sharing aspects of my career and the stories of others illustrating turning points in their personal and professional journeys, my expectation is that you will garner strength in following your passions and realizing ways you can carve out a meaningful career and a meaningful personal life as well.

Overview of the Book

Chapter 1 (Turning Points and Reflections on My Personal and Professional Journey) provides a brief sketch of my personal life from childhood to the present, with implications for the turning points in the evolution of my professional career.

Chapter 2 (The Counselor as a Person and as a Professional) develops the theme of the integration of the counselor as a person and as a professional and shows how our professional life is influenced by who we are as persons.

Chapter 3 (Being Mentored and Mentoring Others) includes six personal stories from graduate students and new professionals who write about their experiences being mentored and how they are giving back to the profession by mentoring others. In this chapter I write about lessons I learned from my mentors, what mentoring means to me, my views on mentoring, and suggestions for getting the most out of a mentoring relationship.

Chapter 4 (How I Developed My Personal Approach to Counseling) describes many of the theoreticians and writers who have influenced me in developing my personal approach to the practice of counseling and psychotherapy. I also share my perspective on the integration of theories and provide guidelines for developing an integrative approach to counseling.

Chapter 5 (My Journey Into Group Work) traces the evolution of my involvement in the field of group work as an educator, facilitator, trainer, supervisor, and writer. I show the connection of lessons from my experiences as a member of various groups to how I developed my approach to group work.

Chapter 6 (Becoming an Ethical Counselor) highlights some of the lessons I have learned about ethical practice. The main emphasis is on my approach to teaching ethics and how I assist students in developing their approaches to thinking through ethical dilemmas.

Chapter 7 (Choosing a Career Path) offers thoughts on creating a meaningful career path. By way of their personal stories, seven individuals present how they identified their passions and met challenges in creating their professional paths.

Chapter 8 (On Being a Writer) offers ideas and suggestions on many different forms of writing—papers for courses, dissertations, conference proposals, case notes, letters of recommendation, journal articles, and books. I highlight my way of writing a book and encourage readers to find a work style that is suited to their personality.

Chapter 9 (Taking Care of Yourself) develops the theme that self-care is not a luxury but is an ethical imperative and a necessity. I talk about my own experiences in self-care and what has been helpful for me, as well as my limitations in taking care of myself. I show how maintaining our vitality is essential if we are to have the stamina to create the professional path we desire.

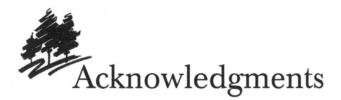

Acknowledgments

Let me give special recognition to Marianne Schneider Corey—wife, colleague, and friend—who read the chapters as I was drafting them, gave honest and critically constructive suggestions, and also brainstormed ideas with me for developing this book. She was a true collaborator on this project and did her best to keep me honest, personal, and focused. I would like to extend my gratitude to a number of other people who read the manuscript and provided me with valuable feedback:

- Jim Bitter, East Tennessee State University
- Patrick Callanan, California State University at Fullerton
- Bob Haynes, Borderline Productions
- Cheryl Haynes, registered nurse and editorial assistant for Borderline Productions
- Mary Kate Reese, Argosy University, Atlanta
- J. Michael Russell, California State University at Fullerton

Special appreciation goes to Carolyn Baker, the Director of Publications at the American Counseling Association. Carolyn liked the idea for this book and encouraged me along the way, reviewing the entire manuscript, providing insightful comments and suggestions, and offering support and guidance at various stages of development. A special note of thanks goes to the copy editor of all of our books, Kay Mikel, who did a marvelous job of making sure the presentation was clear, concise, personal, and effective.

In addition, I want to thank and recognize the 18 individuals who contributed inspiring and honest personal stories about their personal and professional journeys. You can learn more about them in the About the Contributors section.

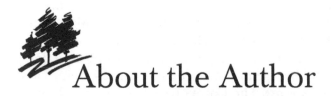

About the Author

$\sim$

Gerald Corey, EdD, is Professor Emeritus of Human Services and Counseling at California State University at Fullerton. He received his doctorate in counseling from the University of Southern California. He is a Diplomate in Counseling Psychology, American Board of Professional Psychology; a licensed psychologist; a National Certified Counselor; a Fellow of the American Counseling Association; a Fellow of the American Psychological Association (Counseling Psychology); and a Fellow of the Association for Specialists in Group Work (ASGW). Both Jerry and Marianne Schneider Corey received the Eminent Career Award from ASGW in 2001. Jerry also received the Outstanding Professor of the Year Award from California State University at Fullerton in 1991. He regularly teaches both undergraduate and graduate courses in the theory and practice of group counseling and professional ethics in counseling. He is the author or coauthor of 16 textbooks in counseling currently in print, along with numerous journal articles. His book *Theory and Practice of Counseling and Psychotherapy* has been translated into Arabic, Indonesian, Portuguese, Turkish, Korean, and Chinese. *Theory and Practice of Group Counseling* has been translated into Korean, Chinese, Spanish, and Russian. *Issues and Ethics in the Helping Professions* has been translated into Korean, Japanese, and Chinese.

Along with his wife, Marianne Schneider Corey, Jerry often presents workshops in group counseling. In the past 30 years the Coreys have conducted group counseling training workshops for mental health professionals at many universities in the United States as well as in Canada, Mexico, China, Hong Kong, Korea, Germany, Belgium, Scotland, England, and Ireland. In his leisure time, Jerry likes to travel, hike and bicycle in the mountains and the desert, and drive his 1931 Model A Ford. The Coreys have been married for 45 years; they have two adult daughters and three grandchildren.

Jerry Corey is coauthor (with Barbara Herlihy) of *Boundary Issues in Counseling: Multiple Roles and Responsibilities*, Second Edition (2006), and *ACA Ethical Standards Casebook*, Sixth Edition (2006); and he is coauthor (with Robert Haynes, Patrice Moulton, and Michelle Muratori) of *Clinical Supervision in the Helping Professions: A Practical Guide*, Second Edition (2010). All of these books are published by the American Counseling Association. Other books that Jerry has authored or coauthored, all with Brooks/Cole, Cengage Learning, include the following:

- *Becoming a Helper*, Sixth Edition (2011, with Marianne Schneider Corey)
- *Issues and Ethics in the Helping Professions*, Eighth Edition (2011, with Marianne Schneider Corey and Patrick Callanan)
- *Groups: Process and Practice*, Eighth Edition (2010, with Marianne Schneider Corey and Cindy Corey)
- *I Never Knew I Had a Choice*, Ninth Edition (2010, with Marianne Schneider Corey)
- *Theory and Practice of Counseling and Psychotherapy*, Eighth Edition (2009, and *Manual*)
- *Case Approach to Counseling and Psychotherapy*, Seventh Edition (2009)
- *The Art of Integrative Counseling*, Second Edition (2009)
- *Theory and Practice of Group Counseling*, Seventh Edition (2008, and *Manual*)
- *Group Techniques*, Third Edition (2004, with Marianne Schneider Corey, Patrick Callanan, and J. Michael Russell)

Jerry is coauthor, with his daughters Cindy Corey and Heidi Jo Corey, of an orientation-to-college book titled *Living and Learning* (1997), published by Wadsworth. He has also made several educational video programs on various aspects of counseling practice: (a) *Theory in Practice: The Case of Stan—DVD and Online Program* (2009); (b) *Groups in Action: Evolution and Challenges—DVD and Workbook* (2006, with Marianne Schneider Corey and Robert Haynes); (c) *CD-ROM for Integrative Counseling* (2005, with Robert Haynes); and (d) *Ethics in Action: CD-ROM* (2003, with Marianne Schneider Corey and Robert Haynes).

About the Contributors
Personal Stories

Honie Abramowicz, MSW, LCSW, received a master's in social work from California State University at Long Beach; she is currently employed in private practice in Huntington Beach, California, specializing in hypnotherapy.

Galo Arboleda, MSW, received his master's degree in social work from the University of Southern California; he is currently employed as a court mediator in Orange County, California, and is a part-time instructor in human services and social work at California State University at Fullerton.

Jamie Bilezikjian, MA, received her master's degree in counseling psychology from Argosy University; she is currently employed at Orange Coast Interfaith Shelter, Costa Mesa, California.

Jamie Bludworth, PhD, is a licensed psychologist working in a counseling center at a large university in the southwestern United States.

Beth Christensen, MA, received her degree in community counseling at Our Lady of Holy Cross College in New Orleans; she is currently a doctoral candidate in counselor education at the University of New Orleans.

Leslie Culver, MS, NCC, is a part-time counselor at a nonprofit agency and a full-time doctoral student in the counselor education program at the University of New Orleans.

Susan Cunningham is in her final year of the master's degree program in counseling at California State University at Fullerton.

Yusef Daulatzai, MA, PsyD, is currently employed as a psychotherapist at Pacific Clinics, a community mental health program; he received his master's and doctoral degrees in clinical psychology at the California School of Professional Psychology.

Mary Jane Ford, MS, is a therapist intern working in a nonprofit community counseling agency in southern California.

Amanda Healey, MA, LPC-MHSP, NCC, is completing her doctoral work in counselor education and supervision at Old Dominion University.

Casey Huynh, MS, MFT, received her master's degree in counseling from California State University at San Francisco; she is currently employed with Pacific Clinics.

Bridget McKinney, MS, NCC, is currently enrolled at the University of New Orleans in a doctoral program for counselor education.

Natalie Mendoza, MS, received her master's degree in counseling and educational leadership from California State University at Los Angeles; she is currently employed as a faculty member and counselor at Citrus Community College District in San Gabriel, California.

Michelle Muratori, PhD, received her doctorate in counselor education at The University of Iowa and is currently employed at the Johns Hopkins Center for Talented Youth as a senior counselor and researcher. She is also a faculty associate at Johns Hopkins University in the counseling and human services department.

Mark Reiser, MS, LPC, is currently a doctoral student in counselor education at the University of Wyoming; he is also an astronomy instructor at the University of Wyoming.

Valerie Russell, PhD, is a licensed psychologist who facilitates groups and supervises interns in a community mental health agency in southern California; she received her doctorate in clinical psychology at the California School of Professional Psychology, Los Angeles.

Julie Tomlinson, MSW, received her master's in social work at the University of Southern California. She is currently working toward her hours for social work licensure; she is a clinical social worker at a Veterans Affairs hospital.

Toni Wallace, LVN, MS, RAS, is currently working as an educator and counselor at Harbor University of California at Los Angeles Medical Center as a part of the Options for Recovery Treatment Program for pregnant and parenting mothers.

Chapter One
Turning Points and Reflections on My Personal and Professional Journey

Introduction

To help you understand my professional path, I begin with a brief sketch of some key events and memories in my life and share some lessons I have learned from my experiences. My aim is to show the connection of past events to my current personal and professional life. I discuss my school experiences from elementary school to graduate school, with lessons I learned regarding how my past contributed to my present and future ambitions as a counseling professional.

Significant Developments Along My Journey

The personal and professional aspects of my life have become intertwined, as the turning points I describe will illustrate.

School Daze

At age 5, I was a kindergarten dropout. On the first day of school I ran down the street after my mother, which was symbolic of my dependency and my fear of being thrust into the world. I was lonely, scared, and insecure and did not want to face the demands of the world. My confidence level was zero!

My entire elementary school experience was one long painful road of frustration and rebellion. I went to Catholic grammar school, and I did not do well. To be blunt, I hated school. We were expected to memorize the Catechism (a book of questions and answers about religious truths), the multiplication tables, and the imports and exports of major countries. I was utterly bored and could not see how any of what I was being taught would be of any use. My resistance in the fifth grade was met with the consequence of being held back in the same grade for another year. I felt humiliated that I could not measure up and that I had let down my parents. I believed I was very different from all the other kids who went on to sixth grade. For the rest of my grammar school years, I played the part of class clown, a trait that is still part of my personality. In elementary school I learned that I must be obedient or else pay the price. My teachers repeatedly told me that I was not working up to my potential and that I could do better if only I would apply myself to my schoolwork. I never listened to these messages!

After 9 years of grammar school, you might think I would have found the road to school success, but my transition to a Catholic boys school at age 15 did not go much better than my earlier schooling. Although I really wanted to succeed, I felt totally overwhelmed and did not have a shred of confidence that I could pass my courses. My life had turned rough and unfriendly, and I wondered if I would ever get through school. I flunked algebra, geometry, and chemistry and passed typing with a D. I endured 4 years of Latin, and all I can now remember is *Mea culpa, mea culpa, mea maxima culpa* (through my fault, through my fault, through my most grievous fault). My high school experiences confirmed what I had learned in my grade school days—that obedience, respect for authority, and compliance are rewarded with approval, good grades, and honors. These adolescent years were particularly painful, and my strategies for staying sane were denial and withdrawal. I felt rather insignificant, and I lacked any sense of meaning or purpose in life.

I began learning to play the saxophone my first year in high school and joined the band. Music is one of the few subjects in any school that is performance based, and improvement is easily noted and recognized. Doing well in music made going to school more enjoyable and brought me my first taste of success. With newfound confidence, I began to apply myself academically. I did fairly well in many of my classes and even decided I wanted to become a high school teacher. A couple of my teachers provided me with support and encouragement; they modeled a caring way of being for young people and were instrumental in my decision to work with adolescents. If I could help other adolescents find their way, I thought I could also learn to understand myself.

My difficult life experiences from kindergarten through high school taught me that it is next to impossible to find success in school if the subjects being taught have no relevance to real life. Finding a few subjects of interest and getting support from some teachers helped me begin to find meaning in school.

Connecting With People

During my early 20s, I attended Loyola University, a Catholic institution taught by Jesuits. My confidence that I could succeed in my goal of becoming a high school teacher expanded, and being a part of the university band added to my self-esteem. I even got a partial scholarship for playing the saxophone and acting as the "property manager" for the band equipment. Although I did not have a modicum of musical talent, I enjoyed being part of a community endeavor. In the academic realm, I was finally finding some direction, primarily because of my excitement over the psychology courses I was taking. These courses were related to life rather than to abstract topics, and I soon chose psychology for my undergraduate degree program.

My decision to major in psychology was greatly influenced by Father Peter Ciklic, founder and one-man faculty of the psychology department at Loyola University. I took all of Father Ciklic's psychology courses, and he became an important mentor for me. I wanted to learn all I could from each course, and Father Ciklic's interest in me was a motivating factor to do well. He encouraged me to pursue doctoral studies, and my best efforts finally started to yield dividends. Eventually, I graduated with a master's degree in counseling and a secondary teaching credential. In addition, I learned an important lesson about the power of a mentor to keep me focused and motivated, even when I had self-doubts. Soon after I graduated, Father Ciklic hired me as a part-time instructor to teach a few psychology courses, which solidified my career decision to be a teacher and a counselor.

In the early 1960s, I began teaching English, social studies, and psychology at Whittier High School in Whittier, California. Teaching was a most rewarding endeavor, and my own elementary and high school experiences gave me a clear picture of the kind of teacher I did *not* want to be. I did everything I could to personalize student learning and to make learning interesting and personally relevant to my students' lives. I was willing to take risks, and I experimented with novel ways of teaching in all of my classes. I loved being a teacher and devoted myself fully to preparing for class. In my English classes, I asked students to write essays on topics such as "The meaning of my life," "What I would do if I had 24 hours to live," and "My values and life choices." I wanted to help students get a clearer sense of who they were and what they most wanted from life. I was finally given a psychology class to teach, which became a passion for me. I was not excited about the textbook for the class, so I wrote my own extensive notes and put them in a booklet for my students.

My 4 years teaching high school students was followed by 2 years teaching psychology in a community college. I found it relatively easy to structure introductory psychology in a way that challenged students to engage in self-exploration and to talk about personal concerns. My courses emphasized discussion and small-group work, which tweaked my growing interest in group counseling. In fact, my doctoral dissertation compared the lecture method with small-group discussion methods of teaching introductory psychology. That analysis increased my interest in using discussion and interactive approaches in all my psychology courses, and I continue to refine this method more than 40 years later. As a high school teacher and community college instructor, my passion was to personalize learning by connecting the subjects I was teaching to the lives of the students. I devised many ways to get students to participate in class discussions and experiential activities. My teaching experience taught me that students do not tend to personalize their learning simply by listening to lectures and taking notes; they internalize their learning by raising questions, sharing their thoughts and experiences, interacting with one another on topics that are personally significant to them, and reflecting and writing about what they experience in life and learn in the classroom.

Mentors Found in Unusual Places

During the 6 years I taught high school and community college courses, I was also attending the University of Southern California's doctoral program in counseling. Although I enjoyed my counseling courses, I loathed statistics and feared I would not be able to pass. My adviser and primary professor, Dr. Jane Warters, was instrumental in putting my fears in perspective. She suggested I read a book on mathematics that was essential for statistics and recommended a professor who was extremely patient. She said, "Jerry, if you take Dr. Welty Lefever's statistics class, I am sure you will pass his course." Dr. Warters did not believe my extremely low graduate record examination (GRE) scores were an accurate reflection of my ability, and she suggested that I take this examination again. I took the GRE twice more, but neither trial elevated my anemic scores. If I were applying for a doctoral program today, I doubt I would be admitted. I don't think exam scores, taken alone, represent an accurate portrayal of our ability or talents, and I do my best to encourage students not to let exam scores get in the way of pursuing their goals. I realize that times have changed, but some schools are beginning to rely less on these scores as the sole criterion for school success.

The semester I struggled with statistics, I came home with a splitting headache after each class. The custodian who worked in my high school classroom, Jim Johnson, was studying to become a math teacher. Taking a special interest in my progress, Jim put math problems on the board and expected me to do this homework each night. Whenever I felt like dropping out of the program because of my math anxiety, both Dr. Warters and Jim calmly assured me that my goals were attainable if I was willing to work hard and to persist. It is easy to feel engulfed by fear and to stop too soon, yet fears can be turned into challenges and overcome. I learned that by exposing my fears they became manageable, and that self-discipline does pay off. Eventually, with the help of a tutor, I *barely* passed statistics. This experience taught me that I needed to acquire the discipline to apply myself to learning difficult subjects. All the encouragement from others would have been for naught had I failed to put in the time and effort necessary to learn.

By the way, Jim and I developed a long-term friendship that continues to this day. In the 1980s he thought it was time I bought a computer to facilitate writing and revising my books. Until that time I had written most of my manuscripts by hand and eventually tediously typed everything on a portable typewriter (remember that D I received in typing class?). Today Jim continues to be my Macintosh mentor, and whenever I encounter problems (which happens frequently) I call and beg for his help. He patiently listens to me complain and laughs when I say, "I never should have gotten a computer. Life was so much simpler when I wrote my books with a pen on a yellow notepad." Don't hesitate to ask for help when you need it, and remember that help often comes in unexpected forms, like meeting a custodian. I hope we all remain open to asking for the help we need throughout our professional journey.

Turning Points in My Personal Life

My late 20s and 30s was an extremely challenging time for me, both personally and professionally. A significant transition in my life occurred when I was 24 and met Marianne Schneider, a foreign exchange student from Germany. We were married in Germany

3 years later, but only after a period of questioning on both our parts. (More about this in Chapter 2.) Another significant turning point in my personal life was the loss of my 70-year-old father when I was 30 years old. A few months prior to his death, I became a new father to our daughter Heidi. About 2 years later I became a father again with the birth of our daughter Cindy. My father often said that he wanted to live long enough to hear Heidi speak German, but he died when she was only 3 months old. He did not live long enough to hear either Heidi or Cindy speaking German, but he would have been proud of them!

Having been married for only a few years and becoming a father to two daughters was a personal challenge for which I was not prepared. I struggled through the process of learning how to be a husband and a father. These were difficult roles for me to learn, partly because I threw myself into my work, somewhat to the neglect of my family. I was overly concerned with the professional path I was pursuing, and I don't think I did a good job of balancing my work life with my family life during these early years of marriage. Despite my devotion to my work, we did go on family vacations, visited Germany for several weeks every summer, frequently headed out to the beach and the mountains, and went on outings with other families. We also made weekend visits to my mother's house, which enabled Marianne and me to have times together as a couple while our daughters spent special times with their grandmother. Taking this time as a family, and also as a couple, was important in helping us to stay productive in our professional lives.

Turning Points in My Professional Life

I landed a new position as assistant professor in the Teacher Education Department and as a counselor in the University Counseling Center at California State Polytechnic University in Pomona (Cal Poly) when I was 30. My professional tasks as a counselor included doing both individual and group counseling and outreach work on the campus. In addition to my work as a counselor, I taught courses in abnormal psychology, adolescent psychology, and educational psychology to students preparing for careers as either elementary or secondary teachers. As before, I encouraged students to review their personal experiences as learners and to decide how they might want to teach differently than how they had been taught. During the time I was a faculty member in the Teacher Education Department, I wrote my first book, *Teachers Can Make a Difference,* which was published in 1973. Although the book was not a bestseller and was out of print after a few years, having a book published was a turning point for me. I learned that writing a book could be a reality if I wrote about a subject I was teaching and if I stayed focused on my interests. In *Teachers Can Make a Difference* I discussed my experiences as a learner (much as I did earlier in this chapter) and the negative impact schooling can have on those of us studying to become teachers. I wrote about several teachers who were making a difference in the lives of students through their innovative classes. My book addressed a humanistic approach to teacher education and the challenge of revolutionizing our schools and how we can make a significant difference in the lives of the students we teach.

Focusing on my goal of completing a book also supplied the motivation I needed to continue when I felt discouraged. I wanted to share my thoughts about creating ways to personalize learning in the classroom. Even though I was motivated to write and blocked off time to reflect and write, writing was not a smooth process. Indeed, I often struggled with getting words on paper and doubted that I had anything worthwhile to say. Here is an excerpt from my journal (in the early 1970s) that illustrates my self-doubt as a writer at that time:

> Today I really wanted to write a chapter in my book. I sat down and just nothing would come. I write and it seems trite and stilted. I just can't organize or develop my thoughts—nothing comes. I feel like junking the whole damn thing! I wasted a whole day—and what do I have to show for it? A few disjointed paragraphs—nothing hangs together, and it seems that I just can't write. I hate that frozen feeling—immobility!

In many of the chapters that follow, I describe my process for writing books, including both the joys and the struggles of being an author.

Along with being involved in writing, teaching, supervising student teachers, practicing individual counseling, and conducting personal growth groups, I was working toward becoming a licensed psychologist. The supervised experience toward getting my license included providing individual counseling with clients in private practice, cofacilitating marathon therapy groups, and working as a counselor at the University Counseling Center.

Designing and Facilitating Groups for College Students

When I began working at Cal Poly's University Counseling Center, I was seeing many students for individual counseling and facilitating a number of groups for college students, but it was difficult to get a sense of my effectiveness. My self-confidence began to erode, which led me to wonder whether I would ever become a skilled therapist. To make matters worse, I did not get much recognition or encouragement from some of my supervisors during my training. One colleague suggested that I might be better off as a teacher and that I should give up on my aspirations of becoming a counseling psychologist. Hearing this feedback was discouraging, but I decided to open myself to new experiences as a counselor and give myself some time to see if I could successfully meet these challenges.

In my work as a counselor in the center, I discovered that many students were not aware of the resources for personal counseling and career development on the campus, so I began speaking at health education classes to inform students about these services. Along with some other counselors in the center, I designed a variety of groups, including process groups, growth groups, and psychoeducational groups, each lasting 10 weeks. My outreach efforts were successful, and our groups began to fill up. My interest in group work increased, and I discovered that working with groups could be more effective than seeing students individually. Sometimes I cofacilitated these groups with other counselors in the center, which enhanced our groups. My coleaders and I arranged time both before and after a group session for planning, processing, and evaluating our groups. I believe it is a good practice to videotape sessions and review them weekly to learn what works and what is not effective. Coleaders can watch these sessions together and offer effective feedback when there is trust and caring in the relationship. This coleadership arrangement with different counselors became a mentoring experience for all concerned and provided a form of peer supervision. After doing these groups for a few years, my confidence as a group leader increased, and my coleaders and I found creative ways to help students explore common themes of interest to them.

A lesson I learned from being a counselor in a university counseling center was the importance of persisting, even with the absence of external validation. It helped to tell myself that I probably would not be as effective as I expected to be when I first began this work. Although it is difficult to persist when reinforcement from significant others is not forthcoming, I gradually began to learn to look to myself for the kind of approval I had sought from others. The personal work I did in my own individual therapy and group therapy provided some insights and perspective. The challenging and constructive feedback I received from friends and family members also helped me to accept some truths and make some significant behavioral shifts.

I hope you do not give up when you experience self-doubts but instead challenge whatever might be holding you back. Sometimes you will be excited about your future as a counseling professional, and at other times you may be discouraged and wonder if it is all worth the effort. If you are willing to continue exploring your personal life, I am convinced that you will be better equipped to assist others as they struggle with their existential concerns.

Taking Risks and Facing Self-Doubts

I had been happy teaching at Cal Poly, and I loved my work as a counselor for the 5 years I was there. Then new opportunities appeared on my professional path. The move I contemplated was certainly risky. One of my former supervisors was beginning an innovative undergraduate human services program at California State University at Fullerton (CSUF), and I visited his classes and was impressed with the students. He encouraged me to apply to teach in the program. The prospect of being part of an innovative student-centered program lured me away from my tenured job to this new and uncertain position. At age 35 I accepted a new position as an assistant professor in the Interdisciplinary Center (known as the ID Center) at CSUF. A professor of English who encouraged the development of innovative courses and programs as part of the university community founded the center, and professors from many different disciplines participated. A few of the courses offered included The Nature of Love From Plato to Joyce; Quest for Self, East and West; Self-Actualization Group; Jazz, Past, Present, and Future; Yoga; and Character and Conflict. The ID Center promoted courses that did not fit in traditional academic departments, and several programs emerged from it, including the Religious Studies Program and the Human Services Program—both of which eventually became undergraduate departments and are still in existence today.

This was a time when I countered the advice I am sure my father would have given me to stay with what was safe and known. A lesson that I relearned was that most professional moves entail risk as well as the promise of new and exciting opportunities. I have typically been willing to choose an unknown path that entailed some risks rather than remaining on a familiar path with less future promise.

The human services program at CSUF was truly unique and attracted some bright and dedicated students. The program involved an integration of both the cognitive and affective domains, which appealed to me. Students majoring in human services found their classes both academically demanding and personally meaningful. Being involved in the controversial ID Center required that I learn strategies for making changes within a program and still surviving in a conservative system that was typically not conducive to innovations. I learned how essential it is to develop and articulate a clear mission statement for a program, as well as a rationale for every course, and to have the courage to stick with a vision, even when this vision is threatened by external factors.

The human services program I had a part in developing at CSUF was also the target of considerable controversy on the university campus. Because the program consisted of many nontraditional courses and involved the personal development of students, professors from some of the more traditional programs were highly critical, suggesting that our program was not academically sound and referring to us as the "touchy-feely" major. Some of our critics did not see a justification for giving students university credit for self-exploration courses, charging that such highly personal courses had little to do with cultivating the intellect and transmitting knowledge. It is a wonder that the ID Center flourished in the conservative political community of Orange County, California. To be sure, there was considerable controversy, and some factions in the university community would have liked to have seen it eliminated.

I quickly learned the value of educating an academic dean about the relevance of the courses in our program. I scheduled time with the dean to discuss the main goals of various courses, addressed any concerns on her part, and invited her to attend some of the classes I was teaching. I found that these efforts paid off, and the dean eventually became a supporter of our program rather than a critic.

Some Challenges and Opportunities in My Forties

In my mid-40s I began conducting workshops in various parts of the United States and also in Europe, often with Marianne Schneider Corey, my wife and colleague. I prefer presenting workshops as a team rather than doing this alone, and Marianne and I have continued this work for many years. We have a similar philosophy but different styles of working. Through my work with Marianne and other valued colleagues, I came to realize that different styles could be complementary and could bring an added dimension to a workshop or a presentation.

I learned a good deal by working with Marianne, and one lesson I have learned and had reinforced time and again is Marianne's way of making a connection with a client or an audience. She demonstrated the importance of being fully present and being herself. At this time, Marianne was an excellent example of a person who demonstrated congruence between her personal self and her professional self, and she certainly influenced me in this regard. These workshops were challenging, exciting, demanding, and enjoyable. These opportunities often came about because of books I authored or coauthored, and they represented yet another way to teach both students and mental health professionals. I continued to find interesting topics for my writing, which I address more fully in later chapters.

This period in my life was in stark contrast to my early years in school when I felt I had no voice. I had finally come to believe that I had a voice and that I could use it to make a difference. This has been my motivation for doing whatever I could to enable students to find their voice and to use it—and to do whatever it takes to stay on course in their personal and professional journey.

My 40s was a demanding time. Not only was I teaching full time in human services, but I also assumed the responsibility of program coordinator (the equivalent of a department chair) for about 9 years. During summers and semester breaks, I was busy writing and revising books, conducting workshops in various states, facilitating personal growth groups, and training students and professionals in the area of group counseling. I had to learn to balance a multiplicity of professional roles, formulate long-range and short-term goals, acquire time management skills, and learn how to create some personal life amid all the fury of my professional life.

Choosing a Road Less Traveled

During my 50s I was doing everything I wanted to do professionally. However, I continued to feel challenged in learning limits and finding a balance with my personal life. I was still attempting to do too many things at once. Many of my personal needs were met from my involvement with so many projects, yet I came to realize that I couldn't do everything that I loved doing. Late in my 50s I decided it was time for someone else to accept the administrative role of directing our undergraduate program, and I also began taking leave-without-pay every fall semester to devote more time to the ever-demanding task of writing. Teaching full time each spring semester kept me active in the classroom and made life less crowded with activity, and this also gave me 8 months to pursue other personal and professional endeavors.

A hard lesson for me to learn was to pause before too readily accepting an invitation for another workshop, a speaking engagement, or a new book. Because I lived with an overcrowded schedule and accepted too many invitations, I needed to learn the value of carefully reflecting on the pros and cons of accepting invitations, no matter how tempting they appeared to be. Although I enjoyed most of what I was doing, I eventually recognized that all of this took time and energy. I had the difficult task of learning to say no to some interesting projects. I frequently had to remind myself that I was one person with limited time, and I could not do everything I might have wanted to do. Now I tell people who make a request that I will seriously think it over and get back to them soon. As tempting as it might be to put more on a plate that is already full, it is essential to learn what you can realistically accomplish within a given time frame. I find that many students have difficulty balancing the costs and benefits of getting involved in certain projects. As I mentor students, I frequently talk with them about establishing priorities and learning practical strategies such as time management and encourage them to think about how their professional or academic life can affect their relationships, family, and personal self-care priorities. I talk more about my self-care practices in Chapter 9.

Over the years I have learned how essential clarity of purpose, motivation, and self-discipline are for engaging in productive work. Realizing that I am the one who decided to commit to these projects keeps me focused and energetic. Let me emphasize that I see myself as having a good deal of discipline (perhaps something I acquired in my Catholic schooling), a trait that is absolutely essential to success. If I were doing what someone else expected of me and was externally motivated, I would long ago have lost my enthusiasm for these projects. This ties into my existential orientation, which emphasizes the role of personal responsibility in shaping our existence. I hope you will strive to discover and pursue your own passions and dreams.

Combining Work and Personal Life

During my early 50s I made some key decisions pertaining to balancing my work life with my personal life. I continued monitoring the number of hours I worked each week and made some changes in my work life that led to less pressure in my personal life. During much of our married life, Marianne and I have made time for vacations, even short times away, but too often we link our professional travels with vacations. For example, one summer we did a couple of 5-day training workshops in group counseling with counselors in Ireland within a 2-week period. We arranged our schedule so we had time both before and after the workshops to see the sights and enjoy the country. We also took the opportunity to spend some vacation time in Germany and Norway. Even when we travel to another state to present at a professional conference, we allow several days before we work to enjoy the natural beauty and sights of that state.

Eventually, we became better at blocking out time exclusively for personal travel rather than sandwiching a vacation into a work situation. For many years we have enjoyed taking cruises to Alaska and the Caribbean, sometimes with our family, other times with friends, and sometimes just the two of us. We have also found renewal on scenic hikes in Hawaii and on the trails in our mountain community. We rarely travel with a computer on our vacations.

Marianne and I take time to enjoy a circle of friends and our family. We have been married for 45 years, which is an accomplishment in itself. Our friends tease Marianne, saying that it was divine intervention that brought her from Germany to California, for there is not another woman in the world who could have been married to me for all these years. And they are absolutely right! Marianne is an exceptional person, as all of our friends would agree, and she is the one person most responsible for contributing to my productivity. Over the years we have collaborated on group work projects, writing, making educational video and DVD programs, and conducting workshops on group counseling. Together we have coauthored five books. Marianne provides significant input on books and chapters for which I am the sole author, and she continues to be my most demanding, honest, and useful critic. The nurturing home that Marianne has created for our two daughters, herself, and me has given me the opportunity to be very productive for many years.

Reflections on My Professional Experiences

In reflecting on my professional experiences, what matters to me most are the rewards of working with students in a teaching career that has spanned almost 5 decades. From the beginning I was motivated by a desire to make a difference. I receive the most satisfaction from helping students move ahead in their personal and professional journey. Getting my students to challenge themselves by questioning life and stretching their personal and professional boundaries has always been more significant to me than merely presenting academic knowledge. My work does not end with me but continues through my students as they accomplish goals they did not dream possible. Mentoring can help us to find our passion and then to follow the direction that passion takes us.

No Retirement in My Picture

I formally retired from the university system as a *full-time* professor at age 63, but every fall semester I teach courses in group counseling and ethics in counseling as an adjunct faculty member at CSUF. Most spring semesters I teach or coteach an intensive 1-week workshop in group counseling for some university or institute in the United States or abroad. In addition, I give a fair number of workshops and keynote addresses at state, regional, and national counseling conferences. With my writing schedule and the teaching I do throughout each year, I am still deeply involved in meaningful full-time work. Currently, I have the opportunity to create my own schedule rather than being linked to a single university setting. My writing schedule now occupies a major portion of my work time, and each year I am involved in the revision of two or three textbooks. At age 72 I still greatly enjoy the various facets of my work life, and I can't see retirement being a part of my future picture until they put me 6 feet under—and then I may continue writing from my new location! Interacting with colleagues on exciting projects is meaningful and enjoyable, and I continue to find joy in working with appreciative and eager students who keep me young in my "advancing" age.

I have had my share of professional accomplishments, but I realize that any talents I have in teaching and writing are ones that God gave to me. I do not deceive myself into believing that without these gifts I could be of significance to others. I feel grateful for being in excellent health and having a good life, which allow me to continue in my pursuit of meaningful goals. Much of what I have achieved professionally is the result of interaction with colleagues and friends in the profession. Our work together and our discussions are the impetus for new ideas and new projects, and I expect that these collaborations will continue in the years ahead.

How Would You Describe Your Personal Journey?

As you read about my personal journey and the evolution of my professional career, I hope you have been thinking about your own personal journey and the kind of professional path you want to create for yourself. If you do not consider your family, other significant relationships, and your responsibilities at home, your professional pursuits may create tension and imbalance in your life. Take time to reflect on some of these questions: What major turning points have you experienced in your life? What most stands out for you when you reflect on your experiences with schooling, from elementary school to graduate school? What have you learned most about yourself? What are your dreams at this time? What is your vision, and who has encouraged you thus far? What challenges do you face in making your vision a reality?

The lessons I have learned from my experiences are the essence of what I hope to communicate to you. Key lessons in this chapter are that failure is not fatal, that we can learn from mistakes and setbacks, and that it is essential to have a vision that guides what we do. Don Quixote dared "to dream the impossible dream," and formulating your own dream can make all the difference. Although I am more than satisfied with my past and present professional life, it is clear that I had trials and tribulations along the way. My hope is that you will not lose sight of your vision, even when you meet with detours along the road. Believe in yourself in spite of self-doubt, find sources of support that can help you get through tough times, and work hard to make your dreams come true.

Chapter Two
The Counselor as a Person and as a Professional

Introduction

We ask clients to look honestly at themselves and to choose how they want to change, and it is essential that we be open to the same kind of self-reflection. Who the counselor is as a person and the quality of the client–counselor relationship are important variables the counselor contributes to success in therapy. The therapeutic relationship is more important than the counselor's theory or techniques. For an in-depth discussion of the factors underlying effective psychotherapy and the paramount importance of the client–therapist relationship, I highly recommend *The Heart and Soul of Change: Delivering What Works in Therapy* (Duncan, Miller, Wampold, & Hubble, 2010).

It is not possible to talk about the counselor as a professional without considering who the counselor is as a person. My experience has convinced me that our beliefs, values, personal characteristics, level of personal functioning, and way of being in the world all influence the way we function as counseling professionals. The theme of this chapter is the reciprocal relationship between the counselor as a person and as a professional.

What's in It for You to Be a Counselor?

In choosing a career in the counseling field, it is important for you to become aware of your motivations for going into the profession and how your personal needs may influence your work as a professional. Take a moment to reflect on these questions: What are your motivations for becoming a counselor? What are your rewards for counseling others? What kind of professional path do you want to create for yourself?

When I first decided to be a high school teacher and counselor, my basic motivation was to help others. I must admit that I was not aware of what I would be getting from helping others. Only later did I realize that self-help motives were operating in my career choice. As a college instructor years later, I found my motives evolving due to mentoring by some key people who made a significant difference in my life. Becoming a counseling psychologist and a counselor educator met my need for being able to make a difference in the lives of others, and this is a basic motivation that keeps me going today. I often see potential in students that they do not recognize in themselves. It means a great deal to me to be instrumental in broadening their vision so they can come to appreciate the talents and gifts they possess.

I imagine that it will be meaningful for you to know that those with whom you will work (clients, students, supervisees) may gain a sense of faith in themselves and hope for their future. You may be the catalyst for others who are making life-changing decisions. Although you may have altruistic motivations for getting involved in the helping professions, it is important that you recognize what you get from helping others.

One reason I entered the counseling field was to better understand my own problems. You too may have entered the field out of a desire to resolve some of your own problems. As you grow in your profession, your motives may change from a need for self-help to a passion for answering a call to be a beacon of light for others. Some other reasons that may be operating underneath your desire for becoming a counselor might include the need to make an impact on others, the desire to give back to society what you have been given, an interest in being a caregiver, the good feelings that come with being needed, the need for prestige and status, and the wish to develop answers to problems and find solutions that help others. Other motivations may be important to you, but I have found that it is not just a single motivation that keeps me going. Instead, my needs and motivations are constantly evolving.

Whatever your needs and motives are, it is important to be aware of them and how they influence you. Satisfying your needs through your professional endeavors is not a self-centered act. In fact, I believe that if you are not meeting your needs through your work, you may lose interest in what you are doing. When meeting your clients' needs also satisfies your own, you are more likely to create a rewarding career for yourself. It becomes problematic only if you are meeting your needs at the expense of your clients' needs.

Concerns Facing Beginning Counselors

Many of us face common concerns as we begin our careers as counselors. In the following pages I share many concerns, both concerns I had as a beginning professional and concerns that have persisted into my later years. I am convinced that we do not have to be stopped by our feelings of inadequacy. Obstacles can be the stepping stones to achieving our goals.

Dealing With Our Anxieties

When I first began seeing clients, I felt lost most of the time. I did not have a clue what the "right" things to say to clients were, and I was sure clients saw me as inexperienced and inept. I was afraid that clients might ask me questions I could not answer. I was uncertain that I could do enough or that I could help clients, and this resulted in anxiety. I eventually learned that having anxieties and self-doubts is normal; what counts is how you deal with them. I did discuss my cases with a supervisor, but I was not very open about my self-doubts, my anxieties, or my effectiveness. If I could do it again, I would talk more about myself and my anxiety, and less about my cases, and I would seek trusted peers and supervisors who could give me feedback. It did not occur to me that my fellow students were plagued with doubts regarding whether they were cut out for the profession, or that they were anxious about their performance. I perceived them as having experience and confidence. As I continue to work with students, I have come to realize that this is an experience many of us share.

Learning to Live With Ambiguity

Many new professionals experience the anxiety of not seeing immediate results. They wonder: "Am I really helping my clients? How can I know if I am effective or not?" As a high school teacher, I had lesson plans for all of my classes, which provided both structure and security against the unknown. As a counselor, there were no lesson plans, and I vividly recall how uncertain I was about the results of my work. I like structure and am uncomfortable when I must tolerate ambiguity. When I began practicing counseling, there was no clear evidence that I was being effective. Even though we might desire clarity, we had better work with our anxiety and uncertainty, along with the lack of comfort this brings.

I found that ambiguity did not have to be a threat and that people can accomplish a great deal through a healing relationship. It took me some time to realize the long-term impact of my work as a counselor. Sometimes we may not find out until years later that we were instrumental in helping a client.

Being Yourself in Your Professional Work

Because I was self-conscious and anxious, I was overly concerned with what the textbooks prescribed and with knowing what techniques to use. Although I wanted to be myself, I was not quite sure what this meant or how to be personal and professional at the same time. I could hear my supervisor's and therapist's voices in my head, and I would find myself uttering phrases they had used. I did not consciously try to hide behind a professional role, but I lost a great deal of spontaneity by trying too hard to do what I thought clients and supervisors expected of me. It is easy to get caught up in maintaining stereotyped role expectations, but when we do so we lose contact with ourselves and with our clients. In my attempt to figure out what to say so that I would appear credible, I rehearsed interpretations in my head, and sometimes clients would look puzzled. It was difficult to be present with clients while paying attention to my internal rehearsal about what to say next. Instead of being with the person sitting before me, I was way ahead of this individual and formulating my responses and questions. Over time I learned that I could be both personal and professional, that I didn't have to have a detailed lesson plan before each session with a client, and that my clients could provide clues that we could explore together—if I would only listen to them. When I became able to be more myself and stopped trying so hard to be what I thought was expected of me as a professional, an important shift took place. This attitude was the beginning of self-confidence for me.

The Appropriateness of Counselor Self-Disclosure

If we are overly concerned about maintaining a professional stance, it is likely that we will remain anonymous to clients, and our clients may view us as hiding behind our professional role. At the other end of the spectrum is engaging in too much self-disclosure. Judging the appropriate amount of self-disclosure can be a problem for seasoned counselors, and it is often especially worrisome for new counselors. In determining the appropriateness of self-disclosure, consider *what* to reveal, *when* to reveal, and *how much* to reveal. Either disclosing too little or disclosing too much can be problematic. If we try too hard to be genuine and self-revealing, we may burden our client with details of our personal life. At times it may be useful to mention something about ourselves, but we must be aware of our motivations for making ourselves known in this way. Assess the readiness of a client to hear these disclosures as well as the impact doing so might have on the client. Remain observant during any self-disclosure to get a sense of how the client is being affected by it.

In my opinion, the most productive form of self-disclosure is related to what is going on between the counselor and the client within the counseling session. The skill of immediacy involves revealing what we are thinking or feeling in the here and now with the client. When done in a timely way, sharing persistent reactions can facilitate therapeutic progress and improve the quality of our relationship with the client. Even when we are talking about reactions based on the therapeutic relationship, caution is necessary, and discretion and sensitivity are required in deciding what reactions we might share. When expressing how we are being affected in relationship to the client, it is important to avoid pronouncing judgments about the client.

Perfectionism Is Not a Virtue

I measured myself against my mentors, therapists, and supervisors, wondering how they ever got to where they seemed to be. In my wildest dreams, I could not imagine myself being as skilled and insightful as I saw them. I burdened myself with the belief that I must never make a mistake. Although I knew *intellectually* that I could not be perfect, *emotionally* I felt far from perfect and did not give myself much room for error. Eventually, I came to believe that it is good to strive to do my best, but this does not equate with perfectionism. It was difficult for me to be fully present with clients or students when I was overly concerned with how I was coming across and what people might be thinking about me. I wanted to be liked and approved of, and I tried to figure out what others expected of me. An important lesson I learned was that if I lived by meeting the expectations of others, I could burden myself with attempting to give perfect peformances.

Because of my own struggles in measuring myself against others and striving for perfect performances, I have always encouraged mentees and students to avoid imposing the unrealistic standard of being perfect. I urge students not to become immobilized by the fear of making mistakes. We can be imperfect and still accomplish a great deal in our personal and professional life. I counsel students to have the courage to be imperfect, to accept themselves as growing and maturing human beings, and to learn what they can from any mistakes. It is freeing at times to say to a client or a colleague, "I don't know—I don't have the answer."

Our imperfections cannot be used as an excuse for being sloppy or being unconcerned about being as competent as possible. As one of my colleagues astutely stated: "Perfection is a direction, not a goal." We can always learn more and get better—if we are willing to accept where we are and take steps to acquire knowledge and skills through supervised experience.

The Place of Humor in Counseling

Although counseling is a responsible and often serious endeavor, it does not have to be devoid of humor and moments of lightness. Laughter or humor does not mean that work is not being accomplished. Humor is an expression of spontaneity, which does not lend itself to planning and rehearsal. It is my job to distinguish between humor that distracts and humor that enhances the situation. Although it is never appropriate to laugh *at* a client, it can be therapeutic to laugh *with* a client. Of course, humor can be used as a deflection or as a way to avoid confronting an unpleasant reality as well. For me, there is a place for humor in the classroom, in the counselor's office, in a therapy group, and at presentations at professional conferences. In fact, when I am not finding some humor in teaching and counseling, I suspect that something is missing. I do not want to take myself too seriously, and finding humor in my foibles keeps me in touch with reality. However, there are times when I have tried too hard to be humorous or to bring it out in people, only to find that it boomeranged and was not therapeutic.

It is important to distinguish between humor and sarcasm, which are two very different entities. Whereas some may use sarcasm as a guise for being funny, I view it as potentially harmful and often tinged with anger. For me, sarcasm is not an honest expression of what we are thinking and feeling. Sarcasm is a way of making an indirect statement, and I hope we can be honest enough with clients to be direct in our messages. I don't see any place for sarcasm in counseling or in teaching, as it can be quite destructive and it is poor modeling.

Dealing With Silence

Encountering silence in a counseling session can be most threatening to beginning counselors. These times of silence can seem like an eternity. When I was doing my first practicum, I brought an audiotape to my supervisor so we could process the session. I still recall his reactions when I interrupted a client when there was a silence, which derailed the session. My supervisor said he would not be surprised if this client did not show up the next week. She did appear, however, and out of my desire not to interrupt her process I said almost nothing. Both of us sat in utter silence staring at each other, waiting for something to happen. I learned that it is important to explore what a silence might mean to a client rather than trying desperately to figure out what to do next.

As I gained experience, I learned that silence can be therapeutic and can mean many things. It certainly does not have to mean that the client is resisting or that nothing positive is happening. Silence can be useful and even necessary for clients to effectively reflect on their experiences. When silence occurs in a session, I try to acknowledge it and talk with the client about what this might mean. If a client says, "I don't know!" I do not give up too easily. I might respond with something like this: "Take a guess. Imagine what your silence might be about. Tune into what is going on within you at this moment and give words to it."

Dealing With Clients We Perceive as Difficult

Understanding and working therapeutically with clients who manifest a range of problematic behaviors is a real concern of many beginning counselors. There are no simple techniques for dealing effectively with clients who pose a challenge for us. If we are overly invested in getting clients who exhibit defensive behavior to change, we may be overlooking our own dynamics and reactions as we interact with these clients. If you understand how you are being affected by certain clients, you can appropriately disclose your reactions without behaving defensively.

I have been facilitating therapeutic groups for many years, but dealing effectively with the problematic behaviors of some members can still be difficult. This also applies to working with students in group counseling courses that I teach. I can become impatient and fail to appreciate that individuals move at their own pace and need time to arrive at certain insights. For example, group members who have fears about speaking in a group may appear to be disinterested and uninvolved. I might be too quick to make inferences and judge them, instead of trying to understand them. Other times I may urge clients to have an insight and to take action that will bring about change. Intellectually, I know that coming to a deeper understanding of ourselves is not always a smooth process and that pushing a group member toward acting in new ways does not bring the desired results. I continue to relearn the lesson of exploring with clients their hesitations, fears, and concerns rather than expecting them to be in a place where they are not. If I can accept people where they are, there is a good chance they will move forward, if they desire to move in that direction.

When a client is reluctant, talking about the difficulties I am experiencing in these situations is a good way to open a dialogue. I do not know exactly what to do in every complex situation, and together we may come to new levels of understanding through this open discussion. I do my best to avoid interpreting client reluctance as a sign of unwillingness to participate in the therapeutic process.

Learning to Work Collaboratively With Clients

Finding the optimum balance of shared responsibility with clients or students can be difficult for me. I have a tendency to assume too much responsibility for the direction and outcomes of a therapy group, a particular class I am teaching, a workshop I am facilitating, or a group supervision situation. I often remind myself that counseling, supervising, and teaching are collaborative endeavors. If I assume full responsibility for outcomes, I am depriving others of their rightful responsibility of becoming empowered. Adlerians suggest that hyperresponsible individuals are often surrounded by irresponsible people. A disempowered client is the last thing any of us want in counseling or therapy. When I am working too hard to achieve certain outcomes, I am not trusting that my students or group members can take care of themselves. Clearly, my childhood fear of failure has never totally gone away.

Clients who are experiencing pain come to counseling seeking to overcome this pain and often request advice on what they should do. It is not our role to assume responsibility for directing our clients' lives. Counseling does not entail dispensing information or giving advice on how to live. Even if we had the capacity to resolve clients' problems for them, this would be ineffective because they would continually need to ask our advice for every new problem that arises. Our task is to help clients make independent choices and develop their own ability to problem solve effectively that will last long after therapy ends. This is empowerment.

Who we are as individuals will influence our functioning as counseling professionals. If this subject perks your interest, you will find good books dealing with the counselor as a person and as a professional. A few that I recommend are *Becoming a Counselor: The Light, the Bright, and the Serious* (Gladding, 2009), *On Being a Therapist* (Kottler, 2010), *On Becoming a Person* (Rogers, 1961), *A Way of Being* (Rogers, 1980), and *Becoming a Helper* (Corey & Corey, 2011).

Personal Therapy for Counselors

I sometimes hear students exclaim that they will not be able to help their clients if they have any problems of their own. From my perspective, the key point is not *whether* we happen to be struggling with personal problems, but *how* we are dealing with them, and what we are willing to do to come to a deeper self-understanding and to resolve pressing problems. Life without problems is a myth, but this does not mean that we must resolve all of our personal problems before we begin a counseling career. By becoming aware of our personal needs, areas of "unfinished business," personal conflicts, defenses, and vulnerabilities we can learn how these issues may interfere in our professional work. Without self-awareness, we can obstruct the progress of our clients. If we are not conscious of our own problems, we will not be able to pay attention to the concerns of clients, especially if their problem areas are similar to ours.

Requiring trainees to have personal psychotherapy is a controversial issue among faculty in graduate training programs. Some faculty strongly support making personal therapy an integral component of the training program, and some doctoral programs require trainees to have a minimum of 30 hours of individual therapy. Other programs offer a nongraded course, called therapeutic group experience, which is facilitated by a practitioner outside of the university to avoid combining the evaluation and therapeutic aspects. Many faculty members in a variety of training programs strongly recommend personal therapy to their students, even if this is not a program requirement.

Other practitioners believe that required therapy will not be effective because therapy entails accepting an invitation to a journey of self-exploration, which cannot be mandated. Others claim that it is an infringement on the student's right to make a free choice in this matter. Some programs are reluctant to require personal therapy out of fear of legal reprisals. This is especially true when students are expected to engage in personal self-disclosure and to get involved in experiential activities in various courses.

Although I echo the soundness of the policy of fully informing students prior to their acceptance into a training program about the value of dealing with their personal issues, I cannot understand how a program can be effective if it does not provide opportunities for the personal development of students. Multiple routes to acquiring increased self-awareness are possible, a few of which include participating in peer groups, participating in a self-help group, taking courses that focus on self-exploration, meditating, and engaging in journal writing. Counselor education programs must do more than impart knowledge and teaching skills; the personal development of trainees is of the utmost importance if trainees are to effectively apply their skills and knowledge in actual counseling situations. For an in-depth treatment of the subject of therapy for therapists, I highly recommend *The Psychotherapist's Own Psychotherapy: Patient and Clinician Perspectives* (Geller, Norcross, & Orlinsky, 2005).

Therapy as a Way to Understand Our Countertransference

Working with difficult clients can affect us in personal ways. Countertransference, defined broadly, includes any of our projections that distort the way we perceive and react to a client. This phenomenon occurs when we are triggered into emotional reactivity, when we respond defensively, or when we lose our ability to be present in a relationship because our own issues become involved. Whether we are students in training or new professionals, we will be challenged to recognize and deal effectively with our countertransference, which can usefully be explored in our personal psychotherapy. We all have personal vulnerabilities that are frequently triggered when we begin working with clients. I don't view countertransference as something that we need to eliminate but as a reality we need to understand and monitor. For example, a potential trigger for me is encountering indifference, apathy, and judgmentalness on the part of clients, students, and workshop participants. I am aware of having to work harder when interacting with someone I perceive as being judgmental. I tell myself that I cannot change a person who may be reacting to me in judgmental ways, but I can change the way I react to such a person.

Another form of countertransference relates to becoming overly involved with a client. One colleague presents her trainees with this guideline to help them detect countertransfence: "When you find yourself working harder than your clients, this is a sign of your countertransference." When we begin practicing, it may be extremely difficult to psychologically leave our clients at the office. We might well worry about certain clients and think of ways they can better cope with their problems. In addition, the emotionally intense relationships we develop with clients can be expected to tap into our own unresolved problem areas. Our clients' stories and pain are bound to affect us, and we must deal with what is opened up for us in supervision and personal therapy. We don't have to numb ourselves to the pain experienced by our clients, and, indeed, we can be touched by their stories and express compassion and empathy. However, we have to realize that it is their pain and not carry it *for* them lest we become overwhelmed by their life stories and thus render ourselves ineffective in working with them.

My Experiences With Personal Therapy

When I began my work as a counselor, I was impatient and anxious about the pace of my counseling clients. I expected clients to get better quickly and to solve all the problems that brought them into counseling on schedule. When clients did not make the progress I expected of them, I interpreted this as being due to my ineptness as a practitioner. If clients complained that they were not getting better or, alas, that they were actually getting worse, my self-doubts were sparked and I was convinced that I had chosen the wrong profession. This was particularly true for me with male clients who complained of depression and anxiety. Many of my unresolved issues stemming from childhood and adolescence reappeared at this time. My father had suffered from depression, and I had done my best to be humorous with him, to get him to laugh, and to cheer him up. I decided I needed to address problems I thought I had worked through earlier in my individual therapy. I think we are mistaken when we believe we have resolved long-standing personality problems. It seems more accurate to say that we get a better understanding of our problems, which can result in healing. By taking control in our life, we are better able to manage our problems.

I accepted the reality that I could not inspire clients to pursue their in-depth personal work if I was avoiding coming to grips with my own problems. I became convinced that I could not take my counseling clients any further than I had traveled on my own personal journey. Thus, I returned for additional personal therapy and attended many different intensive personal growth groups, a topic I discuss further in Chapter 5. Quite frankly, I was not a very good client in individual therapy. I was in my mid-20s and had led a fairly sheltered life. In fact, I didn't think I really "needed" therapy. I went on the recommendation and urging of a friend who said, "Jerry, I really think you could use some individual therapy." When I presented myself in my first counseling session I said to the therapist, "My life is pretty comfortable, and I really don't have any major problems. Because I am going into the counseling field, I thought getting my own therapy might help me get a better understanding of what counseling is about." I think I was looking for reassurance that I was fine the way I was. It was difficult for me to identify and express a range of emotions, and much of my therapy was somewhat of an intellectual exercise, with me trying to figure out my dynamics! Participating as a member of different kinds of groups seemed much more effective in helping me to become emotionally engaged rather than trying to figure out everything on an intellectual level. Both individual therapy and my experience with groups provided me with a better understanding of myself and widened my worldview. These experiences directly contributed to my honing my skills as a practicing counselor and as a teacher.

Seeking Personal Therapy for Yourself

Even if your program does not require any form of personal counseling, I highly recommend that you expose yourself to therapeutic experiences aimed at increased self-awareness. Your participation in your own personal development program can pay dividends in increasing your availability to your clients. Through various therapeutic modes, such as individual and group counseling, you can come to a better understanding of how you operate in your interpersonal world. Personal therapy can help you understand your personal dynamics and will likely enhance your effectiveness as a counselor. If you are open to your therapeutic experiences, you can acquire knowledge, skills, and techniques that are not to be found in textbooks. Simply reading about the counseling process is no substitute for personally experiencing a therapeutic process.

When I promote the value of personal psychotherapy with my students, I often hear that the expense makes this idea prohibitive. I certainly appreciate that students have financial hardships and that paying for tuition, fees, books, and other living expenses is taxing on the budget. If you are interested in counseling for yourself, check out the resources that may be available at your university at little or no cost to you. Both group and individual counseling are often available through your university counseling center. Even though the emphasis may be on time-limited individual counseling, you can experience significant personal gains in a relatively short time. Ask your professors, supervisors, mentors, and peers for recommendations of therapists in the community or in private practice. Many therapists have reduced fees for graduate students in counseling. This investment in personal therapy can pay off in terms of enhancing your personal effectiveness and your skill as a counselor.

Committed professionals engage in lifelong self-examination as a means of remaining self-aware and maintaining their vitality as a person and not just as a professional. Even seasoned practitioners can benefit from personal consultations, peer groups, and personal therapy, all of which are routes to self-care. Your own work as a client can teach you valuable lessons about how to creatively facilitate deeper levels of self-exploration in clients. Through your own therapy, you can gain increased appreciation for the courage your clients display in their therapeutic journey.

Many therapists are wounded healers, having an intimate knowledge of painful life experiences. Through the process of their own healing, they gain a context for understanding their clients' pain. Beth's personal story illustrates how navigating through tumultuous times in her personal life and her own personal therapy have enhanced her ability to be an effective wounded healer.

My Experience as a Wounded Healer

Beth Christensen, MA

I was in my mid-40s when I began working on my master's degree in counseling. I remember wandering around the halls of the small college I attended on the first day of classes, painfully aware of how young the other students looked and how old I was. For a while, I seriously wondered if I had made the right decision coming back to school at this age. When I finally found my classroom and walked in, I realized I was not at all unusual as a graduate student in counseling. My classmates represented a wide array of ages, ethnicities, and experiences, and I began to feel more comfortable. It was then that I took the first step on my journey, and I have had the good fortune to have had wonderful mentors to walk with me along the way. I am now a doctoral candidate in counselor education and a counselor intern. There have been many challenges on this path, and many triumphs, both big and small. But I have never had to go through them alone.

It was not just my age that made me feel unsure of myself as I began this journey. I had made the decision to become a counselor as a direct result of having been through some horrible experiences in my own life. I was the victim of severe sexual abuse as a child and adolescent. It was not until midlife that I began to really remember and deal with my abuse. After several years working with various therapists through immense pain, rage, and grief, I realized that I had an opportunity to create something positive and life enhancing from my abuse and recovery. I believe that meaning is not inherent in life events; instead, it is what we create in response to those events. I chose to use the experience of my own healing to assist in the healing of others.

Of course, nobody gets to adulthood without some degree of psychic pain, but some of us get a bigger dose of it. I have come to know several wounded healers who have created successful professional lives out of their own pain. This kind of professional development, grounded in having survived trauma of some sort, can hold both great promise and great risk. I am fortunate in having had several wise, compassionate, and ethically grounded people to support me as I have navigated the perils of transforming my experiences into a source of something positive. I would like to reflect on some of those perils here.

I have found that as a wounded healer I must have a clear sense of purpose. I need to be aware of what I hope to achieve in terms of who is to benefit from my actions. When I am engaged in a counseling relationship with a client, I must be able to make choices that benefit the client and contribute to the therapeutic process. If the interaction also results in something positive for me, that is fine, but it is not the primary goal. It is my responsibility as an ethical counselor to make sure that my own needs are met in appropriate ways, and never at the expense of a client's well-being.

I have to maintain a clear purpose as well in my interactions with peers, supervisors, professors, and supervisees. I want to use my experience and my presence to dismantle some of the inappropriate shame that is associated with sexual abuse and trauma-related emotional problems. I decided early on that it was not enough for me to *say* that I reject inappropriate shame; I have to *act* on that conviction as well. Therefore, I have decided not to hide the fact of my abuse; the damage that it has done; or the difficult, painful, and often baffling processes involved in recovery. I want my colleagues to see the person beneath the pathology and the potential that lies in some of the most distressed of clients. I want to be an advocate for survivors by becoming an educator and researcher in the subject area of surviving and recovering from childhood sexual abuse. Again, I am fortunate to have mentors to lead me in that endeavor.

Another important issue for wounded healers is the need for balance and replenishment. Sometimes the needs of clients are so immense, and the desire to help them so intense, that I run the risk of being sucked into the client's agony. That kind of enmeshment is detrimental for both the client and me. The best way for me to prevent this kind of entanglement is to have open, honest, and thoughtful supervision sessions and to be willing to maintain a high degree of self-awareness. I also maintain balance by continuing to receive counseling for myself, so that I minimize the risk of using my sessions with clients or with other professionals as a way to meet my own needs. Even when the subject of my own abuse is part of a professional encounter, such as a discussion with my supervisor or dissertation chair, I have to be aware that these people, however caring and knowledgeable they are, are not my therapists. This boundary is important in that it allows me to grow and flourish as a professional while continuing my healing work with my own therapist. These processes are parallel and, I think, should remain so.

As a doctoral student and counselor intern, I know that I have a lot to learn, and I am eager to continue to do so. As a person who has successfully navigated the rocky terrain of recovering from serious emotional distress, I think I have a lot to teach. In my emerging career as a counselor and a counselor educator, I hope to do both.

∼

Commentary

I appreciate Beth's honesty is describing some very difficult experiences in her journey. Most of us do not reach adulthood without experiencing some psychic pain and some psychological wounding. Beth's lesson is that negative events do not determine us; we can choose to bring new understanding and meaning to past events. Beth is aware that being an ethical counselor requires that she be able to focus on what is in the best interests of the client. If she had not dealt with the pain of her own trauma, she would not be in a position to be present for her clients. Fortunately, Beth encountered people who were instrumental in her ability to transform some of the traumatic experiences she endured. She realizes that if she had not explored and worked through the effects of this trauma, she would be highly vulnerable to being engulfed in the painful stories of her clients. Beth learned that the best way to prevent becoming entangled with her clients is to have open, honest, and thoughtful supervision sessions. She learned the value of receiving counseling for herself as a way to maintain a high degree of self-awareness and to minimize the risk of using her clients to meet her own personal needs. Beth avoided making her professsors into her therapists, for she realized appropriate boundaries. Her journey has made it possible for her to become a wounded healer.

Questions for Reflection

- What aspects of Beth's story most affect you?
- Does any of her pain relate to the pain you have experienced in your life?
- What does being a wounded healer mean to you? In what ways, if any, might you be a wounded healer?
- To what extent could you demonstrate empathy and understanding for a client like Beth if you have not shared similar experiences?
- Do you think participating in personal therapy could eventually completely resolve most of your problems? If you were to pursue therapy for yourself, what would your expectations be?

My Introduction to Multicultural and
Diversity Perspectives

A key dimension of the counselor as a person and as a professional involves coming to a better understanding of how our own cultural background influences our lives. In the following pages, I describe some salient aspects of my cultural and family background and how these experiences have influenced me. In addition, two contributors (Yusef Daulatzai and Casey Huynh) share how their cultural backgrounds have been significant influences in the professional work they are doing.

In my years in graduate school, there were few discussions of how culture influences the assessment and treatment process, and no multicultural courses were offered. When I began my university teaching, I focused on counseling from an individualistic perspective and studying internal psychodynamics, with little discussion of the cultural context of the therapeutic process. In the early 1980s, our human services faculty expanded to include two people of color with expertise in multicultural perspectives and backgrounds in social work. Soraya Coley and Jerome Wright both served mentoring roles for me, helping me to recognize the limitations of counseling strictly from an individualistic perspective. They broadened my view of helping to consider the person-in-the-environment. In fact, Soraya and Jerome did a great deal to broaden the scope of our human services program to encompass the clients' culture and the impact of the community on the individual. They also served as mentors to many of our students and supported them in their vision of pursuing graduate school.

The Influence of My Family on
Understanding How Culture Affects Us

I am a first-generation Italian American, and I learned about cultural diversity first from my family of origin. Both of my parents were from Italy, yet neither of them seemed to think it important that I learn how to speak Italian at home. I do not remember conversations about cultural matters, and there did not seem to be an interest in passing along cultural traditions to my brother or me. When I was a child, we spent almost every Sunday at a family gathering with my grandparents. I felt lost because most of the conversation was in Italian, as my grandparents never learned to speak much English. I didn't feel that I fit in at these gatherings with uncles and aunts. In some ways, a theme of my early years was that I did not fit in any place!

My father, Joseph, was a brilliant and sensitive man, but he wrestled with anxiety and depression for much of his life. Sent from Italy to New York when he was 7 years old, he was raised in an orphanage. Eventually he became a dentist, and he practiced dentistry during the Great Depression. Because he was convinced that many people would not want to come to an Italian dentist, he changed his name from Cordileone (meaning "heart of the lion") to Corey, denying his heritage in some ways. My father's depressive condition had a major impact on me as a child, adolescent, and young adult. He died shortly before I received my doctorate in counseling. His message to me was to choose the safe path and not to take risks. When my father died, I made a decision that I did not want to follow his path of choosing safety over venturing into new territory. I also did not want to let depression ever dominate my life. It may well be that keeping myself busy for most of my life is partly related to keeping depression at bay.

My mother, Josephine, lived to be 94, and she was a great teacher for me by modeling her way of living. From her early childhood years, she worked hard on her father's peach orchard and learned the values of a simple life. Although she loved school and had a keen desire to learn, she was not encouraged to pursue education beyond high school. Despite having a hard life, she retained her wit and sense of humor. She taught me the value of hard work and showed me that one can change even in old age. Unlike my father, she was a risk taker and was interested in many facets of life. She was especially interested in our daughters' lives and greatly enjoyed spending time with them, as they did with her. My mother got very impatient with me at times and had no trouble letting me know this. I remember one time her telling me: "Jerry, all you can talk about is your books and school! Can't you talk about anything else?" My mother realized that my interests were somewhat narrow, and she challenged me in caring and humorous ways.

My brother and I had the same parents, but you would never know we were brothers. Bob was 13 years older than I, and we had very little in common. He was in World War II when I was a child, and after the war he went off to college to study business and eventually went into the business world. We were polar opposites in terms of values, perspectives on life, and religious and political views. Although we had the same parents, it seems as though we grew up in two vastly different cultures. In spite of our differences, we had a cordial relationship and kept in contact until he died at age 83. It pleased me that he seemed proud of Marianne's and my accomplishments in the professional world. He often joked that it was hard to believe I had ever finished school based on my track record in grammar school!

Being around a nuclear and extended immigrant Italian family, I learned at an early age that people see the world through different eyes and express themselves in different ways. I came to appreciate differences rather than judge them. Because of my father's experiences, I became aware that people were discriminated against because of their heritage. My extended Italian family encountered some discrimination, yet some of these family members harbored their own prejudices as well. I observed some of my relatives making disparaging remarks about certain other groups of people and learned that racism can be both subtle and blatant. Somehow I developed compassion for people who were the target of any form of discrimination. Perhaps this was partially due to my own childhood experiences of feeling I was on the outside and not wanted by my peers. I am not sure how I developed compassion for others and a nonjudgmental way of being, but somehow I moved toward becoming a caring person.

I also learned about cultural diversity from Marianne, who had immigrated to the United States from Germany at the age of 19. We were married in Germany when I was 27, but both of us, especially Marianne, experienced some turmoil about whether or not to get married. We were from two different cultures: She grew up in a rural town on a farm, and I grew up in the city of Los Angeles; she was Protestant and I was Catholic. Marriage meant that Marianne would leave her family in Germany and make her home in California. At that time cultural and religious differences were more significant in society than they are today. With some helpful mentoring from several people, we were able to work through the differences that almost separated us. We realized that we had many core values in common, which helped to put our differences into perspective. We were married in the Worms Cathedral in Germany (*Wormser Dom*), and both of our families attended the wedding, which was a clear endorsement for us.

Each summer we spent time in Marianne's village in the Rheinpfalz, which gave me an opportunity to experience the values associated with living in a small, rural town in another country. Living in two cultures has helped me to appreciate the complexities of culture and various ways of perceiving the world. Without a doubt, Marianne has been my primary mentor in teaching me about culture—and she has been one of the major forces in challenging me to think about ways of understanding diversity and how to incorporate this understanding into counseling practice.

Our daughters, Heidi and Cindy, were greatly influenced by their experiences both in Germany and in the United States. Both of our daughters are bilingual and bicultural. Cindy earned a PsyD in clinical psychology, with a specialization in multicultural and community counseling. She currently teaches multicultural counseling in a highly diverse university graduate program. We share common interests and concerns about multicultural issues, and she has challenged me to reexamine some of the assumptions underlying my clinical practice. Along with Marianne and me, Cindy has copresented at several conferences, has cofacilitated several weeklong residential groups, and has recently become involved in coauthoring some books with us. Cindy has taught me valuable lessons about how culture influences the therapeutic process and affects teaching in the field of counselor education. Heidi took another route in the healing arts, that of teaching yoga. Heidi's influence is a reminder of the importance of paying attention to the body and not getting lost in words, which certainly has relevance in counseling.

Marianne and I both expanded our horizons considerably through our travels to other countries. We have conducted workshops in Mexico, Hong Kong, China, Korea, Scotland, Germany, Belgium, Canada, and Ireland, as well as in many regions of the United States. Our group counseling workshops have shown us how cultural variables influence an individual's functioning within a group. Each of these experiences has provided Marianne and me with a different way of looking at what counseling is all about and has offered powerful avenues for learning about the interface between counseling and culture.

The immigrant stories of Yusef Daulatzai and Casey Huynh that follow demonstrate how early life experiences were the foundation for their decisions to complete graduate programs and to work with culturally diverse client populations. As you read their personal accounts, identify some aspects of their stories that could help you in your journey toward becoming a culturally competent counselor. Consider how Yusef's and Casey's earlier experiences relate to what they are accomplishing in their professional careers today.

 ## Academic Analysis Versus Direct Social Activism

Yusef Daulatzai, MA, PsyD

I strongly believe that who I am as a person influences my work as a therapist, and this view is confirmed by clinical research. My interest, my passions, and my intellectual and spiritual development contribute to my effectiveness as a therapist. My career path was partially inspired by life events that occurred during my first year of undergraduate studies. I am an immigrant and a man of color, and my early experiences of racism and discrimination had made issues of race, class, and inequality a topic of interest to me. I began a process of critical self-evaluation and identity development, as many college students do. As this analysis was occurring within me, a larger action was occurring outside of me in the form of the Los Angeles riots in the spring of 1992. This was my first year in college, and I happened to be taking a sociology course on race and inequality. I spent my 4 years at UCLA as a sociology major studying the structures of racism and inequality while developing my passion and commitment to social justice issues.

As graduation approached, I was searching for a way to interweave this commitment into a career. I am grateful to have had a mentor in and close relationship with Professor Jerome Rabow in the Sociology Department at UCLA. I loved the climate he created that encouraged us to analyze issues of social inequality in the classroom and to participate as activists through our work at community centers and schools. The combination of academic analysis and social activism served as a wonderful experience, but it created a thoughtful debate within me in terms of a future career. I was considering pursuing a PhD in sociology, with a career in teaching and writing on social justice issues. However, I struggled with the lack of direct contact I would have with the community outside the walls of academia if I chose this path. I was concerned that a university career involving academic analysis of social issues would not be as fruitful as more direct forms of social activism. I wondered how I could forge a career combining both the academic exploration of social issues and direct involvement in social activism, because both had meaning for me.

After graduation I obtained a teaching position at an underserved middle school in East Los Angeles. I enjoyed the hands-on approach of teaching but knew in my heart that I wanted to attend graduate school. Encouragement from my family and professors helped me pursue this path. Questions I asked myself were: "Am I ready for the stress of graduate school? What kind of work do I want to be doing? What career path will make me happy?" Although I did not enjoy research and statistics, I knew this was part of a doctoral program. A friend suggested that I check out the California School of Professional Psychology (CSPP), a graduate program that appeared to have many of the things I was looking for. The program offered specializations in various fields of clinical psychology. One of the tracks was the Multicultural Community Clinical Psychology option, designed to focus on the impact that culture and context have on communities and the individual. They offered both a PhD (emphasizing research) and a PsyD (focused more on practical clinical work). After much consulting and investigating, I enrolled at CSPP, where I believed I could continue to develop my skills in the academic analysis of social justice issues as well as be empowered to work in the community as a clinical psychologist. Through this program, I found a way to combine my interest in the academic analysis of social justice issues with applied social activism.

My current position at a nonprofit community mental health program is funded by the Los Angeles Department of Mental Health. I work with at-risk youths throughout the San Gabriel Valley, all of whom are on parole or in a foster system. Many of the youths experience multiple levels of oppression from poverty, being the victims of physical, sexual, or emotional abuse or disrupted family support. I work with a multidisciplinary team to help connect young people to needed community support. I also work with schools to increase educational support services. In addition, I provide intensive individual and family therapy and serve as an advocate for youth.

My advice to current graduate students in the helping professions is to reflect on your interest and passions and consider how those passions can be tied to your professional careers. Be active in developing yourself. Graduate school can be very stressful and can leave little time for focusing on personal development. In the helping professions, you are the instrument. Who you are as a person, your character, your intellect, your level of self-awareness, and your love and capacity for deep emotional connections with others may be your most powerful ally in helping others. Never stop working on developing yourself; continue to be a work in progress. I encourage you to develop and maintain relationships with others in the field who do similar work. It is important to have a community who nurtures and encourages you. Take good care of yourself so you will be in a good place to help care for others.

∽

Commentary

As an immigrant and person of color, Yusef had personal experiences with racism, discrimination, and unequal treatment. His story demonstrates how such negative life experiences can be transformed into a vision of wanting to engage in social justice and advocacy work. His personal and professional lives are intertwined, and he has an experiential understanding and an academic understanding of pressing social problems that are a basic part of his professional life as a clinical psychologist working in the community. Yusef suggests that you reflect on your passions and see how they can be linked to your professional career. Yusef had two different but related career paths and found a way to combine the academic exploration of social justice issues with direct engagement in social activism.

Questions for Reflection

- In what ways can your life experiences be transformed to create the professional path you most want?
- Have you experienced unequal treatment, and if so, how have these experiences influenced you?
- To what extent do you agree with Yusef that your character, your intellect, and your level of self-awareness are your most important instruments for effectively working with others?

A Journey From Darkness to Light

Casey Huynh, MS, MFT

I was 6 years old when my family decided to escape from Vietnam by boat in 1981. After failing during our first attempt, we succeeded on our second attempt. I was subjected to many horrific events, including seeing people being killed, having a gun pointed at me, being vulnerable to abuse, and being separated from all of my relatives. I stayed in a Thailand refugee camp for 6 months, fighting to survive and be reunited with my family. Eventually I was reunited with my family who arrived before me in America. A wonderful American family who sponsored us gave me hope and light.

I was 15 years old when I made a conscious decision to become a therapist and to work mainly with Asians, especially with the Vietnamese population. When I was in therapy, my counselor wanted me to forgive the people who were abusive to me, but I was far from being ready to forgive. I vowed to myself that I would be a different kind of therapist. This memory helps motivate me to be the best therapist I can be, and it is largely responsible for me persisting in graduate school in spite of difficulties.

During graduate school I did not pass my second year of practicum because I struggled with applying the theories I was learning to working with Vietnamese-speaking clients. Repeating this practicum cost me an extra year in the program, but I came to realize that this was a gift in disguise. I learned that graduate school was a time to learn, to practice skills, and to master the basics of the counseling field. This extra year gave me the opportunity to spend time learning skills and acquiring knowledge that I would need to realize my dream of becoming a professional counselor.

After 3 years of overcoming some obstacles, I obtained my master's degree in counseling. I then worked for 2 years to complete the hours required for licensure as a marriage and family therapist (MFT). It then took me another 3 years to pass my licensing exam, after three attempts with each of two sections of the exam. I was ambivalent about passing the exam because I was afraid of becoming successful. I wanted to give up, yet a number of people who knew me encouraged me to continue pursuing my professional goals. I focused on what I needed to do to pass the exam, which eventually paid off. Many times in my life I had faced adversity, felt powerless, and was limited by my environment, both personally and academically. Obtaining my license gave me a sense of accomplishment and independence. I secretly believed that I could be a good counselor, but I had been too afraid to admit it before. Getting my license fulfilled my lifelong dream, and I realized that the possibilities were endless. I felt a sense of empowerment that I had not allowed the adversity and detours in my path to get the best of me.

I am currently working for a private nonprofit agency providing therapy to mostly monolingual Vietnamese-speaking children and their parents. Most of the Asian families I see are referred by the Department of Children and Family Services, Regional Center, the court, school counselors, and family doctors. The majority of my clients are children, ranging in age from 5 to 18. These children have symptoms relating to depression, anxiety, posttraumatic stress disorder, identity formation, parent–child conflicts, and substance abuse. Some of these problems within a family are intensified because of language and cultural barriers between monolingual Vietnamese-speaking parents and their English-speaking children. Because I can speak Vietnamese, I am able to break through the language barrier and help family members feel understood. I am also able to reduce the threat associated with negative mental health stigmas. I use genogram work with family-of-origin issues to aid the family's comprehension of multiple generational experiences and understanding of different cultural perpectives. Through these therapeutic interventions I notice a pattern of reduced emotional reactivity, healing of psychological wounds, and greater open communication among family members. A few of the benefits that accrue from our work together include the greater capability of children to manage their symptoms well enough to achieve in school; their being able to establish and maintain friendships; and their increased engagement with their caretakers. When parents pratice the skills they learn in therapy, they experience an improvement in their family dynamics.

My journey has led me to an appreciation of life and a mission to contribute to the Asian community in much the same way as did the many who cared for me during the difficult times in my life. I am proud to be a part of the progress my clients are able to make. My journey from darkness to light has been most difficult at times, yet it has been instrumental in my being able to make a difference in working with Asian clients. For me, navigating my journey has been like passing the Olympic torch. I had to find my light, ignite it, and learn how to keep it burning.

∾

Commentary

One of the striking elements of Casey's journey is how she not only survived unbelievable odds but has thrived in creating a professional life devoted to assisting people in her community find hope and light in their lives. It is apparent that Casey had her share of failures in graduate school and in the licensure process, yet she did not let these setbacks deter her from following her childhood dream of becoming a counselor.

Questions for Reflection

- What elements of Casey's story are most significant for you personally?
- What can you learn from Casey about meeting with setbacks? What will be helpful for you when discouragement sets in?
- What do you think will be required of you to work effectively with culturally and racially diverse client groups?

Becoming Culturally Aware Is a Continuing Journey

Regardless of our cultural background, I believe that as counselors we need to examine our expectations, attitudes, biases, and assumptions about people from diverse groups and reflect on how these influence our view of the counseling process. It is possible for us to carry our bias around with us yet not fully recognize this fact. It takes a consistent effort and vigilance to monitor our biases and values so they do not interfere with establishing and maintaining effective relationships with our clients.

I have expanded my cultural awareness through direct contact with a variety of groups, through reading, through special course work, through consultation and discussions with colleagues, through in-service professional workshops, and through providing services in various settings. One lesson I have learned is that expanding your cultural awareness and becoming a diversity-competent counselor does not end upon your graduating from a program. Instead, it is a lifelong developmental process that requires continuing education, training, reflection, discussions with trusted colleagues, and the willingness to seek supervision and consultation. In this arena we are called to be a work in progress rather than a finished product.

I live in California, where it is hard to ignore the cultural diversity that is all around us, but I recognize that in some parts of the United States and in some parts of the rest of the world, the communities in which people live are more homogeneous. There is less evident diversity, and the diversity that is part of the community may have to be sought out. I encourage you—no matter where you live—to go on a search for difference. If you can, travel to different parts of the world. If you can't do this, go to a different part of your town or to an area in which people from various cultures congregate. Do everything you can to stretch beyond the comfort zone of what you have always known. Be willing to challenge yourself personally in the same way that you might encourage your clients to broaden their horizons.

Chapter Three
Being Mentored and Mentoring Others

Introduction

The theme of this chapter is the circular process of being mentored ourselves and eventually mentoring others. Students and new professionals have generously shared their personal stories, identifying lessons of support, encouragement, and guidance from mentors that provided them with the impetus to reach their goals. The 18 stories you will read in this book illustrate how individuals faced and overcame obstacles, either internal or external, that could have blocked their professional journey. For most, a mentor who believed in them provided the motivation they needed to pursue their dreams. They have achieved heights that they did not think possible and have expressed a desire to give back to others through their own mentoring activities.

All of us are called to be mentors in some fashion, regardless of the stage of our personal and professional development. The president of the American Counseling Association (ACA), Dr. Lynn Linde (2009), wrote an article challenging professionals to mentor and described how many people have encouraged and mentored her over the years in her graduate program, her career, and her work as ACA president. She raised some key questions that deserve reflection: How many of you succeeded in graduate school or a new career because of someone who eased a transition or paved the way?

How many of you became a counselor because somebody saw something in you that you did not see? How many of you have had a person broaden your vision to think about becoming a counseling professional? Dr. Linde believes she has a responsibility to mentor others, and she suggests that every counseling professional find one person during the next year to mentor. I like her notion that we establish an ongoing relationship with a student, a family member, or a colleague and help this person on his or her journey into the profession. The people whose personal journeys you will read about in this book are all following Dr. Linde's advice and providing direction to others. They understand the value in giving back to others what was given to them.

Lessons I Learned From My Mentors

Some of my own mentoring grew out of experiences that may have seemed negative at the time. My own fear of failing, feelings of inadequacy, and struggles to define who I am have been my best teachers. Although I had my share of failure, I came to realize that failing in some endeavor does not mean that I am a total failure as a person. I also learned that making a mistake is not the same as being a failure. In fact, I came to believe that not being willing to venture out and try new things might well be the biggest failure of all. I had to realize that there is no perfect security in pursuing a professional endeavor. Alfred Adler's idea that feelings of inferiority are the wellsprings of creativity is a notion that I find significant. Along with the Adlerians, I believe that our striving for superiority, or a sense of personal competence, stems from our feelings of inferiority. I hope that you do not look upon your perceived failures or inferiority as weaknesses. As strange as it seems, you might find creativity within you if you embrace all aspects of your being, including your sense of inferiority. Several of the personal stories you will read contain themes of worrying about making mistakes, experiencing the fear of failure, and struggling with feelings of not being adequate. The authors of these stories attribute their present successes to facing their self-doubts and anxieties about being personally and professionally competent.

What Mentoring Means to Me

I recognize the power mentors had in inspiring me to strive for my dreams. Having people who believed in me gave me a sense of hope when discouragement set in. Passing this belief along to others is one of the most rewarding aspects of mentoring and teaching for me. Encouragement is a vital source that can help you combat the inclination to give up. I remember how much I valued my mentors' belief in me and their nudging me to persist, especially in difficult situations. Each of us has unique gifts, and we can make a powerful impact on facilitating change in individuals, groups, and society. Our influence can extend far beyond the simple actions we may take today.

Over the years I have made it a priority to include friends and colleagues in many of my projects, and these projects have become joint ones instead of solo endeavors. I believe there can be a great deal of power in the collaborative spirit, and I have consistently included colleagues when writing books and articles, creating educational video programs, coteaching various courses, giving workshops, and giving presentations at professional conferences. Because I strive to be inclusive, projects become more meaningful to me. I view mentoring as a way to involve others in collaborative relationships in which we both benefit. I have gained much from initiating these relationships with both colleagues and students, and those whom I have been fortunate enough to mentor often have become important sources of mentoring for me.

I view mentoring as an advocacy process that involves helping mentees to discover their voice and to be able to use it. In my mentoring relationships, I try to do more than advocate *for* mentees. My goals are to teach those I mentor to think for themselves, arrive at their own conclusions, and speak for themselves. I do not want to create clones, nor do I want disciples. Instead, I hope to be a guide for their journey. I want to empower them to eventually mentor themselves so that they can create their own professional path.

How can you find a mentor? Potential mentors are friends, peers, family members, counselors, professors, and supervisors. Many will offer you guidance and suggestions as you navigate through your educational and professional career. Ask for the help that these individuals can provide. Your personal and professional journey will have many paths, so you have a lot to gain by recruiting several mentors, for different people can be resources for you in different ways. If you become dependent on any one mentor or group of mentors, you will be limited in what you can become. Think of questions you can ask of your mentors and consider the answers they give you.

Experiences of Others in Being Mentored

I have talked about turning points in my own personal and professional journey. Now I want to share some lessons about being mentored and mentoring others through the personal journeys of six individuals. As you read about the personal and professional journeys taken by Natalie Mendoza, Susan Cunningham, Jamie Bludworth, Galo Arboleda, Valerie Russell, and Mary Jane Ford, identify the parts of their stories you can relate to and the lessons you can derive from their experiences. Following each story, I present a commentary on the lessons that most stand out for me about being mentored and mentoring others.

People Make All the Difference

Natalie Mendoza, MS

I am employed by a community college in Southern California as a tenured counselor and faculty member. I work for a counseling retention program that supports, motivates, and encourages first-generation students, especially those who are educationally and economically disadvantaged. We assist students in earning their associate's degree or certificate and with transfering to a 4-year institution to earn a bachelor's degree and beyond.

My passion for higher education began when I was a high school student. I was an average student, and my counselors did not encourage me to pursue postsecondary education. However, a turning point occurred when I was introduced to Mr. Sal Castro of the Los Angeles Unified School District, Chicano Youth Leadership Conference. He enlightened me to the importance of getting a higher education, and with hard work and dedication I eventually earned a bachelor's and a master's degree. It was the best decision I had made in my life, and it set the foundation for my future career—helping others fulfill their educational and career goals. I also learned how I could mentor others through this experience.

My journey has taken an incredible amount of effort and self-confidence. When I was first establishing my professional relationships at the high school, I felt I was being "tested" to see whether I could handle my job. For example, when I worked as a high school counselor, I observed several parents with perplexed looks on their faces. I imagined they were saying, "You look very young to be a counselor. What could you tell me that I don't already know?" Although this was challenging for me, I took steps to carry out the tasks required in my position. By not being defensive and by focusing on my job, I eventually gained the respect of parents, students, school administrators, and community members. I was clear about my purpose, and I had a passion for education. Most of all, I came to believe in myself and what I had to offer.

As a younger looking Latina counselor, I have had to work hard to gain the respect of colleagues and administrators. However, this has been a catalyst for utilizing my strengths and empowering others around me to do the same in their chosen career fields. By the end of my first academic year as a school counselor, the principal informed me that I had a record number of requests from students and parents to be on my caseload for the following school year. Had I allowed intimidation from some parents to derail me, I would not have experienced this success. I continue to learn the value of challenging myself by dealing with difficult situations.

My vision in becoming a counselor has always been to give back to the community and help people in the way in which I was helped. As a Mexican American woman with a graduate degree, I believe I have a responsibility to do my best to help students reach their educational, career, and personal goals. I continue to assume this responsibility because Latinos have the highest high school and college dropout rates in the United States. This motivates me to do whatever I can to make a positive difference in the lives of the students with whom I work.

I have a few recommendations for graduate students preparing for a career in the helping professions. Believe in yourself and what you have to offer, and build professional relationships with people, even if you are shy. No one will take notice of you if you do not put yourself out there. Be willing to introduce yourself to people and to take risks. Tap into the resourceful people around you who are willing to provide you with tips in establishing your career path. Participate in ongoing personal and professional development activities, and stay informed about current research and practices in your field. Create an identity outside of your work so you don't depend on work to fulfill all of your needs.

Having an "expert" support system was especially helpful for me in pursuing my career aspirations. For example, to prepare for an interview, I set up a mock interview panel, had them ask me questions, and did an oral presentation to get their feedback. I also had several people look at my resume and cover letter and give me feedback before I submitted it for a position. My support system includes individuals with whom I have established trust over the years and who are honest with me. This has been immensely helpful when feelings of doubt hover over me.

I currently mentor students by conducting "The Leader in You" workshops. I go the extra mile to explain the benefits of pursuing a graduate degree and help students to see the power they have in themselves to give back to their own communities. It is very rewarding when students write a letter, send a card, or meet with me in person to tell me how significant I have been in their personal and professional journey. It is truly gratifying to know that I have influenced a person's life for the better and that I have made use of my talents. I experience a sense of pride when clients or mentees tell me how much they have grown to believe in themselves, respect themselves, and have learned to overcome obstacles in their path. Seeing that they appreciate how far they have come as a result of our work together is my reward, and this is the legacy I will continue to pursue.

~

Commentary

A number of key lessons stand out for me in Natalie's journey. Although she was not encouraged to set her sights beyond high school graduation, Sal Castro expanded her vision and inspired her to pursue her bachelor's and master's degrees. Natalie deserves credit for deciding to do the hard work involved in getting to her present position as a community college counselor who makes it her mission to motivate first-generation students to expand their horizons. She is doing for so many others what her mentor began with her when she was in high school.

Natalie has been steadfast in her desire to give back to the community and to influence others in the way in which she was helped to discover the talents and resources within her. I like the recommendations that she gives to graduate students of being willing to take risks and of tapping into the resourceful people around them. Regardless of whether you face obstacles similar to those of Natalie, you will benefit from reaching out to others who can provide support and direction for your professional aspirations. Natalie's ceative use of her support system reassured her when feelings of doubt hovered over her.

Natalie also recommends creating an identity outside of work rather than depending on work to fulfill all of your needs. I believe it is important to identify the sources of meaning in your personal life and to nurture those relationships. Natalie's passion for giving back to the community keeps her focused on helping those she counsels and mentors to learn ways to overcome obstacles in their path. Her reward is hearing from her mentees that they increasingly believe in themselves.

Questions for Reflection

- What kind of support system do you have to help you stay focused? What steps are you willing to take in creating a support system, whether at home, at school, or in the workplace?
- Are you willing to ask for the help you need?

- Does a particular person stand out for you who inspired you to pursue your dreams? How did this individual influence you?
- How have you challenged yourself and already overcome some road blocks?
- In what ways might you want to give back to the community?

A Difficult Journey to an Amazing Beginning

Susan Cunningham

As I begin my final year in a graduate program in the counseling field, I am halfway through my practicum program, seeing clients 2 days a week and attending classes 2 days a week. The journey I have taken to reach this point in my life has been difficult at times. I am a single mother of two teenage sons and an adult reentry student. I decided to return to school when my divorce was final in order to support my children.

When I started my educational journey, my vision was to complete nursing school, but I was unable to enter a nursing program because my prerequisite classes were completed out of state. As I looked within myself to determine what road to take next, I remembered a colleague and friend who is a licensed professional counselor whom I had worked with for many years. I enjoyed her enthusiasm about life and about helping others. She had once mentioned that I would make a great counselor because I am able to truly listen to others. This person is the reason I entered an undergraduate human services program and continued into the counseling graduate program.

I want to help people through the difficult times in life, and I have focused on the preteen and teenage population, mainly because they are facing so many difficult decisions in life. They are dealing with hormonal changes, and most of the time they do not understand what is happening. These children need someone they can count on to listen without judgment and to be there consistently for them.

When I finished my undergraduate program, I was unsure whether I had what it would take to complete a graduate degree. I dreamed of becoming a counselor, but I didn't think I was smart enough and thought I would fail. Discussing my fears with a friend who truly knew me, I was able to realize I was placing obstacles in front of myself because of my fear of failure. This gave me the strength and help I needed to apply to the graduate program. Having someone who could be my mentor during the difficult times made all the difference in the world to me and to my educational journey. I have now become a mentor to two individuals attending graduate programs as well. Both of these individuals are English language learners, and when they have difficulties writing papers or understanding the information, I am there to help. Part of my journey involves giving back to others because so many people have helped me.

Many things motivated me along my educational journey. Being able to support my children without depending on others was the biggest motivation. My goal is to have my own home, and completing a graduate program is the first step. My friends have also motivated me to continue my education. Having friends who understand the difficulties I face has been especially helpful as I pursue my career aspirations. Taking the time to truly understand my fellow students has given me a support group who understand the difficulties I am facing. These friends help me study, and when burnout hits, they are there to push me to continue. I am able to return this help when my friends are suffering from their own bouts of burnout.

As a single mother I had to overcome many obstacles to get where I am today. Finances were the most difficult obstacle. The graduate program requires 1 year of unpaid practicum service. To complete this requirement I had to quit my part-time employment and increase my student loans. Living with my mother allowed me to continue my education without having to pay the numerous bills required when living on my own. Another obstacle I have had to face is being away from my children four nights a week. The teenage years are truly important, and because of my school schedule I do most of my parenting on the phone. Being a mother is the most important thing to me, and not being there to help with school work every night has been extremely difficult for me. It has been a difficult adjustment for my children as well. As they started high school and junior high this past year, their school work provided many difficult challenges. Once I was able to adjust my time with my boys, I noticed an improvement in their grades. I want to be there for my boys whenever I am needed; however, attending school and working during the evening hours has made this a difficult obstacle to overcome.

Throughout my journey I have learned some things that would have been helpful to know in the beginning. The first and most important is that it is okay to make a mistake. It does not mean I am a failure, and I can learn from the experience. Having a good support system is also very important. Making friends with classmates gives you the opportunity to lean on people who understand just what you are going through. The journey through an education program in the helping professions requires in-depth self-discovery. Surrounding yourself with people who are on the same path can ease some of the pain and frustration. The last important piece of advice I would like to give is to have fun. Letting loose once in a while allows my brain to reboot and my body to let go of the stress it is carrying. Laughing with family and friends creates healing within my soul.

～

Commentary

A striking feature in Susan's story is how she initially restricted her dream of becoming a counselor because of her belief that she was not smart enough and her fear of failing. Susan eventually realized that she was blocking her path with her fears, and she decided not to let them continue to stop her. Not only did Susan have internal obstacles in the form of self-doubt and worries over making mistakes, but she had to deal with external obstacles as a single mother and figure out how to support her family and pay for her education. I suspect that Susan's story is one that many students can identify with, especially the part about balancing her responsibilities as a mother with doing what is required of her in school.

Susan reminds us how important it is to make time for fun, to reengergize ourselves, and to laugh with friends and family. Her notion that laughter creates healing within her soul is an idea that I certainly want to keep in mind. If you are not enjoying yourself and don't laugh very often, this can be an invitation to evaluate how you are living.

Questions for Reflection

- If you have fears of failing, what do you think would be helpful for you in dealing with them?
- Do you have a support group to help you put your difficulties into perspective?

Self-Doubt and High Expectations

Jamie Bludworth, PhD

When I was an undergraduate student, I took a course with a professor who had the reputation of a real taskmaster. I was intimidated by this person. He expected excellence from his students, and this motivated me to produce my best work. Over time I learned that he was approachable and cared about me as a person. He mentored me regarding career decisions and encouraged me to pursue a PhD at a time when I was less than self-confident. He helped me to overcome self-doubt by placing the graduate school application process in its appropriate context. I eventually accepted an offer of admission to my top-choice program and moved out of state to start life as a graduate student.

I was so nervous the first day of my doctoral program that I nearly lost my breakfast when I sat down for my first class. Again I was faced with a professor who had very high standards and was highly respected in the field. I thought I had gotten over being intimidated by professors, but here was the old feeling of uncertainty again. This time I "knew" I could never do anything that would be good enough for this guy. I had heard that first-year doctoral students had actually been reduced to tears when presenting their research proposals to him.

Toward the end of the first semester I presented my first research proposal in his class. He destroyed it. By the end of the presentation I had sweat beading off my forehead. Afterward, he pulled me aside and said something that I will never forget: "You are not your ideas. When you can truly get that my feedback to you is not a personal attack, but rather a critique of ideas, you will be able to *respond* to reviews from editors and feedback from clinical supervisors rather than react. You can do this." The exchange was warm and caring; I had found another mentor. That first bit of advice served me well throughout my career as a doctoral student in psychology.

When I finally sat for the national licensing exam for psychologists, I thought back on the more than 7 years that had led up to that pivotal day. Inside the nervousness and anticipation about taking the final step to becoming a psychologist, I became aware of how grateful I was to my wife. She had carried me on her back while I fretted over pleasing my clinical supervisors or tried to learn structural equation modeling. She had taken every step with me and demonstrated remarkable endurance, loving kindness, and a willingness to hold my feet to the fire when I wanted to give up. She had supported me in every way, and the recognition of her support calmed me when it came time to answer the first question on that unholy exam.

I now practice as a licensed psychologist at a fast-paced university counseling center, providing individual therapy, group therapy, psychosocial assessment, community outreach, after-hours crisis intervention, and consultation to the broader university community. I also have the great pleasure of providing clinical supervision to master's students and doctoral-level trainees. In my role as clinical supervisor, I often find myself thinking back to what it has been like to have had mentors who challenged me and held me to high standards while also respecting and believing in me as a person and as a professional. I strive to provide to the trainees I supervise the same combination of challenge, support, and structure that has been so instrumental in my career journey. This often looks like helping them be with their uncertainty about their clinical choices and using my own experience as a possible example of how they might approach the ambiguity of the task with which they are faced.

The best thing I ever did in my journey to becoming a career psychologist was to seek mentors who would push me to move past my self-imposed limitations. I chose mentors who initially scared me, and I learned that they weren't scary. It was I who was scared. It had nothing to do with them. To this day, my mentors seem always to call me to be better than I believe I can be. They push me to move outside my comfort zone and support me in navigating unfamiliar territory. As I gain more experience as a supervisor and mentor, I am learning that my trainees also push me to grow into a larger view of myself. The growth in these relationships is reciprocal. For these things I am grateful.

∾

Commentary

One of the lessons that most stands out for me with Jamie is how mentors can provide us with both the support and challenge to move outside our comfort zone and to take the risk of choosing to explore the unknown. Jamie certainly followed this advice from several of his mentors, and he was able to create a unique professional path that he would not have envisioned when he began his undergraduate studies. The role that Jamie's wife played in keeping him focused on his journey demonstrates how critical it is to have support from family members in meeting and coping with what may seem like Herculean tasks. Certainly his mentor in the doctoral program challenged him not to let his fear of writing a research proposal get in his way of doing quality work. As a relatively new professional, Jamie is giving back to others through his work at a university counseling center.

Questions for Reflection

- What lessons from Jamie's story might help you?
- How willing are you to move out of your comfort zone?

- Do you ask family members to encourage you in pursuing your dreams?
- If you allow professors or supervisors to intimidate you, what can you do to put your fears into perspective?
- Have any of your teachers or mentors called upon you to be better than you believe you can be?

Take Advantage of Your Opportunities

Galo Arboleda, MSW

In my position as a court mediator, I have had the opportunity to learn about family law and its procedures. I help parents come to an agreement regarding a parenting plan for their children and help them devise a custody arrangement that is in the best interests of the minor children. As a child custody investigator, I interview the parents, interview collaterals, interview the children (if age appropriate), and review police reports and social services reports (if applicable). Then I write a report with an evaluation and recommendations of what type of custody arrangement the parents should have with their children. The job can be stressful, but it is rewarding because I can be the voice of the children involved in the dispute.

I have an opportunity to educate the parents on how their divorce or separation will affect their children. I explain the major adjustments the children will face pertaining to a new home, a new school, and not having both parents in the home. I inform the parents they can help their children adjust to these changes by maintaining a mature and respectful coparenting relationship with each other. Most important, I try to have the parents discuss what is in the best interests of their children.

I met my current supervisor at a professional conference, and he informed me that a position was available. A few months later I applied and was fortunate enough to be hired. This taught me how important it is to network with other professionals in the field at every available opportunity.

Prior to working with the court, I was a counselor at a nonprofit agency for approximately 7 years, working with individuals, children, families, and groups. I facilitated mandated groups for child abuse, domestic violence, parenting, anger management, and substance abuse treatment. Working with mandated group participants is challenging but also can be rewarding. When working with individuals who are forced to do something against their will, I often encountered resistance.

When clients begin the group, they may not be ready to take responsibility for abusing their spouse, children, or drugs and instead blame everyone else for their current situation. To work effectively with this population, I have found that I must be assertive in helping clients redirect their lives. My task is to get them to focus on what they have done and begin to take responsibility for their actions.

One positive aspect of facilitating mandated groups is having the opportunity to help people view their situation from a different perspective. In working with the batterer's intervention group, my goal was to help the individuals in the group see the situation through the eyes of the victim. I also had the opportunity to work with a large number of Spanish-speaking clients, which I found to be very rewarding, as I am Latino. It was fulfilling to be able to educate these clients about the therapeutic experience. What I truly enjoy and find satisfying is being able to interact with so many different individuals from different races, ethnicities, socioeconomic statuses, and life experiences.

I found that I have had to motivate myself and not wait for others to motivate me. I like to challenge myself to try new activities and experiences. However, I have had to challenge my fear and not allow it to control my thoughts and decisions. Self-doubt has also been an obstacle I have had to learn to control. I now challenge those thoughts of fear and self-doubt and ask myself, "What is the worst that can happen?"

I have had to learn to discover my voice and use it. Growing up I was very shy and quiet and would not express my thoughts and feelings. When I began my undergraduate studies, I didn't take advantage of the resources that were available to me. At the time I didn't have the assertiveness skills to ask for guidance and support. Eventually I began speaking in class and asking for help that I knew was necessary to achieve success. By taking these steps, I learned that I had the ability to express myself. Most important, I realized that if I didn't speak up for myself, nobody else would.

I would encourage those of you who are in graduate programs to take advantage of your resources. The professionals you will be working with at school and at your placements have a wealth of information to offer you, and they are willing to share their experience and knowledge if you challenge yourself and ask them questions. Meet with your professors during their office hours, and express your thoughts and opinions in class. Allow yourself to have a voice, and learn to express yourself. I hope you take full advantage of the position you are in to obtain a quality higher education.

∽

Commentary

Galo's story illustrates the importance of networking and learning to ask for the help you need to succeed. Like so many others, Galo had to push himself to find his voice and to use it. During his youth, Galo was not encouraged to express his thoughts or feelings, and it took some doing for him to begin expressing himself. A lesson he learned was that if he did not speak up for himself, others would not do this for him.

Galo facilitated and found it satisfying to interact with diverse client populations. If you were to work in a nonprofit community agency with involuntary clients, consider what this would be like for you, and the possible challenges you would expect to face. As you think about your future work, assess the knowledge, skills, life experiences, and personal characteristics you will need to work effectively with a diverse range of clients.

Questions for Reflection

- Do you take full advantage of the opportunities that are available to you? Have you been willing to do the networking that could enable you to achieve your goals?
- To what degree do you allow yourself to have a voice and use it?
- If you are currently a student, what can you do to become even more actively involved in your education?

I Wish I Had Been Mentored More!

Valerie Russell, PhD

Providing supervision and assisting in the mentoring process of doctoral- and master's-level interns has been a particularly rewarding part of my career. In addition, working with involuntary clients has provided meaning in my professional life. It is interesting for me to reflect on why I chose to become a therapist in the first place and why I have gravitated toward mentoring interns and working with such a challenging population. Perhaps, as Freud would suggest, answers to these questions can be found in part in the formative years of my childhood.

My younger brother Ben, who was born with a developmental disability and spent the first half of his life in an institutional setting, has been one of the most influential figures in my life. I attribute the underpinnings of my interest (desire) in helping others to my feelings of powerlessness at being unable to "help" my brother. In my youth I often visited the institution where my brother lived, and I remember feeling a combination of confusion and compassion toward these unusual "patients" who were cut off from the rest of society. I also felt a sense of curiosity about the people who worked with them. I expressed my interest in the helping professions as a future career choice to my second-grade teacher. "I want to help others," was my reply to Mrs. Phillips's question "What do you want to do when you grow up?" Various volunteer experiences throughout my adolescence were rewarding and served to fuel my interest in choosing the helping professions as a future career.

As an undergraduate psychology student choosing my first clinical internship population, I was not interested in working with the developmentally disabled, as I had too many raw nerves associated with my brother. Perhaps with my brother in mind, however, I was drawn toward working with adolescent males. My clients were similar to my brother in that they lived in a residential facility, separated from the rest of society. They were different from my brother, however, in that they were not developmentally disabled; rather, they were incarcerated as a result of having been arrested for various infractions.

Choosing to work with adjudicated adolescent males was an eye-opening experience for me. It introduced me, a Caucasian female who had grown up in an intact white-collar household, to the very different lifestyle typically experienced by my young charges. It helped me understand how the cards you are dealt as a child can play a crucial role in shaping your future. Had the circumstances of these young men's lives been different, perhaps they would have been preparing for their SATs rather than struggling to complete their GEDs. This rewarding experience was the impetus for my future interest in working with involuntary populations.

Once I entered graduate school, I chose a community mental health agency as my first practicum experience. It was here that I began working with adult court-mandated (involuntary) populations. I was able to draw from my clinical experience with adjudicated adolescent males and see that both experiences were rife with similarities. I also saw the potential for imparting change in a difficult population, the impact of which would be felt by the vast numbers of victims (both children and adult females). My interest in working with involuntary populations was solidified as a result of my experience at this agency. Today people oftentimes ask me how I can work with a population that many would shun, and I reply that I see myself as an advocate for women and children.

My interest in the helping professions developed at an early age, and my focus on working with involuntary populations seemed to follow a fairly straightforward path. But my journey toward graduate school and my eventual profession as a clinical psychologist in a community mental health setting was anything but direct. It was long-winding and circuitous, much like a sailboat tacking to the left and then to the right, interrupted by many stops and starts along the way, and depending on the capricious nature of the wind. The critical missing ingredient that stands out for me as I reflect on my overall academic experience was the absence of positive and meaningful mentoring experiences.

One undesirable experience that significantly affected my academic focus occurred when I took an Introduction to Psychology course my first semester in college with the intention of majoring in psychology. When my psychology teacher began asking me out on dates, I quickly became disenchanted with psychology and switched my major to business. It wasn't until 15 years later, while working in a financially rewarding but personally unfulfilling job in corporate America, that I began to contemplate resuming my study of psychology, accompanied by the thought of graduate school.

As a returning undergraduate psychology student, I had the energy, drive, and intellect to embark on this new and exciting academic quest, but I sorely lacked information and direction. For one thing, it became apparent to me that a schism existed between research psychologists and clinical psychologists. I remember a particularly unpleasant experience when I asked for a letter of recommendation for a clinical graduate program from a professor I had been assisting for the past year. He lambasted the clinical psychology profession and made it clear he thought I was making a terrible mistake to study clinical psychology. Even though I was no longer an impressionable young coed and knew I was not interested in pursuing a career as a researcher, this was still a damaging experience for me. My sense of self-worth suffered, and I began questioning my desire to become a clinician as opposed to a researcher. If there ever was a time when I needed someone to talk with about my confusion, that was the time!

I eventually muddled through my confusion and entered a graduate clinical program. My belief that my struggles were behind me and that it would be smooth sailing from then on couldn't have been further from the truth. I worked with four dissertation chairs before finally completing my dissertation: Two were fired from the university and a third one died. So much for the idea of having an academic role model to provide consistent mentoring throughout my graduate school experience! In addition, the support that might be expected from one's cohort was unfortunately undermined by the fiercely competitive nature of our particular group. I found myself once again craving support from faculty and peers that seemed to be unavailable.

Although these examples stand out in my mind as damaging, painful, and discouraging, they have unwittingly played a role in igniting my passion for mentoring others. It's somewhat analogous to those wounded parents who develop their parenting style based on what their parents didn't do for them, as opposed to what they did do for them. What I didn't get in preparation for my profession has led to what I now try to provide to others.

My lack of mentoring during my academic career has prompted me to actively seek out mentors as a developing professional, and I have had the good fortune to develop rewarding and enriching relationships with positive role models since completing graduate school. I certainly could have used better mentoring while preparing for my own career, but I find it fulfilling to pass along to others what I have learned on the path I took.

∼

Commentary

Valerie's story shows the power that a lack of mentoring can sometimes have on a person's desire to strive for excellence. Even in her doctoral program there was a lack of a cooperative spirit among her peers. Instead, she had to deal with competition and lack of support from both her peers and the faculty. It is striking to me that her lack of mentoring from others did not kill her spirit. My guess is that many of you who are reflecting on Valerie's story can point to a number of your own negative mentoring experiences and encounters with negative role models. You cannot change the reality of negative experiences in your past, but like Valerie you can change how you interpret these experiences and how they continue to influence you today.

Questions for Reflection

- What are some elements of Valerie's story that most catch your attention? What lessons can you apply from her story to your own journey?
- In what ways would you want to mentor others, either similar to or different from how you were mentored?

- If you wished for better mentoring, what would you want to give to others that you did not get?

The Hidden Gifts of Graduate School

Mary Jane Ford, MS

Even though it has been only 3 years since I received my master's degree in counseling, graduate school seems like another world. The difference between learning about counseling and experiencing clients every week continues to surprise me. I have completed all but 50 of my required 3,000 internship hours, and when I pass the state licensing exam I will feel that I have worked very hard to become a therapist. It is a long road, and many times along the way I have wondered whether the end is worth the effort. However, I love the work, and in the final analysis that is enough for me. When considering what helped me through graduate school and working as an intern, several thoughts come to mind.

Make Friends at School

I was 47 years old when I entered graduate school, and I was among the oldest students. But in my first semester, I was lucky enough to meet two women who were near my age. By the end of our 4 years in the program, the three of us had taken nearly every class together. We studied together, we laughed and cried and shared disappointments, and we celebrated success. More important, we became friends. Although each of us has taken a different path since graduation, we stay in contact and try to make time to renew our connections. I am not sure that I would have persevered through graduate school without the support of peers who understood my frustrations and encouraged me as I encouraged them. Certainly having friends at school helped me to enjoy the experience more fully.

Reach Out to Instructors and Supervisors

While attending school to obtain my undergraduate degree, I often observed other students seeking out instructors as mentors. I avoided doing this and adopted a strategy of remaining aloof and independent. I regret not extending myself, as I am sure I could have learned much from those who have been in the counseling field for many years. Fortunately, I have not repeated my mistakes when interacting with supervisors. I have made a point of staying in touch with supervisors whom I admire and respect, and I know they have much to teach me. It is through supervisors that I have been able to make connections that have led to jobs and internship placements.

Be Prepared to Sacrifice

Graduate school is expensive. Working as an intern does not pay very much, and it is easy to become discouraged about money. Before entering graduate school, I worked in the accounting field and earned a reliable, steady paycheck. Becoming a therapist often requires working many hours for little or no pay. Clients do not stay in therapy forever, and cancellations are common. Being a therapist is full of economic uncertainty, particularly if you pursue private practice. Without the financial support of my husband, I could not have completed my internship hours in 3 years. I have found myself working for close to minimum wage just to accumulate hours. I do not believe that graduate school does enough to prepare students for the economic reality of being an intern, particularly because many students are also faced with paying back student loans upon graduation.

Be Open to Serendipity

While in graduate school, I vowed that I would not work in the field of substance abuse. I had no desire to work with addiction. When it came time to select a field placement, I had my heart set on working in a community counseling center. I ended up working at a residential treatment center for intravenous drug users, and that became my favorite internship placement. I was allowed to conduct groups, I had clients for one-on-one sessions, and I was able to see most clients weekly for the entire length of their stay in this 6-month treatment program. Most important, I received supervision from a brilliant psychologist who had 20 years of experience working with clients suffering with personality disorders and attachment issues. I was exposed to many challenging clients but received amazing support both emotionally and academically. My role as a therapist was changed by this experience, particularly when it came to setting boundaries and having the expectation that I would "change" a client.

Had I been stubborn in my refusal to work in the field of addiction, I never would have met the supervisor who has most influenced my style and conceptual beliefs about therapy. In addition to being guided by a talented supervisor, I was introduced to other agencies and community organizations that helped me obtain the intern hours I needed working with children. As I continue working toward my licensing goal, I will not ignore the chance encounters that sometimes change my path.

Stay Connected

Many times in graduate school I would hear professors warn that being a therapist can be a lonely and isolating experience. I have now experienced what they were saying. Never have my therapist friends been more important. In most professions one can go home and vent or celebrate the workday with family. Therapy requires confidentiality, which makes talking about clients to others unethical. Even if I took great pains to disguise the identity of clients, friends and family do not really understand the need I have to explore the motivations and strengths of my clients. It has been my experience that getting together with other therapists is helpful. I try to have dinner at least once a month with a group of therapists to process our own feelings of success, inadequacy, frustration, and joy. I feel so much less alone knowing that my colleagues struggle with many of the same thoughts and feelings that I have.

Allow Yourself to Be Inspired

Early in graduate school I began to notice that if I was interested in something I worked harder, retained the information, and had less stress about passing the class. I feel the same way about working with clients. I look forward to the moments when clients teach me something about what it is like to be them. Although I like being the person who knows what to do and continue to give too much advice, I am a better therapist when I let my clients give me direction about their journey.

Mentoring also involves inspiration. My struggle has always been to let go and let another guide me. To the extent that I can make room for another point of view, I can allow myself to be mentored and thus be inspired. The best mentors I have known have had the ability to point me in the direction that most interests me. They have been available but not hovering, encouraging but not patronizing. Mostly they have had passion; so much passion that it overflows and invites one to participate. That is the kind of mentor I would want as well as the kind of mentor I would want to be.

〜

Commentary

At age 47 Mary Jane was employed in the accounting field and doing well financially, yet she embarked on graduate studies so that she could become a counselor. She identifies passion as something that her best mentors had in common. There are several key lessons in the journey that Mary Jane took that probably apply to many of you. As you read her story, I hope you will consider the degree to which you have developed friendships as a support system to help you persist in your goals, especially during difficult times. Mary Jane's story offers lessons for all of us regarding the advantages of remaining open to working with various client populations.

I especially like Mary Jane's comments on allowing yourself to be inspired by clients and mentors. Her best mentors were passionate individuals who provided her with direction, were available, offered inspiration, and encouraged her.

Questions for Reflection

- Who have been your best mentors, and what qualities did they possess? How did these mentors influence you?
- From your contact with mentors, what did you learn about being a mentor to others?

Concluding Comments

The personal stories in this chapter demonstrate how important it is to find people who can serve mentoring functions as you follow your passions. Several graduate students and new professionals discussed how their friends, family members, and peers served as mentors and kept them focused on their professional path. They also acknowledged their commitment to giving back to others as a way of paying a debt of gratitude for what others had given to them.

As a way to bring together some of these ideas, I want to ask you to consider that you and I are in a mentoring relationship. Imagine the kind of professional career that you would most desire. This may not be easy because you might not allow yourself to see all the possibilities. I encourage you to search for and identify your passion in life. What really matters to you? What is it that you most want to achieve and accomplish? What legacy would you want to create? How do you want to use the unique talents you have? In what ways would you most like to help others? If you could imagine any kind of career that you might carve out, what would this look like before you retire?

If you ask me for recommendations about how to successfully navigate a graduate program and your career path, I might be willing to make some suggestions. However, before giving you suggestions, I would want to know what kind of advice you have already heard or given to yourself. Here are a few messages for you to consider from my own mentoring experiences:

- Don't strive to copy anyone else's style; rather, experiment and create your own unique style of helping that fits you.
- Follow your heart and know that you can trust your intuition.
- Although you may learn lessons from your mentor, put these lessons through your own filter.
- Be open to assistance and support from many different sources.
- Ask for help when you need it, and be assertive in asking for what you need in your mentoring relationship.
- Seek out multiple sources for mentoring, including your peers, friends, and family members. Don't underestimate what you can get from others in your program.
- If you have your sights set on graduate school, be willing to do the research necessary to select the right kind of program for you.
- Be willing to examine your fears, doubts, and negative self-messages.
- Be willing to stretch your boundaries by moving outside your comfort zone.
- Take risks, both personally and professionally, and see what this might bring you.
- Ask yourself where you can best put your unique talents to work and where you can make the greatest contribution.
- Develop self-discipline, be willing to work hard, and don't give up when the road is rough.
- Find a group of supportive people to offer you encouragement when you are inclined to give up.
- Regardless of where you are on your academic or career path, look for ways to teach others what you have learned.
- Network with peers, reach out to instructors and supervisors, and make connections that can lead to internship placements and jobs.
- Realize that you will probably have to make financial sacrifices during graduate school and as a new professional.
- Give thought to what kind of mentoring you want for yourself and the kind of mentor you want to be to others.

You may be interested in learning more about the process of being a mentor and what this entails. I highly recommend two books as being among the best available presentations on mentoring. In *On*

Being a Mentor: A Guide for Higher Education Faculty (Johnson, 2007), the author explores topics such as why mentoring matters, what functions mentors perform, the mentoring relationship, and the ethical mentor. In *The Elements of Mentoring* (Johnson & Ridley, 2008), the authors identify what excellent mentors do and the skills required of mentors, discuss personal traits of excellent mentors, focus on establishing and maintaining the mentoring relationship, and address matters pertaining to the integrity of mentors. This is a concise and readable guide for both new and seasoned mentors.

Chapter Four
How I Developed My Personal Approach to Counseling

Introduction

Let us consider how theory fits with practice, with emphasis on developing a theoretical framework that is personally compatible. Much of my writing has focused on helping students understand the basic concepts of the contemporary theories of counseling so they can apply them to actual practice. I have come to view theory as a road map that provides a context for understanding client behavior, knowing where the therapist and client are going, and making sense of what therapists are doing in their counseling practice. Attempting to practice without having an explicit theoretical rationale is like trying to build a house without a set of blueprints. The foundation of a house needs to be sturdy and strong to support the rooms. Theory is the foundation for your work in the counseling process, providing you with a blueprint that gives direction to what you do and say. If you cannot draw on theory as a framework to support your interventions, you may flounder in your attempts to help people change. Theory is not a rigid set of structures that prescribes what and how you should function professionally but a road map with general directions.

When I began my work as a counselor, I asked myself "What theory best fits who I am?" and "How can I develop my own framework and use it in my work setting?" In this chapter I describe the experiences that led to my understanding and appreciation of the different theories. One of my areas of specialization for about 38 years has been teaching the theory and practice of counseling, writing a series of books applying theory to practice, and in recent years making CD-ROM and DVD programs demonstrating an integrative approach to counseling practice. I will share the highlights of this journey, which led to the evolution of my integrative approach to counseling practice.

My First Opportunity to Teach Theories and Techniques of Counseling

When I began a doctoral program in counseling at the University of Southern California in 1962, I took two courses devoted to "counseling procedures" but no comprehensive course on theories of counseling. I was exposed to only two major approaches to counseling: the directive approach and nondirective counseling. That was the extent of my formal course work dealing with counseling theories and procedures. Clearly, I had to do extensive reading in the various theories of counseling after graduating from the doctoral program.

In my early teaching years at CSUF, I contributed to the development of an undergraduate human services program. The faculty decided this major needed a course in Theories and Techniques of Counseling. A course proposal was written that successfully went through the curriculum committee. In 1973 when I began to teach this course on a regular basis, there were few textbooks available that described the current theories and their practical uses. Two of these books were *Theories of Counseling and Psychotherapy* (Patterson, 1973) and *Current Psychotherapies* (Corsini, 1973), which was an edited volume in which a key person from each of the theories contributed a chapter in his or her area of expertise. Because I wanted something that expressed my thoughts, I wrote articles on each of the theories I was teaching at that time: psychoanalytic approach, existential-humanistic approach, client-centered approach, Gestalt therapy, transactional analysis, behavior therapy, rational emotive therapy, and reality therapy. These articles contained a summary of the key concepts and some major techniques associated with each of the theories, along with my personal commentary on what I found most useful about each approach. I don't think I intended to write a book on counseling theory at that time, but I wanted students to be able to read my summary and critique of the theories before we discussed them in class. In preparation for teaching the theories course, I did a great deal of reading on all the theories and attended many workshops and conferences to get a better grasp of how these theories could be applied to practice. My study of theories of counseling really began *after* I had completed my doctoral program, and this study continues to this day.

Overview of the Theories of Counseling

In addition to my research, I sought out colleagues and mentors who could deepen my knowledge of the different theoretical orientations. In this section I identify specific aspects of each theory that I value most and mention some people who were especially influential in the development of my theoretical orientation. My aim is not to teach you about these theories but to describe what I have taken from each theory in designing my own counseling perspective along with noting some significant influences that shaped my therapeutic style. Many standard textbooks present a detailed discussion of the key concepts and techniques of each of these theoretical models; among them are *Current Psychotherapies* (Corsini & Wedding, 2008), *Systems of Psychotherapy: A Transtheoretical Analysis* (Prochaska & Norcross, 2010), and *Theories of Psychotherapy and Counseling: Concepts and Cases* (Sharf, 2008).

Psychoanalytic Therapy

My own childhood experiences have shown me how important it is to understand how our past influences our present personality. My friend and colleague Michael Russell, who is steeped in the psychoanalytic tradition, has taught me how this approach has been transformed since Freud's time. Michael has been instrumental in broadening my understanding of the approach, especially in calling to my attention the newer formulations of relational psychoanalysis. From this perspective, I especially value the attention given to understanding the role of transference and countertransference in the psychotherapeutic relationship. This model provides a unique way of understanding how resistance is a basic part of therapy and how to deal with resistance therapeutically. I tell my students that they may not use many psychoanalytic techniques in their work as counselors, but they can learn to think in psychoanalytic terms and conceptualize a case from this valuable perspective.

Adlerian Therapy

There is much from the Adlerian approach that I greatly value. Perhaps Adler's central contribution to the field is the influence his thinking has had on the development of many other therapy systems. As I have studied the contemporary theories, many of Adler's notions have reappeared with different nomenclature. I owe a debt to my friend and colleague Jim Bitter, who has mentored me in the Adlerian way of thinking about counseling practice and has been instrumental in my understanding of practical ways to apply these concepts to individual, group, and family therapy. The Adlerian approach has given me an appreciation of how thinking influences feeling and actions. I am intrigued by the notion of exploring one's lifestyle to discover patterns in one's life.

Years ago when Jim and I were teaching at CSUF, he did a lifestyle assessment with me, with a small group of our students observing the process. Actually going through this process was revealing to me and demonstrated the value of this approach to assessment much more than simply reading about lifestyle assessments. This reinforced my belief in the value of involving students in a personal way in learning about theories of counseling.

Studying the Adlerian approach has convinced me that our past does not determine how we presently behave; rather, it is our striving toward the future that motivates us. We can best be understood by noting goals that we are pursuing. When I think of my own development from childhood to adulthood, I see how Adlerian ideas of interpreting my early experiences within my family of origin shed light on my present behavior. Adler's ideas on social interest—going outside ourselves and striving to make society a better place—hold special significance for me. I agree with the Adlerian notion that happiness is not based on individual achievements but is rooted in our connection with others. In many ways, the process of mentoring fits within the concept of social interest.

For a comprehensive overview of Adlerian therapy in contemporary practice, I recommend *Adlerian Therapy: Theory and Practice* (Carlson, Watts, & Maniacci, 2006).

Existential Therapy

My interest in existential psychology, which began in graduate school, has developed into the foundation of my theory. What draws me toward this approach is its emphasis on choice, freedom, responsibility, and self-determination. For much of my early years, I did not trust that I could be the author of my life. Freedom of choice was associated with anxiety, which I wanted to avoid. Instead of looking inward and accepting responsibility for making choices in my life, I looked for external authorities to tell me how to live. My personal journey has shown me how basic the key existential themes are in understanding myself. Existential notions that I find especially valuable, both personally and professionally, include the following: meaning in life is not static, for we re-create ourselves through our projects; anxiety goes along with the freedom to choose our way and needs to be explored, not eliminated; and the reality of death gives significance to life and is the source of finding meaning in life. I appreciate the fact that the existential approach is not based on a set of techniques. As an existential therapist, I can draw on techniques from many therapy systems, as long as I remember that what is primary is understanding the client's world. One of the best sources for information on the existential approach is *Existential Psychotherapy* (Yalom, 1980). A concise and readable book on a range of existential topics is *The Gift of Therapy* (Yalom, 2003).

Person-Centered Therapy

My respect for Carl Rogers and his contributions to the field of counseling and psychotherapy dates back to a course in counseling procedures that was part of my doctoral studies. Through Carl Rogers's writings I came to appreciate what it means to trust in the client's capacity to provide the direction of counseling. Listening carefully to the client and following his or her lead is essential. My job is to provide a climate that will allow clients to tell their story. Rogers taught me that the quality of the therapeutic relationship is at the heart of counseling. The core therapeutic conditions of the therapist showing respect for the client, assuming a nonjudgmental position, being genuine, and showing empathy are basic qualities that must be present in any therapeutic relationship, regardless of the therapist's theoretical orientation. I have come to realize that the basic attitudes of a person-centered therapist have relevance for creating an effective relationship.

A few years ago I was fortunate in meeting Carl's daughter, Natalie Rogers, at a humanistic psychology conference. I was giving a keynote address on my perspective on humanistic psychology, and Natalie was in the audience. We talked for a while, and she graciously agreed to review my chapter on person-centered therapy in my theory book. Although she shares the philosophy of the person-centered approach with her father, Natalie believes that clients also can be helped in their personal journey through person-centered expressive arts therapy. She has taught me how the expressive arts can be effectively incorporated into a person-centered approach to group work.

If you want to learn more about the influence of Carl Rogers on the counseling profession, I recommend *The Life and Work of Carl Rogers* (Kirschenbaum, 2009). For more on person-centered expressive arts, see *The Creative Connection: Expressive Arts as Healing* (N. Rogers, 1993).

Gestalt Therapy

Both Marianne and I have had the good fortune of participating in workshops led by Dr. Erv Polster and the late Dr. Miriam Polster, two key leaders in Gestalt therapy but each with a different therapeutic style. This taught me that there is great variability within a given theory, even among the masters of a theory. At one of the Polsters' workshops, Marianne said to Erv, "You don't sound like a Gestalt therapist or Fritz Perls." He replied, "Thanks for the compliment. Fritz was my mentor, and I had to find my own way. While a theory provides structure, we each have to create our own therapeutic style." The Polsters influenced Marianne and me in gaining a deeper understanding of ways to create an effective therapist–client relationship. The personal way of being exhibited by both Miriam and Erv demonstrated that effective therapy entails much more than using techniques. The Polsters agreed to do a 1-day workshop at which they each demonstrated their own unique style as Gestalt practitioners through live demonstrations. The students were impressed with how they blended their presence and human touch while working with volunteer clients in a highly creative manner. The Polsters taught us how therapists with the same theoretical orientation frequently have diverse styles of applying the theory to working with clients. They reconfirmed my belief that what counts is the counselor's presence, which is fundamental to establishing contact with a client. Through my study of Gestalt therapy I have come to value the power of being as fully present as possible with a client.

The Gestalt approach is characterized by many key concepts that can be usefully blended into other theoretical orientations. Gestalt therapy techniques encourage clients to bring early memories and feelings pertaining to both past and present events to center stage. I like the way Gestalt therapists speak of experiments rather than prefabricated techniques. Experiments are unique to what is happening in the context of a therapeutic session, and they are tailored to helping a client gain insight, trying on a new behavior to see how it fits, or taking what the client is learning in the therapy office into his or her daily life. In collaboration with the therapist, clients devise experiments that can lead to decisions that change the course of their lives. Gestalt therapy utilizes experiments to move clients from *talking about* to taking action. There is a creative spirit of suggesting, inventing, and carrying out experiments aimed at increasing awareness. What I especially value with this approach is the emphasis given to the relationship between client and therapist, which is shared with the existential and person-centered approaches.

A classic book that I highly recommend is *Gestalt Therapy Integrated: Contours of Theory and Practice* (Polster & Polster, 1973). Another useful resource for learning more about Gestalt therapy is *Gestalt Therapy: History, Theory, and Practice* (Woldt & Toman, 2005).

Psychodrama

I was introduced to psychodrama in my mid-30s when I attended a workshop on this therapeutic modality. In the spirit of the psychodrama approach, I learned about this form of therapy through my personal involvement as a participant. Psychodrama and Gestalt therapy share some of the same attributes. Both therapies are action oriented, focus on the here and now, place value on the therapeutic relationship, encourage clients to enact life situations rather than talk about them, and emphasize experiential learning. A motto in psychodrama is "Don't tell me, show me!" Using psychodrama, the client dramatizes past, present, or anticipated life situations and roles to gain a deeper understanding, explore feelings and achieve emotional release, and develop behavioral skills. Significant events are enacted to help members in a psychodrama group to connect with unrecognized and unexpressed feelings, to provide a channel for the full expression of these feelings and attitudes, and to broaden the roles that they might play in everyday life.

When I was a participant in a psychodrama, I experienced how intense it can be to bring a past problem into the here and now and explore facets of a life situation. For me, there was a big difference between trying to analyze a problem intellectually and actually experiencing the situation. This experiential work tends to result in both emotional and cognitive insight, which can lead to new behaviors. Through participating in psychodrama groups, attending psychodrama conferences and workshops and reading about the approach, I learned many useful techniques that I could apply in groups I was facilitating. I also saw how valuable role-playing techniques can be in my work as a counselor educator. Psychodrama concepts and techniques provide the basis for the integrative approach I use in group work.

I did not meet the founder of psychodrama, J. L. Moreno, but I have been fortunate in attending workshops presented by his wife and colleague, Zerka Toeman Moreno, who has played a key role in the development of psychodrama. She typifies a sense of presence, engagement, and creativity in her work with participants in her psychodramas. Observing her work in action and studying her writings have been influential in teaching me more about psychodrama. For more on Zerka's contributions, I highly recommend *The Quintessential Zerka: Writings by Zerka Toeman Moreno on Psychodrama, Sociometry and Group Psychotherapy* (Horvatin & Schreiber, 2006).

I have learned a great deal about psychodrama from Adam Blatner, a psychiatrist who has written extensively on the theoretical foundations and methods of psychodrama. In his workshops, Adam has highlighted the value of play, creativity, and spontaneity. Not only did I enjoy his workshop on play, but it showed me how play and humor can be effectively integrated into intense personal work in a group. Adam has worked closely with me for every revision of the psychodrama chapter in *Theory and Practice of Group Counseling* (Corey, 2008) and has generously offered suggestions for updating each edition. If you are interested in an introduction to psychodrama, see *Acting-In: Practical Applications of Psychodramatic Methods* (Blatner, 1996).

Recently, I was invited to give the keynote address at the annual conference for the American Society for Group Psychotherapy and Psychodrama in St. Louis. My talk dealt with ways that I use psychodrama from an integrative perspective and how psychodrama techniques can be incorporated into many other therapeutic systems. During this 3-day conference I attended several experiential workshops and was again impressed with the power of this approach and the willingness of participants to get personally involved. This conference reaffirmed my belief in the value of the philosophy underlying psychodrama and the usefulness of integrating concepts and techniques from this approach into other therapy orientations.

Cognitive Behavior Therapy

When I first studied behavior therapy in the 1970s, it was my least favorite approach because it seemed too structured and in some ways mechanistic. However, it is abundantly clear that cognitive behavior therapy (CBT) has broadened considerably since my early encounter with this model. Traditional behavior therapy has been greatly expanded to include what has been called the "third wave" of behavior therapy. My sense is that there are not many traditional behavior therapists today, as behavior therapy has made room for cognition and other nonobservable phenomena. New facets of CBT have emerged that emphasize considerations that would have been out of bounds at an earlier time. Some of these newer trends are mindfulness, acceptance, the therapeutic relationship, spirituality, values, meditation, and being in the present moment. In addition to reading about these recent developments, I have learned more about them by attending workshops at the Association for Behavioral and Cognitive Therapies conferences and at the Evolution of

Psychotherapy conferences. To learn more about the evolution of behavior therapy, I recommend reading *Contemporary Behavior Therapy* (Spiegler & Guevremont, 2010).

Presently, the cognitive behavioral approaches are most commonly used in working with diverse client populations in clinical settings. Under this general category are specific approaches such as behavior therapy, cognitive therapy, and rational emotive behavior therapy (REBT). With respect to cognitive therapy, I have been influenced by both Aaron Beck and Judith Beck. Attending presentations at conferences by Judith and Aaron Beck has taught me a great deal about the contributions of cognitive therapy and has brought their writings to life for me.

Albert Ellis, the founder of REBT, has had a significant influence on my thinking about therapy practice. Indeed, he was a mentor to me in learning about REBT. In his workshops he seemed to enjoy peppering his speech with four-letter words. He also had a reputation for being rather confrontational, abrasive, flamboyant, and eccentric, but I saw a side of Al that was often not noticed. When our daughter Heidi developed Type-1 diabetes, he wrote her a lengthy letter expressing his regret over hearing this news. He was a diabetic for 30 years, but he reassured Heidi with these words: "By using the philosophy of Rational Emotive Behavior Therapy to the hilt, I do very little whining, keep very busy, and enjoy life in a highly active manner. Similarly, I am sure you can do the same." He also admitted, "It is a royal pain in the ass having this condition!"

Marianne and our daughters dropped in to the Ellis Institute to see Al on a trip to New York, but he was off doing a workshop in another country. Marianne wrote him a note and joked that she and our daughters were deeply disappointed that he was not at the Institute, but they would try to get over this rejection! Al wrote to Marianne saying that he was sorry he wasn't available but asked them to drop by again if they found themselves in the neighborhood. He was attentive and responsive, and I had numerous delightful human exchanges with Al Ellis from the late 1970s until he died in 2007 at the age of 93.

Ellis was devoted to his work and to helping others learn about REBT, and he was not afraid to speak his mind. I invited him to present a daylong workshop at CSUF, and the students loved him and enjoyed his manner of presenting. As busy as he was, Al always made time to read the REBT chapter in each new edition of my theory book, and he was not shy about suggesting changes.

I respected Al's capacity to live by what he taught. He was certainly committed to the REBT way of life, especially as a way to deal with adversity, including coping with his many health problems well into his 90s. *Rational Emotive Behavior Therapy: It Works for Me—It Can Work for You* (Ellis, 2004) illustrates how he applied his theory to his own life. Most of what I learned about REBT came directly from contact with Al Ellis and his writings. I appreciated both him and his work and have incorporated many of his ideas into my personal life and my own style of counseling.

Although the cognitive behavioral approaches are quite diverse, they place thinking at the core of emotional and behavioral problems. My study of CBT has convinced me that if we change the way we think, we can also change our feelings and our behavior. I especially like the emphasis of CBT on a collaborative partnership between therapist and client. For change to come about, clients must assume an active role, both in the therapy office and in outside life. I also appreciate how homework can be designed collaboratively and how clients are expected to practice new skills in their daily lives.

For more on these subjects, see *Cognitive Therapy for Challenging Problems* (Beck, 2005) and *Rational Emotive Behavior Therapy: A Therapist's Guide* (Ellis & MacLaren, 2005).

Reality Therapy

I was initially introduced to reality therapy through the writings of its founder, William Glasser, and learned about this approach by attending many of Glasser's lectures and workshops. We also had a collaborative relationship, and he reviewed chapters I wrote on reality therapy. Like Al Ellis, Glasser was quite able to express his thoughts. I found his books easy to read and was able to glean ideas from each of them that I wanted to apply in my work with clients and students. Glasser did pioneering work in counseling, beginning in the mid-1960s, and he wrote in a way that appealed to counselors working with difficult-to-reach clients. He also influenced elementary and secondary school teachers and devoted considerable time to workshops for teachers and administrators who were interested in alternative forms of teaching and learning. Reality therapy is grounded on an existential philosophy, which I like. I value the basic notion of the need to assume personal responsibility for our feelings that reality therapy stresses. William Glasser accepted an invitation to present a 1-day workshop on reality therapy at CSUF, and by doing this he mentored students and faculty on ways to apply reality therapy to many counseling situations.

A colleague and friend, Robert Wubbolding, is Director for the Center for Reality Therapy in Cincinnati and also Director of Training for the William Glasser Institute. He has done a great deal to advance the development of reality therapy, and he presents workshops in the United States as well as around the world. Bob has had an even greater influence than Glasser did on my understanding of the practice of reality therapy. I have attended a number of Bob's workshops, and from this I have learned how to apply reality therapy concepts to many different kinds of counseling situations. In fact, Bob and his wife, Sandie, joined Marianne and me for a cruise in Alaska, and we spent countless hours discussing reality therapy on the deck while watching the ocean slide by beneath us. He has been most helpful not only as a teacher but also as a reviewer for everything I have written about reality therapy.

I appreciate the emphasis of reality therapy on focusing on what we are doing. This approach does not ignore the role of feelings or thinking but incorporates these aspects as a way of understanding behavior. Bob Wubbolding has shown me the importance of asking clients what they want, asking if what they are doing has a good chance of meeting their needs, and asking clients to evaluate their current behavior. If clients determine that what they are doing is not working for them, the reality therapist then helps them design an action plan and make a commitment to implementing their plan as a route to change. This emphasis is useful for any therapy, and I see value in using this framework as a basis for practice. I like the focus on what we are doing and our ability to control our actions. For a more detailed presentation of this approach, see *Reality Therapy for the 21st Century* (Wubbolding, 2000).

Feminist and Systemic Therapies

I included a discussion of issues pertaining to gender, culture, and family in my early years of teaching, but my main emphasis was on an individual perspective and on understanding models that could be applied to counseling individuals. Most of the individual counseling theories do not place a primary focus on the influence of systemic factors on the individual, and my knowledge of the importance of integrating systemic factors as a vital component of counseling practice was slim. A number of colleagues suggested ways to broaden my understanding, which led me to study feminist therapy, family therapy, multicultural perspectives, and postmodern approaches. Again, by attending conferences and workshops on these topics I gained a clearer understanding of how an individual's dysfunctional behavior grows out of the interactional units of the family, the community, and society. One of my colleagues from the University of New Orleans, Barbara Herlihy, has been instrumental in helping me gain a better understanding of the principles and applications of feminist therapy. Our collaboration resulted in a coauthored chapter on feminist therapy that is part of my theories of counseling book.

I came to appreciate the commitment of feminist therapists to actively breaking down the hierarchy of power in the therapeutic relationship. Therapists with a feminist orientation understand how important it is to become aware of typical gender role messages, and they are skilled in helping clients identify and challenge these messages. Both feminist and systemic therapies operate on the premise that an individual's problems cannot be understood by focusing solely on the individual's internal dynamics. Individuals are best understood within the context of relationships.

For a comprehensive treatment of feminist therapy, I recommend *Feminist Theories and Feminist Psychotherapies: Origins, Themes, and Diversity* (Enns, 2004) and *Feminist Therapy* (Brown, 2010). For an excellent overview of systemic therapies and the various theories of family therapy, I recommend *Theory and Practice of Family Therapy and Counseling* (Bitter, 2009).

Postmodern Approaches

I began including a chapter on the postmodern approaches to counseling in my theories book in 2005. Postmodernism is a philosophical movement across a variety of disciplines that critically examines many of the assumptions underlying established truths in society. The heart of the therapeutic process from the postmodern perspective involves identifying how societal standards and expectations are internalized by people in ways that result in narrowing their quality of life. Therapists with a postmodern orientation invite clients to think of themselves as being separate from their problems so that they do not adopt a fixed problem-oriented identity. With the assistance of a therapist, clients come to view their life stories from different perspectives and eventually create alternative life stories. What I particularly like about the postmodern therapies is the notion that clients know more about their lives than the therapist does. The therapist-as-expert is replaced by the client-as-expert. Working together, therapist and client collaborate on ways to open up a range of possibilities for present and future change. One of the best ways to create this collaborative therapeutic partnership is for therapists to show clients how clients can use the strengths and resources they already possess to find solutions. This therapy involves a movement from problem-talk to solution-talk. Attention is paid to what is working, and clients are encouraged to do more of this. I particularly like the emphasis on viewing people as being competent, resourceful, and oriented toward growth.

Attending workshops helped me understand that the postmodern therapies provided an alternative perspective to the traditional therapy models I had been writing about for years. I was fortunate enough to meet and develop relationships with Gerald Monk and John Winslade, both of whom are steeped in the postmodern tradition. We have had many fruitful discussions about the field of psychotherapy. I have been mentored through an association with many talented people over the course of my career. If you want to learn more about the postmodern perspective, I recommend *Narrative Therapy in Practice: The Archaeology of Hope* (Monk, Winslade, Crocket, & Epston, 1997) and *Narrative Counseling in Schools* (Winslade & Monk, 2007).

Writing a Textbook on the Theory and Practice of Counseling

Much of my writing has been devoted to helping students understand the basic concepts of the contemporary theories of counseling so they might be able to apply these concepts to actual practice. My emphasis in both writing and teaching is on the practical applications of the various theories. Creating materials for my classes led me toward a more formal writing career, and I learned a great deal from these projects.

Many years ago two executives from Brooks/Cole Publishing Company came to my office for a routine visit and asked if I was doing any writing. I quickly presented them with a copy of the articles I had created as handouts for my students and let them know I was excited about teaching Theories and Techniques of Counseling and would be open to publishing possibilities. We talked about their publication process, and they indicated I would hear from them soon. Almost a year later Claire Verduin, an acquisitions editor, called to apologize for the delayed response, saying she had just discovered my articles on a desk amid other papers. She expressed interest in a book contract because Brooks/Cole did not have a book on counseling theory and practice at that time. In 1975 I drove to Monterey, California, to meet with Claire Verduin and Terry Hendrix to talk about the process of translating a manuscript into a book. They said that before I submitted the final manuscript for the publication process, reviews would be necessary. This included both general reviews of the entire book and expert reviews by a leading person in each of the theories. Most of the reviews were positive and supportive, but a few reviewers gave some very harsh, critical, and discouraging feedback. Others thought my style of writing was too informal and not empirically sound. These negative reviews were difficult to hear, but I considered their specific criticisms and decided they had made some valid points.

An important lesson here is that critical reviews should not stop us from pursuing projects we believe have merit. It would have been easy to let discouragement get the best of me, but I continued to see the value of persistence, hard work, and self-discipline as a route to reaching my goals. I also learned to persist in the face of self-doubts. The editors I worked with had faith in the overall book and were supportive and helped me apply the comments of reviewers toward making this a better book. From these early experiences in writing, I learned that a textbook involves the collaborative efforts of many. In December 1975 I delivered the final manuscript; *Theory and Practice of Counseling and Psychotherapy* was published in 1977 and is now in its eighth edition (Corey, 2009c).

I have frequently been asked how I decided which theories to add over the various editions. Early on I felt that Adlerian therapy deserved a chapter of its own because Adler's ideas were visionary and his core concepts are found in many contemporary counseling models. Later I decided to add chapters for various cognitive behavioral approaches, feminist therapy, the postmodern approaches (solution-focused brief therapy and narrative therapy), and family systems therapy. I also gave increased attention to the movement toward psychotherapy integration. Prior to revising a new edition, my publisher and I conduct a survey of university professors to determine which theories they most want to include in their courses. The results of these surveys guide my choice of theories for the new edition of the book.

Developing the Theory and Practice of Counseling Course

I continued to experiment with various approaches to teaching the Theory and Practice of Counseling. Students were now using my theory textbook, so I did not see it as the best use of class time to lecture on the assigned readings. I did some lecturing on key concepts and practical applications of each theory, but I frequently used live demonstrations to illustrate my way of working with a "client" (a volunteer from the class) using a particular theoretical approach. This seemed to bring to life the readings and the discussions in class. I also made use of the Case of Stan, which has been in all eight editions of

Theory and Practice of Counseling and Psychotherapy. At times I would have a student "become Stan," and I would demonstrate how I would counsel him from the perspective of the particular theory we were studying that week. This gave students a glimpse of some ways of applying principles to an actual case. In small groups, students took turns "counseling Stan" for a few minutes, and they had the opportunity to process what it was like to be the counselor and the client.

Students had an opportunity to apply some of the ideas of each theory to themselves in small-group work in class. Rather than just learning about the theory, students spent some time in personal reflection and discussed with one another how each theory could be applied to their own concerns. For example, when learning about Adlerian concepts such as the family constellation, students were asked to share in a small group what they had learned from their family of origin and how this might be influencing them today.

Creating a Casebook for Counseling Practice

During the summer of 1980, my family and I went to Germany for 7 weeks, which we did most summers. I love to walk in the forests and on the many walking paths near my wife's hometown. While on one of these walks, I began to think about writing a book that would apply all the theories I discussed to a single case. This idea became a reality when *Case Approach to Counseling and Psychotherapy* (first edition) was published in 1982. I thought of common themes in the lives of many clients with whom I had worked and came up with a composite client who would illustrate the kinds of problems a client might bring to psychotherapy. As I was writing in Marianne's family courtyard, their neighbor Hans drove up to his entry gate on a tractor and began calling for his wife Ruth. His routine was to have Ruth open the large gate so he would not have to get off his tractor to open the gate himself. He called Ruth's name several times, and each time his voice escalated in volume. I decided then and there to name my fictitious client Ruth.

In this book, I wanted to show how I would work with Ruth from each of the theoretical perspectives that were featured in my theory book. During that summer most of the days were cold and rainy, which helped me stay focused and allowed me to write the first draft in 2 weeks. Marianne was a practicing marriage and family therapist who did a good deal of individual counseling, so I recruited her to read what I wrote each day. Marianne provided insightful comments that I incorporated into the manuscript, and she was especially helpful in providing a focus for the clinical work and for making sure that my work with this client was a realistic portrayal. She has been a vital part of this project from the day I first got the idea for the book to when I wrote the current edition many years later. In fact, Marianne has always played a significant role in the development of my books by reading drafts and providing ideas and feedback, even for those books we have not coauthored.

The first edition of this casebook had its limitations because I was the only therapist counseling Ruth, but it provided me with another tool for conceptualizing cases in my classes. In subsequent editions I invited experts in each theory to write about how they would work with Ruth from their theoretical orientation, and the seventh edition of *Case Approach to Counseling and Psychotherapy* (Corey, 2009b) has expanded considerably from the original version. This book retains my approach to counseling Ruth from the vantage point of each theory, but it has benefited from including the therapeutic styles of other contributors as well. In the latest edition, 26 colleagues, all of whom possess expertise in a particular theory, demonstrate techniques they would use when counseling Ruth. For some theories two experts present their style of counseling Ruth. For example, in the chapter on reality therapy William Glasser describes his perspective on Ruth and provides sample therapist–client dialogue to illustrate the key points of therapy sessions, and then Robert Wubbolding writes about his style of counseling Ruth as a reality therapist. I included two therapists to show that there is often great variation in therapeutic styles even among practitioners who share the same theoretical orientation. Collaborating with the 26 theorists and practitioners in my current casebook has been a great way for me to learn more about the nuances of each theory and about a multitude of therapeutic styles. These contributors have been mentors to me in understanding practical applications of therapy.

Reminiscing about the evolution of this particular book reminds me of how a project can develop over the years. The casebook was a simple idea that evolved into a comprehensive treatment of diverse ways of assessing and treating a single client. With all the counseling that Ruth has received from 26 different expert therapists and from me, you would think she would be cured by now! Sadly, she is still working through the life themes that brought her into therapy back in 1982! Years later while chatting with the real Ruth when I was in Germany, I told her how I came about borrowing her name for the main client in my book. She laughed and said she wanted some royalties, so I reached into my pocket and found one Euro and gave it to her for the use of her name, which delighted her.

My First Educational Video
on Integrative Counseling

The theory books that I developed all served a purpose, but one component was missing. I began thinking of the value of doing an educational video in which I could actually apply my therapeutic style in counseling Ruth. Robert Haynes, a colleague and friend, was producing educational video programs as a part of his work as director of professional education at a psychiatric hospital. Bob and I talked about the possibility of creating a video program that would involve me demonstrating an integration of various theoretical approaches in working with themes from Ruth's life. Once we determined that this was a worthwhile project, the next step was to find a person to role-play Ruth with me as her therapist. I asked a former graduate assistant, Lynn Henning, if she was interested in assuming the role of Ruth for this video program, and she was eager to participate. Although a great deal of preparation took place in advance of the filming, I did not want us to use a rehearsed script. Both Lynn and I tried to make our interactions as real as possible, even though my "client" was role-playing; we relied on improvisation to elaborate on themes we identified. We did have clear objectives and a general plan of what we wanted to demonstrate in each of the 13 counseling sessions, yet we wanted to create the space for spontaneity in these sessions. Some of these sessions included creating a therapeutic relationship, establishing therapy goals, understanding diversity, working with resistance, exploring how the past influences the present, and termination. The emphasis was on illustrating how I counseled Ruth by drawing on cognitive, emotive, and behavioral techniques in an integrative way.

We did the filming over a 4-day period in January 1995 with a full technical crew, a producer and director, and consultants. Everything went relatively smoothly during the counseling sessions and the process commentaries following each session. Toward the end of the last day I was to introduce the program. My prescribed lines were simple, yet I stumbled over each sentence again and again. The camera crew was growing exhausted, as were the director and producer. Try as I might, I just could not recite memorized sentences in a way that seemed natural. Once the filming was over, the work continued because the producer (Bob Haynes), the director (Tom Walters), Marianne, and I had the tedious job of editing 4 days of filming into a 1-hour educational video on integrative counseling. We eventually converted the program and expanded some commentaries, and it became *CD-ROM for Integrative Counseling* (Corey, with Haynes, 2005). Lynn Henning is now a licensed marriage and family therapist in private practice, and she recently earned a doctorate in psychoanalysis. She is a vibrant and enthusiastic woman with a rich personal and professional life. Although she convincingly played the role of Ruth, she is nothing like this character in her real life.

Doing this program taught me that creating an educational video involves as much work as writing a book. I learned how important preparation is, and I became aware of the importance of being flexible and dealing with the unexpected. Lynn and I worked well together, which calls to mind the importance of a good relationship, whether it is in an actual client–counselor relationship or when working together to film the counseling process. This video proved to be helpful for visual learners, and it was the forerunner for four other video programs on different aspects of counseling, three of which Marianne and I did in consultation with Bob Haynes and Tom Walters.

Making a DVD Program on Counseling Stan

Having successfully completed the Ruth video applying my integrative perspective, I was motivated to create a video in which I would counsel Stan (the central case in my theory book) demonstrating 11 different theoretical orientations. The Stan program also consisted of 13 separate "counseling sessions," and in each of these sessions I applied one or two selected techniques to illustrate a particular theory.

The idea for a video with Stan originated in the spring semester of 2000, when I invited one of my advanced undergraduate students, Jamie Bludworth, to coteach the Theory and Practice of Counseling course with me. Both he and I presented brief lectures on each of the theories, and we both facilitated small discussion groups aimed at helping students to personalize each theoretical approach. Each week Jamie became the client "Stan," and I counseled him utilizing the theory we were studying.

In 2006 I approached my publisher with a proposal for a DVD program with Stan, who would be role-played by Jamie. The publisher was interested in a different kind of program, one that would feature various therapists with different clients. Ed Neukrug was interested in this idea, and *Theories in Action: Counseling DVD* (Neukrug, 2008) was made featuring different therapists demonstrating counseling with different clients. I recommend Neukrug's video program for getting a sense of how various practitioners apply their respective approaches with diverse clients.

I had written about how therapists with various theoretical orientations might work with Stan, but I did not yet have a vehicle to show how I would apply each theory to my work with Stan. I wanted to demonstrate my interpretation of each of the theories in my work with Stan, and I was convinced this would be an effective way for students to learn practical applications of these theories. My publisher eventually agreed to the project I was proposing, which resulted in *Theory in Practice: The Case of Stan—DVD* (Corey, 2009d).

To prepare for the filming, Jamie and I spent a couple of days during the summer of 2006 hiking and talking about the different segments. Together we identified a topic for exploration for each session and a specific technique to illustrate a given theory in action. For example, for the Gestalt therapy session we decided Stan would bring in a dream to explore. Although we identified topics and what we wanted to accomplish for each session, we did not rehearse the specifics, as we had faith that we could both improvise, which provided a more natural quality to the sessions. We filmed all 13 sessions in one day, which was a real improvement over the 4 days of filming I did with Ruth in 1995.

Designing Your Integrative Approach to Counseling Practice

Ultimately, I hope counseling students will learn the fundamentals of the various counseling models and begin to develop their own integrative approach. Whether you are a student-in-training or a counseling professional, it is good practice to familiarize yourself with what the diverse theoretical orientations have to offer you.

It is important to develop a style of counseling practice that reflects your uniqueness as a person. Your theory of counseling needs to be congruent with what complements you personally. Some counselors base their practice on a single theoretical system. Other counselors recognize the value of integrating various therapeutic approaches or drawing on a diverse range of techniques. Even if you work within the framework of a single theory, it is unlikely that you will use the same techniques with all of your clients. We need to be flexible in applying the techniques that flow from a theory as we work with different clients. For myself, I draw from a thinking, feeling, and behaving model. Thinking, feeling, and acting are interactive, and a complete therapeutic approach needs to address all aspects of human functioning. I attend to what clients most need at a particular moment in a session. I attempt to address what clients are thinking, how their thinking affects how they feel, and what they are doing. Paying attention to what clients are experiencing provides clues to which dimension is the most salient to explore.

By accepting that each theory has strengths and weaknesses and is, by definition, different from the others, you may find some basis to begin developing a counseling model that fits for you. As I illustrated in my overview of the various theories, by direct contact with proponents of different theoretical positions and a comprehensive reading program, I eventually discovered aspects of all of the therapeutic systems that I wanted to incorporate into my personal therapeutic perspective.

Learn About Many Theories of Counseling

All these theories have unique contributions as well as some limitations. It is useful to study all the major contemporary theories to determine which concepts and techniques you can incorporate into your approach to practice. It is my bias that because there is no "correct" theoretical approach, you would do well to search for an approach that fits who you are and to think in terms of working toward an integrated approach that addresses thinking, feeling, and behaving. This kind of integration implies that you have a basic knowledge of various theoretical systems and counseling techniques. Developing an integrative perspective requires being thoroughly conversant with a number of theories, being open to the idea that these theories can be unified in some ways, and being willing to test your hypotheses to determine how well they are working. Functioning exclusively within the parameters of one theory may not provide you with the therapeutic flexibility you need to deal creatively with the complexities associated with diverse client populations.

Some research indicates that therapy outcomes are roughly equal regardless of the theoretical orientation of the practitioner. The trend over the past couple of decades has been away from single-theory practice and toward an integration of therapeutic approaches. Psychotherapy integration is best characterized by attempts to look beyond and across the confines of single-school approaches to see what can be learned from—and how clients can benefit from—other perspectives. The integrative approach is characterized by openness to various ways of integrating diverse theories and techniques.

Identify and Master a Primary Theory

For those of you who are beginning your counseling career, I recommend that you learn a theory as thoroughly as you can, and at the same time be open to examining other theories in depth. If you begin by working within the framework of the primary theory that comes closest to your worldview, you will have an anchor point as a foundation for developing a personal therapeutic style. It is possible to select concepts and techniques from many of the contemporary theoretical approaches and strive to see how these concepts and techniques can fit within the general spirit of a given theory.

Recognize Diversity as a Part of Effective Practice

One of the major challenges you will face as a counseling professional is understanding the complex role cultural diversity and similarity plays in your work. All counseling interventions are multicultural. Clients and counselors bring a great variety of attitudes, values, culturally learned assumptions, biases, beliefs, and behaviors to the therapeutic relationship. From both an ethical and a clinical perspective, it is essential that your practices be accurate, appropriate, and meaningful for the clients with whom you work. This entails rethinking your theories and modifying your techniques to meet clients' unique needs and not rigidly applying interventions in the same manner to all clients.

Give Yourself Time

If you are currently a student-in-training, it is unrealistic to expect that you will already have an integrated and well-defined theoretical model. An integrative perspective is the product of a great deal of reading, study, experiential personal work, supervision, clinical practice, research, and theorizing. With time and reflective study, you will develop a consistent conceptual framework that you can use as a basis for selecting from the multiple techniques to which you will eventually be exposed. Developing a personalized approach that guides your practice is a lifelong endeavor that is refined with clinical experience, supervision, and continuing study.

Because I am drawn to the value of integrative approaches to counseling practice, I wrote a book that describes the basis of my integrative approach. If you are interested in more on this subject, see *The Art of Integrative Counseling* (Corey, 2009a). For a more comprehensive and in-depth treatment of the topic of integrative approaches, I recommend *Handbook of Psychotherapy Integration* (Norcross & Goldfried, 2005). Another useful resource is *A Casebook of Psychotherapy Integration* (Stricker & Gold, 2006).

Chapter Five
My Journey Into Group Work

Introduction

In this chapter I trace the evolution of my involvement in the field of group counseling—as a group member, group practitioner, group educator, consultant in group training, and author of books on group counseling. My interest in small groups began more than 40 years ago when I began experimenting with various ways of teaching Introductory Psychology so students could apply what they were learning to their lives rather than just learning about a subject intellectually. I begin with what I learned from being a participant in many groups, for these experiences prompted me to do further study in the field of group work and eventually led to my specialization in this area of practice, teaching, and writing.

Lessons From My Experiences as a Group Member

During my 30s and 40s I was a member of many different groups, a few of which included overnight marathons, traditional weekly therapy groups, and a variety of residential personal growth workshops and encounter groups (ranging in length from a weekend to 10 days). My first group experiences had provided insight and were instrumental in leading me to make some changes in my personal life, so I continued to seek out varied experiences as a group member. Although my primary motivation for participating was not to learn techniques or specific ways to conduct groups, I received indirect benefits that I could apply to my professional work. Whether I agreed with a style of group leadership or a way of structuring a group, I learned important lessons about conducting groups from my experiences as a member.

Marathon Groups

For several years in the late 1960s, I attended a number of overnight marathon groups with the same group therapist, but with different participants making up each marathon group. These were intense experiences that enabled me to integrate feeling with cognition. These groups were personally meaningful for me because it was not possible for me to sit back and observe or to engage in abstract cognitive excursions. Instead, I was emotionally engaged, not only in my own work but also through the sharing of other members. I found marathon groups and other group experiences to be much more useful for me than was my own individual therapy. I learned the value of a sustained format that created a sense of community and fostered intensity. All of this had applications to my work as a group practitioner.

At this time I was also part of a traditional therapy group that met weekly for about a year. We met for 90 minutes with a group therapist and then continued to meet for another hour on our own in what was called an "after-group session." Although I generally found this group to be of value, I tended to be a relatively quiet member and did not ask for my share of time. It was easier to be a listener in this group than was the case in the marathons I attended. However, the combination of these marathons and weekly groups was instrumental in my personal development.

Residential Workshops

During the late 1970 and early 1980s, I attended three weekend and weeklong residential workshops held at the Esalen Institue in Big Sur, California, where many innovative programs were being developed. These kinds of workshops were in vogue during the encounter group era. Over an 8-day period I participated in a 5-day workshop consisting of a Neo-Reichian body approach to deep emotional release and reintegration and a 3-day workshop on meditation, breathing, growth activities, and centering. These workshops gave me an opportunity to explore personal issues, experience body work, and learn to quiet my mind through meditation practices and centering techniques. About 5 years later, I participated in a 5-day human potential group that consisted of a synthesis of Gestalt therapy, interactive group work, body work, and meditation. I had an opportunity then to do interpersonal work, explore personal concerns, and practice body work and meditation.

I participated in many other growth groups during this time. Although I approached most of these groups with some apprehension, I was excited about the prospects of putting myself in new situations. I was open to experimenting with new avenues for broadening my horizons. Taking these workshops collectively, I gained personal insights and found aspects that I could apply to my personal and professional life. I learned how important it is to pay attention to my body, and I learned of the important connection between the body and psychological functioning. Although intellectually I knew that stress and my psychological state had an effect on my body, I needed to experience this through body work and by observing the work of other members to make the emotional connection come alive. Experiencing and releasing emotions can be freeing and can lead to insight and to behavioral changes. I observed how repressing feelings leads to havoc in our bodies, and I experienced the healing power of catharsis. However, I also learned that emotional release is not enough for transformation to occur. Cognitive work is an essential part of increased self-awareness and the healing process. For an interesting account of the encounter group movement, see *Carl Rogers on Encounter Groups* (C. Rogers, 1970).

In the early 1990s I participated in a 10-day workshop emphasizing personal transformation with Brugh Joy, MD, on a ranch near Sedona, Arizona. This was not an interactive group, nor was it an encounter group, a process group, or a therapy group. This workshop focused mostly on individuals working one at a time with the leader in a group setting. We met as a group before sunrise each morning for meditation, which certainly helped in quieting my mind and centering me. This experience led me to a new appreciation of meditative practices and to recognize how meditation can be incorporated into both individual and group therapy. After breakfast we met for several hours as a group to share and explore our dreams with the workshop leader. Again, this was one-on-one work with the leader with the rest of the group being observers. I had often said that I did not have many dreams or that it was difficult for me to remember them. As I shared some dreams and as I observed others doing individual dream work in this group, I revised my thinking. I learned how my dreams were an expression of my unconscious dynamics, and I developed a framework for understanding some of the patterns and messages in my dreams. Although this experience was personally meaningful, it was certainly a different kind of group from the ones I was accustomed to facilitating. At times I caught myself thinking about how I would do things differently if I were leading this group, and then I would remind myself that I was not here to critique the workshop leader but to open myself to new experiences, deepen my self-understanding, and experiment with more spontaneous behavior.

Brugh Joy said to expect some surprises, and one morning we were driven to Sedona to board hot-air balloons and soar into the air to watch a spectacular sunrise. I acquired significant personal learnings by moving out of my comfort zone and opening myself to new experiences. I am fond of routines, and I was uncomfortable much of the time because I did not know what to expect, yet I needed to be shaken up a bit. I learned that at times experiencing anxiety and dealing with the unknown can be catalysts for personal growth. This workshop provided a sense of personal renewal and helped me to broaden my range of experience.

Personal and Professional Lessons

As valuable as these group experiences were for me personally, I also learned a great deal that I could directly apply to the groups I was creating and developing in the university setting. I learned new skills and was exposed to new ideas that were useful in my professional work even though I might function differently as a group leader and structure the group differently. I had concerns about the way some groups were set up or facilitated, but I also learned lessons from them that provided a framework for designing therapeutic groups. For example, I place more emphasis on screening, selecting members, conducting a preliminary orientation session for members, and giving more information about the group and how the participants can get the most from their group experience than did the leaders of most of the groups I participated in as a member. I have come to believe in the value of the group leader providing a structure that will lead to a climate of trust and encourage members to take risks. As I did not have much training in group work in my doctoral program, these experiences filled this gap by giving me practical lessons in group process, both as a member and as a facilitator.

A Self-Exploratory Course: Character and Conflict

When I first began teaching in the human services undergraduate program at CSUF in 1972, my main task involved teaching a self-exploratory course that had become popular on campus during the late 1960s. This course, known as Character and Conflict (or simply C&C), was created by William Lyon, a clinical psychologist and an early founder of the Human Services Program at CSUF. The C&C course is an experiential, theme-oriented group exploring life choices in the struggle toward personal autonomy. Themes include review of childhood and adolescence, adulthood and autonomy, work and leisure, body image, gender roles, sexuality, love, relationships, marriage and other committed relationships, loneliness and solitude, death and loss, and meaning and values.

When Bill Lyon initially offered the course, the room was overflowing with students and professors who wanted to enroll. Bill found a creative way to accommodate everyone. He would lecture on a theme for the first hour of class, and then he invited some of the professors who had enrolled in the class to function as discussion leaders for small groups for the remaining 2 hours. He observed each of the small groups each week, and he met with the group facilitators after each session for a supervision session. He eventually designed another course called Practicum in Group Leadership, which consisted of eight students who were interested in learning how to become group facilitators. During these early days of the program, it was not uncommon for professors from many different disciplines (biology, psychology, political science, philosophy, engineering, religious studies, mathematics, to mention a few) to enroll in both C&C and the Practicum in Group Leadership training program. Many of these professors found creative ways to apply what they were learning as group leaders to their own classrooms.

Practicum in Group Leadership began with a 25-hour weekend training workshop, which gave students an opportunity to do their own personal work and provided many opportunities for students to function both as group members and as coleaders of their own small groups. The workshop focused on sharing one's personal journey on the assumption that the ability to understand the struggles of others is rooted in the ability to find counterpart struggles within oneself. Those who were in the Practicum in Group Leadership course functioned as coleaders for the small groups that became an integral part of the C&C course. Both of these courses have endured as a part of the Human Services Program for more than 40 years, despite numerous challenges over the years about the legitimacy of experiential self-exploration courses focused on personal and interpersonal learning. Eventually, C&C

became a general education course and attracted students from diverse majors on campus. Multiple sections are offered each semester, and the course provides a context in which students can better understand themselves and others.

When I first began teaching at CSUF, simply being on the faculty with Bill Lyon was a challenge in itself. He was a charismatic person with definite ideas of how the program should be designed and how the courses should be taught. Some of the group leaders who enrolled in my C&C class had worked with Bill, and they compared us, letting me know that I was doing things differently. I struggled to find my own way and eventually developed my own way of structuring and teaching this course, but I retained the basic idea of providing supervised training for student leaders in a small-group interactive format. I presented C&C as a growth-oriented experience that consisted of an *invitation* to self-exploration and personal development. I encouraged students to think seriously about how each theme (relationships, meaning in life) applied to them personally. I believed that if I could create an atmosphere in which participants could openly and honestly explore their feelings, thoughts, and actions pertaining to these personal themes in their small groups, they would be better able to make significant choices that could alter the course of their lives. Each topic was introduced through a brief lecture, and students then engaged in discussion in small groups for most of the session. Students completed assigned reading on the themes of the course, wrote reaction papers each week, worked on their personal concerns in a small group, and learned how to listen to the stories of others and relate to them in this interpersonal group. At the end of the semester they wrote about their experience in C&C, including what they had learned about themselves and others and their plans for continuing their personal development once the course ended.

This is still a 3-unit course that is required for human services majors and is an elective for students with varied academic and career interests. Students are not evaluated on the quantity or quality of their self-disclosure or their participation in their small group. However, there are clear standards for receiving credit, including class attendance, doing the readings, and turning in weekly papers addressing the readings and students' experiences in their group.

I did *not* view the C&C course as a substitute for intensive psychotherapy, nor was it intended to provide group therapy. Rather, it focused on exploring students' personal concerns and experiences and encouraged them to talk in personal ways about these subjects. Students were able to realize their strengths and the ways in which these strengths may be blocked.

As I taught C&C over many years, I observed how students who were timid in speaking about themselves in a small group at the beginning of the semester gradually became active verbal group participants. For many students, being part of such a personal class was a new and valuable experience. It was common to hear students describe how they began sharing what they were learning about themselves with family members and friends. I learned that a classroom context can be connected to personal learning that extends beyond the classroom walls. A fair number of students in each C&C class expressed their desire to become group leaders in future classes, and they subsequently enrolled in the Practicum in Group Leadership course.

I often reflected on topics addressed in the C&C course, and I read many books as well. I also began writing on the topics students explored in their small groups. I was motivated to write a book that expressed my own experiences and thoughts on the themes we explored each week, which resulted in *The Struggle Toward Realness: A Manual for Therapeutic Groups* (Corey, 1974). I sent the manuscript to many publishers, but all I received were letters indicating that the manuscript did not fit into their publication scheme. Although I received no encouragement to persist in my efforts, I did not abandon the idea and eventually self-published this book.

In collaboration with Marianne, I continued to expand on our treatment of the topics covered in *Struggle Toward Realness,* which eventually led to a new book, first published in 1978, titled *I Never Knew I Had a Choice,* now in its ninth edition (Corey & Corey, 2010). The title for this book occurred to me as I listened to a client describing his own therapy experience: "One thing that my therapy taught me—I never knew I had a choice!" Many of the ideas for chapters in the *Choice* book came from reflecting on themes expressed by members in groups Marianne and I were coleading, especially the residential personal growth workshops we were doing at the time (which I describe shortly). Some themes we have been developing for more than 32 years are reviewing your childhood and adolescence, adulthood and autonomy, body image and wellness, managing stress, love, relationships, becoming the woman or man you want to be, sexuality, work and recreation, loneliness and solitude, death and loss, and meaning and values. *Choice* is perhaps our most personal book.

Creating a Residential Therapeutic Group Course

I developed several innovative courses in the early 1970s at CSUF, one of which was a weeklong residential therapeutic group course held in a mountain setting. My colleagues (Marianne Schneider Corey, Patrick Callanan, Michael Russell, and others) and I offered two sections of this therapeutic group course every summer for 25 years through the Extended Education Office at CSUF. The group was limited to 16 students and four licensed professionals who facilitated the groups. The facilitators included marriage and family therapists, social workers, psychoanalysts, and psychologists. Being part of these residential groups as cofacilitators each summer was one of the most rewarding activities of our professional careers. Most of what we learned about the power of groups came from being involved with these therapeutic groups, and they were of immense value to us both in our personal lives and as counseling professionals.

A great deal of preparation, on the part of both students and facilitators, made this a successful experience. Unlike most of their classes, students could not simply sign up for this summer class. Successful completion of the C&C course was a prerequisite for the weeklong group course, and I interviewed everyone who applied to determine whether such an experience would be appropriate for them. Here are a few of the questions I asked: "What was your experience in C&C like for you? How did you hear about the weeklong group, and what did you hear about it? What are your expectations? What are some of the personal issues you want to explore in this group? What questions do you have about this group?" If students were in personal therapy, I asked them to check with their therapist about the advisability of being involved in an intensive residential group experience. I wanted to make sure that this particular group would be appropriate for each participant and not counterproductive. For example, those who were currently in a crisis situation, were on medication to allay symptoms of depression and anxiety, or were psychologically impaired would not benefit from such a group. I viewed this screening as a two-way process, for I also wanted applicants to interview me to determine whether this kind of group would be in their best interests. In making selection decisions for the group, I did my best to assemble a group of 16 participants who were heterogeneous with respect to age, culture, race, interests, and other background factors. The majority who applied for this group experience were students in one of the helping professions who were interested in their own personal development but who also hoped to apply what they learned to their professional work.

A pregroup meeting was held about 2 months before the intensive workshop for members to get acquainted and to introduce themselves and their goals to the group. All four group leaders were present at this initial session, and we went over topics such as confidentiality, ground rules for the group, and how to prepare for the workshop. We also addressed members' concerns and questions and made it clear that anyone could withdraw from the course within 2 weeks after the pregroup meeting by simply contacting us. Prior to the intensive work, students were expected to read several books that applied to their lives, write a paper about themselves, and keep a personal journal. During the weeklong group, we encouraged members to continue to write in their journals. They were also asked to write another paper after the weeklong group that discussed their significant learning from this experience and how they were applying what they had learned to their everyday lives. A follow-up group meeting was scheduled about 3 months later to help members put this experience in perspective and to evaluate longer term benefits of the group experience. This postgroup session gave participants a chance to share how they were using what they had learned in their significant relationships.

I believe it is important to create guidelines and safeguards so that members can benefit from their learning experience. Most of these procedures can be applied to other kinds of groups, but from my own group experience I had discovered that these procedures often are not practiced. When I am not careful in screening, selecting, and preparing members, problems tend to develop later. If members are not given enough information prior to joining a group, they will not have a basis for knowing whether the group is appropriate for them. The informed consent process protects the rights of individual members and benefits the group as a whole. By my giving careful thought to why I am organizing a group and what I hope to accomplish, I believe the chances are greatly increased that members will engage in productive work. Regardless of the kind of groups you may facilitate, preparing the members for a group shows them that you are interested in their welfare.

I realize that in some residential treatment facilities or outpatient clinics screening and pregroup meetings are not realistic. Even in these cases, however, I urge you to think of alternatives to screening and preparing members. If I worked in a setting where I could not screen and select members, I would still strive to meet participants even briefly before convening the group. I would also do my best to teach members what the group's purpose is and how they might personally get some benefit from their participation.

The intensive part of this course provided opportunities for participants to engage in significant exploration of personal concerns, and having an opportunity to retreat from the demands of daily routines for this week added a dimension that increased the cohesion and sense of community within these groups. A typical day was from 8:00 a.m. to 10:00 p.m. We had group sessions until lunchtime at 1:00, with unstructured time in the afternoon for members to rest, write in their journals, or simply enjoy what the mountain setting had to offer. We convened again for an early dinner and then held group sessions from 6:00 to 10:00 p.m. For more on how the sessions were structured, the kinds of topics explored, techniques that were used, and stages of the group's development, see *Group Techniques* (Corey, Corey, Callanan, & Russell, 2004).

Although each person in the group was unique, some common themes and life experiences became apparent. We hoped that participants would leave the group with an increased awareness of how they typically initiate and respond in their world, how they want to renew significant relationships, and steps they can take to make changes in their daily existence. One of our tasks was to assist group members in gaining insights into some of the ways they might limit themselves and how they might have allowed others to unduly influence them. To use a metaphor in wide use today, the group experience gave participants opportunities to *reauthor the story of their lives*. In essence, the intensive group evolved into a dynamic community that encouraged interpersonal honesty and gave the participants encouragement to be themselves.

We did our best to provide boundaries and to create a climate of safety that permitted participants to take the risks necessary to build trust and to reveal themselves in significant ways. At times participants said that they experienced the group as an ideal family. In this new family, the members felt safe, felt understood, trusted one another, expressed themselves without fear of being judged, felt accepted and protected, and were encouraged to try out new behavior.

Many of the principles of these residential weeklong groups can be applied to a wide range of groups that you may design and facilitate in various settings. If properly designed, groups have the power to create a caring community in which members can offer hope and can encourage one another to take steps to bring about significant changes. Certainly, groups that meet on a weekly basis in an office can be very productive. In fact, such groups have the advantage of involving members in designing homework that enables them to practice the skills they are learning at work and at home. I encourage you to find a way to express your creativity in designing projects that are meaningful for you, even if they are outside the traditional realm of practice.

On several occasions over the years I had to convince university administrators to allow us to continue offering this unique residential course, but in 1998 the course was discontinued because of the university's concerns regarding liability. I felt a keen sense of loss for this special kind of group experience that I had valued so much.

Making Educational Videos on Working With Groups

When Marianne and I presented workshops at universities and professional conferences, people often asked us why we had not made a video demonstrating our way of working with an actual group. For several years we thought about making such a video and carefully considered the ethical and practical matters involved in this kind of project. Issues of confidentiality and privacy gave us cause for concern, and we consulted with colleagues to design safeguards to protect the eight people who eventually agreed to be group members for this program. After resolving our concerns, we decided to embark on this new project.

First we looked for candidates who would be willing to explore their genuine concerns in a videotaped group for a 3-day weekend. We did not want to use actors or scripts or have group members merely role-play; rather, we wanted the people we selected to be members in the context of an actual therapeutic group. Members had to agree to be videotaped for more than 24 hours of group interaction, and participants signed a waiver allowing the publishers to use any aspect of the program that was deemed appropriate. This waiver took care of the legal aspects, but we still had ethical concerns and devised several strategies for safeguarding the rights of those who would participate. At a preliminary group meeting several weeks prior to doing this weekend workshop, we clearly explained what would be expected of members and addressed any of their concerns and questions. Throughout the 3-day weekend workshop, we reminded members several times that they could inform us if they did not want something that was filmed to be in the final program and that we would honor their request. At a follow-up meeting some weeks after the filming, group members viewed a draft of the 2-hour video program, and they were again given the opportunity to have some of their personal work edited out. This initial program, *Evolution of a Group,* would not have become a reality had we not sought consultation to address our ethical concerns.

Evolution of a Group focused on group characteristics at the various development phases—initial, transition, working, and final stages—and the feedback we received suggested that we had made group work seem too easy. Some professors and practitioners asked if we could make another program that depicted work with a wide range of challenges that group counselors often face. We conducted an informal survey to identify the kinds of problems professors would most like to see illustrated with us as cofacilitators and decided to arrange for a group that would demonstrate working with various problematic behaviors in groups. This second program, *Challenges Facing Group Leaders,* consisted of improvisational enactments of problematic scenarios and critical incidents in a group. We asked the participants of this second program to be themselves as much as possible, even though they were enacting different roles of problematic members at times. A few of the scenarios that were role-played were working with members who do not want to be a part of the group, dealing with a group when members are making little progress, addressing conflict, dealing with silence, exploring a member's reactions to being left with unresolved feelings about a prior group session, working with members who are uncomfortable with expressing emotions, addressing a member's concern over feeling pressured to talk, managing a member who assumes a role of assistant leader, dealing with trust issues and concerns about confidentiality, working with a quiet member, and addressing the ways in which diversity influences group process.

This second program was completed in 2006, and the publishers converted both programs to a DVD format with a workbook to accompany each program. The combined project was called *Groups in Action: Evolution and Challenges—DVD* and *Workbook*(Corey, Corey, & Haynes, 2006). This group program entailed considerable work in preparing, cofacilitating, filming, editing, and writing a workbook to accompany the DVD, but we found the work meaningful and satisfying.

For both Marianne and me, creating these programs was as time-consuming as writing a book, yet we believed we had a useful product for enhancing instruction and teaching group facilitation skills. Marianne and I spent countless hours prior to filming exchanging ideas and choosing the major lessons pertaining to group work that we wanted to develop. A successful outcome was dependent on this kind of collaboration as we planned these projects.

Teaching a Course in Theory and Practice of Group Counseling

Since the early 1980s I have offered an undergraduate course in the Human Services Department in Theory and Practice of Group Counseling. This course is a corequisite with Practicum in Group Leadership, and students enrolled in these two undergraduate courses serve as cofacilitators of small groups in the C&C course.

The Theory and Practice of Group Counseling course entails a critical evaluation of 11 contemporary theoretical approaches to group counseling and basic issues in group work, such as group leadership skills, the group leader as a person, ethics in group work, and stages in the development of a group. I emphasize developing skills under supervised conditions and applying theories and techniques to actual group situations. Each week is dedicated to learning and applying concepts and techniques from one of the following theories: psychoanalytic group, Adlerian approach, psychodrama, existential approach, person-centered groups, Gestalt group, transactional analysis, cognitive behavioral approaches, rational emotive behavior therapy, reality therapy, solution-focused brief therapy, and comparison and contrasts among the theories. A prerequisite is the Theories and Techniques of Counseling course. In Theory and Practice of Group Counseling, students build on the overview theory course by applying each of these theories to group process.

The Theory and Practice of Group Counseling course meets once a week for 3 hours over the duration of the semester. During the first half of the class, I present a lecture focusing on aspects I find most useful from the theory, address student questions, discuss practical applications of the theory to groups, and conduct a live demonstration in which I do my best to stay true to the spirit of the particular theory we are studying. Students are assigned to one of two smaller groups for the semester, and during the second half of the class, small-group discussion gives students a chance to learn how to apply these basic ideas and techniques to group work—from the perspective of both a member and a leader. The experiential practice is primarily for learning about group process and is not a therapy group. I ask students to choose small and realistic goals to guide their active participation. Students are encouraged to think of a personal issue relative to each model that has relevance to their effectiveness as a group facilitator. For example, for the cognitive behavioral approach, students might identify beliefs that sometimes get in their way of effectively participating in a group as members or as facilitators. For the week we deal with reality therapy, students might talk about whether what they are doing is getting them what they want in their lives. When students are studying solution-focused brief therapy, they may reflect on how life might be different if a miracle happened and a particular problem they had no longer existed. Students are asked to consider what they know about themselves that may influence their ability to facilitate a group. By keeping the focus on their personal strengths and limitations as they apply to being a counselor, the groups have some structure.

Patrick Callanan, a close friend since we first met at CSUF in 1972, volunteers his time to supervise the small groups with me. Students sign up to colead their small group using a particular theory twice during the semester. Student coleaders meet before the group session to prepare and to get to know each other. They have 45 minutes to facilitate their group, with supervision. During the next 30 minutes, Patrick and I facilitate processing of the group, which includes our observations and commentary on the session. Patrick and I alternate between the two groups each week, so that by the end of the semester students have experienced both of us as supervisors every other week. We typically begin the processing of the group by asking the coleaders to talk to each other in the group about what the previous 45 minutes was like for them and also what they especially noticed as they were leading the group. As supervisors, we strive to be sensitive in the way we give feedback to the coleaders, for we realize there may be anxiety in cofacilitating a group. Students often hear us say that they are there to learn about group facilitation and that no matter what happens in the group there are important lessons to learn. Students are not graded on how well they facilitate the group, nor are they graded on their participation as a group member. In addition to the ethical difficulties involved in such grading, we also are trying to minimize the possibility that students will be performing for a grade.

Having taught this course for almost 30 years, I have seen certain themes emerge. Although students have some anxiety over coleading with a supervisor present, they are typically very willing to challenge their fears of making mistakes. Patrick and I use an inner and outer group approach, working with one group while the other group is observing. This arrangement, called a *reflecting team*, allows those in the outer group to observe group process and to learn about interventions from this observation and from the discussion after each group has had an opportunity to be in both the inner and outer circles. Another advantage is that students are able to experience and observe our coleadership interventions.

In one of these demonstration groups we ask students to identify their anxieties pertaining to being a member of the small group and to coleading their group with supervisors present. Some commonly expressed anxieties pertain to not knowing the theory well enough to lead within a theoretical framework, making mistakes in front of their peers and the supervisors, getting stuck and not knowing what to say, not being able to work effectively with a coleader, and getting emotionally involved and not being able to lead their group. As students express their fears related to being a member and a leader, they often say they feel more grounded and less anxious. In another session we ask students to identify personal goals they want to explore as members in their small groups. Goals students have suggested include wanting to find their voice and not being afraid of using it, being less concerned about what others might think of them, exploring some aspect of countertransference that could get in their way in their work as a group counselor, not being stopped by the fear of conflict, and exploring self-limiting beliefs (such as not being smart enough to go to graduate school). By the end of the semester, students generally find that the experiential part of the course has been extremely valuable in helping them learn both about being a member in a group and about facilitating a group.

Training Workshops and Intensive Group Counseling Courses

During the early 1980s, Marianne and I began conducting 5- and 6-day training workshops for group workers. Typically, these intensive training and supervision workshops were for advanced students or for practitioners in the mental health field who were interested in learning more about group process and gaining supervised experience leading groups. Many of these workshops were part of continuing education for addiction counselors, professionals who were working in the military, and counselors who wanted advanced training in group counseling. We did several of these training workshops in Germany, Belgium, Mexico City, and Ireland. Most often the workshops were residential, which gave participants a chance to be able to be away from work and home for 6 days and to focus on what they could learn from participating in a group and from leading a group with supervision.

I also coteach and cofacilitate intensive 6-day graduate group courses with a few trusted colleagues at a number of U.S. universities. My colleague is generally on the faculty at the university and invites me as a visiting professor for the week. My colleague organizes and prepares the students for this special kind of group counseling course. We emphasize to students that advance preparation is essential for this course. The course is generally limited to 16 students, and informed consent is a key consideration. Students are expected to read *Groups: Process and Practice* (Corey, Corey, & Corey, 2010) and to view the *Groups in Action: Evolution and Challenges—DVD* and *Workbook* (Corey et al., 2006) and complete the workbook exercises prior to the weeklong course. They know that this course involves a major commitment both personally and academically and serious thinking and writing both before and after the intensive portion of this group course.

I depend on the faculty member at the university to set up a 3-hour preliminary meeting with students for orientation several months prior to the intensive week. At this meeting students are given a syllabus, and all of the personal and academic expectations are explained. It is essential that students be fully and adequately informed about the specific nature of this course. The basic policies are explained, such as the nature of confidentiality as a major responsibility, the importance of making a commitment to attend all sessions, the willingness to participate in a self-exploration group, the academic requirements, the basis for grading and evaluation, and clarification that the small-group experience in the afternoon is not used as a basis for determining the course grade. Although we expect students to actively participate in their small groups in a personal way, we emphasize that it is their choice to decide what aspects of their personal lives they will share. It is up to them to decide on the level of self-disclosure they are willing to make.

The course meets from 9:00 a.m. until 5:00 p.m., with the morning session being devoted to discussion topics in the assigned readings, short lectures by the coinstructors, and a live demonstration that we cofacilitate with students who volunteer for the demonstration group. After the live demonstration, we ask students to identify specific interventions that we made and we explore with them the rationale behind our interventions. We also show portions of the

DVD program *Groups in Action,* stopping the program at many points and using what they just saw as a basis for discussion and teaching about group process.

In the afternoon sessions students colead their group with supervision from either my colleague or me. There are two 90-minute sessions, with 1 hour allocated to group interaction that is facilitated by two student coleaders. The next half hour is set aside for processing the group and giving feedback to the facilitators, which is conducted by the supervisors. After a short break, the groups resume for another 90-minute session, but this time with the alternate supervisor. With this structure, we are each able to supervise both groups every afternoon.

Students are informed that the purpose of their small groups is not to provide group therapy, yet it can be a therapeutic and personally significant learning experience. We encourage students to focus on the here and now and to concentrate on the reactions they are having to what is happening in the group. We suggest that part of this here-and-now emphasis pertains to their fears, concerns, hopes, and goals regarding being in the small group. Participants are encouraged to share how they are being affected rather than judging others in the group. The focus is on what it is like for them to be a part of the experiential group and issues as they emerge within the context of the small groups. Students are expected to participate in a personal way, and we try to provide a safe climate that allows for interactions to be real and for students to explore concerns that they choose to talk about.

I have encountered students in these courses who were there mainly because they were required to take a group course as part of their master's degree program in counseling. Teaching this course to even a few students in a class who do not want to be there can be as challenging as working with mandated clients. To be honest, I have always found it difficult to deal with students who are reluctant to involve themselves both academically and personally. I do my best to prepare students for the group training experience, including by providing informed consent and striving to create a safe climate, yet it does negatively affect me when I encounter less than enthusiastic responses from students. I continue to learn that I can invite students to be open to learning in a group course, but I cannot make them learn in this context. Through my experience teaching some required group courses, I have an increased appreciation for counselors who work with involuntary clients on a full-time basis.

Group Training Workshops in Korea

A few years ago Marianne and I were invited by the Korean Society of Group Counseling to conduct a series of three intensive workshops for professionals in the mental health field and for graduate students in counseling programs in Korea. Before we accepted this invitation to conduct training workshops and teach our approach to the practice of group counseling, we considered carefully whether our philosophy and many of the basic concepts and assumptions underlying the practice of group work in the United States would be appropriate for the Korean culture. After deliberation, we decided to present a series of workshops in Korea.

Our main objective was to share an attitude toward group counseling that might be useful to both students and professionals alike. Working with the Korean audience was a very meaningful professional experience, yet it was also a demanding and challenging endeavor. In addition to getting used to working with translators, we had to think of effective ways to present both concepts and practical applications of group work without imposing our approach on the Korean participants. We encouraged those who attended our workshops to discover ways that they could adapt what we were teaching to their cultural context and work settings.

As an example of how we taught about group process, one workshop consisted of a 4-day group that Marianne and I cofacilitated with eight volunteers who served as members of the group for the entire time. These group sessions were videotaped and projected into a nearby (but separate) room where they were observed by about 80 university professors, counseling professionals, and graduate students in counseling psychology and social work. The eight volunteers were screened and selected by the person who hired us and were given an orientation to what they could expect from us and what would be expected of them. They knew that they would not be role playing, and they agreed to explore some of their personal concerns. They were informed that the sessions would be videotaped and that a large group of observers would be in another room. One criterion for selecting these eight members was that they all could speak English, as we conducted the small group in English. Although we were not involved in the selection and preparation of these group members, Marianne and I met with them a day before the sessions began. This seemed to ease their anxiety to a great extent.

The small group was clearly a fishbowl experience, and two translators gave the observers an ongoing summary of the proceedings.

This was certainly a challenge for these capable translators, both of whom had doctorates in counseling psychology and both of whom were university professors in Korea. Admittedly, Marianne and I were somewhat anxious prior to this workshop and felt considerable pressure and responsibility to both the members of our small group and to the 80 observers who had come to learn practical applications of group counseling. During the last hour of each day, we ended the small group and joined the large group to process the day and take questions about our interventions. We emphasized that we did not think it would be appropriate to talk about any individual's work or his or her dynamics. Instead, we focused on discussing and clarifying group issues and what the people had observed us doing as coleaders. These sessions were frequently quite lively, and often we found that some who were observing were emotionally affected by the work of members in the small group.

As we do in all our groups, we strived to adopt a not-knowing position as we approached these culturally different group members. We were hesitant in making assumptions about our clients, and we did not impose our worldview or values on them. Instead, we met group members with respect, interest, compassion, and presence. We worked collaboratively to discover how to best work with these group members to resolve the difficulties they experienced internally, interpersonally, and in the context of their social environment. We maintained an attitude of respect and appreciation for differences and were challenged to be culturally sensitive on an emotional and behavioral level, and not just intellectually.

This experience made it clear to us that there was an interest in Western approaches to group work and to counseling practice in general. We discovered that many Korean cultural values complemented a range of ideas embodied in our practice of group work. We learned that although our approach to group counseling had been developed in the United States, the basic philosophy reflected in our books was well received by the students, professors, and mental health professionals who made up the audience.

Both of us were positively affected by the respect and gracious attitudes of the Korean people. Those we met had warm and open hearts and were very kind, accepting, and gracious. Our experiences in Korea confirmed our belief that we all share certain values and life themes. In working with the pain and joy that people experience, we understood that what causes pain or joy in one culture may have a different cause in another culture. However, the experience of certain human emotions is universal.

Based on this cultural experience, the main message that I want to convey is the importance of approaching people with whom we work with an open mind and an open heart. We need to put our personal agendas aside and work with any differences we encounter in an individual or a group in a respectful way. It is easy to forget that our way of thinking is not suitable for everyone we meet. By exploring the meaning of differences, we deepen our work as counselors.

Writing Several Group Counseling Textbooks

Being steeped in group work seemed to naturally flow into writing about different facets of group counseling. I would like to share a brief story behind three different group counseling books and some lessons that might be gleaned from these writing experiences.

Groups: Process and Practice

As we cofacilitated residential workshops, Marianne and I began to see patterns in the stages of groups and developed many ideas about facilitating therapeutic groups. We wanted to share our ideas about group process and practice, so we drafted a proposal for our first group counseling textbook with Brooks/Cole, *Groups: Process and Practice*. Claire Verduin mentored us in our early days and remained part of our book team for 25 years until she retired. The first edition of *Groups: Process and Practice* in 1977 dealt with topics we had been thinking about based on our work with groups and included the group leader as a person and as a professional, ethical issues in group work, facilitating special types of group, and the evolution of a group (from initial stage to termination). We continued to refine our ideas about group work with each new edition, and our daughter Cindy Corey joined us as a coauthor of the eighth edition of *Groups: Process and Practice* (Corey, Corey et al. 2010), bringing her experience and expertise in the areas of diversity and multiculturalism to this latest edition.

Theory and Practice of Group Counseling

In the late 1970s as I hiked along a mountain trail I began to think about the individual theories I had written about and how they might apply to group counseling practice. We had a book that dealt with group process, but I had done little writing about the theory of group counseling. My mind was full of ideas for a new book as I finished my hike, and upon returning home I said to Marianne, "I'm pregnant again! I have a plan for another book." She replied,

"Oh no, don't tell me! Not again." I wrote a proposal that entailed translating 11 theories with applications for practice with various kinds of counseling groups. *Theory and Practice of Group Counseling* (Corey, 2008) is now in its seventh edition and is the textbook for a course I described earlier in this chapter.

Group Techniques

Group Techniques (Corey et al., 2004) is now in its third edition, but the idea for this book was born spontaneously after a conference that Michael Russell, Patrick Callanan, Marianne, and I attended. We had given a presentation on ways to develop and use techniques in groups, and many in the audience seemed keenly interested in learning more about how to create techniques that could enhance the diverse groups they were facilitating. Since the four of us began working together in 1972, we had been involved in almost every aspect of group work in our roles as members, leaders, teachers, and workshop conductors. In the course of our long association, we found ourselves frequently faced with questions about techniques in groups—their place in a group, their usefulness at various stages in a group, and their potential misuse. In many of our training workshops we observed beginning leaders having difficulty using techniques appropriately and effectively. This got us talking about writing a book based on our ideas about how to design, use, and evaluate techniques in a group. We soon drafted a proposal and worked on the project as a team in 1980. We did much of the initial writing when the four of us met to formulate ideas and case examples for separate chapters. We had our own intensive group for about 2 weeks, recalling specific scenarios that had occurred in our groups over the years and brainstorming what we had in mind for a particular technique and ways the technique might be adapted for different situations. We also talked about alternative techniques for each situation. Michael was the best typist among us, so he typed as we all shared our ideas. I did some further writing and editing, and then we each went over the chapters individually and incorporated our changes and new material. Later, the four of us met again for collaboration on the entire book.

We had some concerns about writing a book on techniques because we did not want to put together a cookbook of prefabricated techniques. We were guided by our assumption that techniques are not the main course in any group, and we focused on the members and the leaders and on the quality of the interactions between them. From our perspective, techniques are meant to fit the needs of the group participants, not the needs of the group leader, and we are not inclined to use structured exercises or group activities to stimulate group interaction. We also wanted to express our unique personal styles as group leaders, and at the same time we wanted to present ideas regarding how group leaders could develop their own leadership style and unique approach to drawing concepts and techniques from various theories. As we were creating vignettes and describing techniques we had used in our groups, we often thought about the importance of considering members' readiness to confront their problems, their cultural background, their value system, their trust in us as leaders, and the stage of development of the group.

Certainly, many group practitioners do use structured activities and exercises when working with children, adolescents, and adults in a variety of settings, and other writers have different and useful perspectives on how to use preplanned exercises to promote interaction within a group. If you are interested in learning more about choosing, planning, conducting, and processing exercises and activities in groups, I recommend the following books:

- *Group Counseling: Strategies and Skills* (Jacobs, Masson, & Harvill, 2009)
- *Group Techniques: How to Use Them More Purposefully* (Conyne, Crowell, & Newmeyer, 2008)
- *Active Interventions for Kids and Teens: Adding Adventure and Fun to Counseling!* (Ashby, Kottman, & DeGraaf, 2008)
- *Group Work Experts Share Their Favorite Multicultural Activities: A Guide to Diversity-Competent Choosing, Planning, Conducting, and Processing* (Salazar, 2009)
- *School Counselors Share Their Favorite Group Activities: A Guide to Choosing, Planning, Conducting, and Processing* (Foss, Green, Wolfe-Stiltner, & DeLucia-Waack, 2008)
- *Group Work Experts Share Their Favorite Activities: A Guide to Choosing, Planning, Conducting, and Processing* (DeLucia-Waack, Bridbord, Kleiner, & Nitza, 2006)

Final Thoughts

My professional passions are teaching group counseling courses, conducting training for professionals who want to refine group leadership skills, and writing books on group counseling. I find that all of these aspects of my work are integrated and that the writing about group work that Marianne and I do is informed by the training workshops we have done. Teaching is a main area of professional interest that began with what I learned experientially by being a member in many groups. I continue to find teaching and practicing group work to be very challenging and rewarding.

Chapter Six
Becoming an Ethical Counselor

Introduction

Becoming an ethical counselor is a large theme for a brief chapter. I want to share what I think is involved in the process of becoming an ethical professional and explain my thinking on many topics pertaining to ethics that students often grapple with in their training and that new professionals face in their careers. Many books on ethics in counseling practice provide in-depth discussion of the topics I will introduce here.

My interest in ethics was sparked by discussions my colleagues and I had beginning in the mid-1970s about practices within the profession. Marianne Schneider Corey, Patrick Callanan, and I gave presentations on ethics in counseling at some professional conferences, and we began to meet frequently to discuss a wide range of issues. These discussions resulted in the first edition of *Issues and Ethics in the Helping Professions* in 1979. The three of us have been meeting regularly for more than 30 years now to discuss ethical and legal issues in counseling. The field of ethics has evolved over the past 3 decades, and we have deepened our knowledge and refined our thinking in just about all areas of ethics during this time. The eighth edition of *Issues and Ethics in the Helping Professions* (Corey, Corey, & Callanan, 2011) is the result of our discussions and reflects the evolution of our thinking about ethics.

Today more prominence is being given to ethics in all aspects of practice. When we began writing about ethics in 1977, few counseling books or journal articles addressed ethics. Today a separate course in ethics is required in most counselor education programs, and textbooks and other information on all aspects of ethics in the mental health professions are widely available. I believe one of the reasons for this attention to ethics is the fact that ethical violations are not an uncommon occurrence among mental health professionals. The increase in malpractice actions against helping professionals has been a contributing factor in requiring a course in law and ethics in graduate programs and in requiring a 1-day continuing education workshop on law and ethics for the relicensing process for counselors, psychologists, and social workers.

When I reflect on some shifts in my thinking about ethics over the years, I realize I have come to a much greater appreciation of ambiguity and a realization that ethics involves far more than finding the one best answer to an ethical problem. However, such was not always the case. Being a structured person, I initially preferred having direction and clear answers, but my exposure to dogmatic versions of religion from grade school through graduate school left me with an aversion to dogmatic pronouncements that discourage independent thinking.

Ethics codes sometimes are interpreted in dogmatic fashion, which defies what I view as the spirit of these professional codes. Ethical practice does not entail finding simple solutions to the complex dilemmas we encounter at various times in our careers. Ethics codes are not intended to be blueprints that remove all need for judgment and ethical reasoning. Formal ethical principles can never be substituted for an active, deliberate, and creative approach to meeting ethical responsibilities. Ethics codes can provide a framework for us to do what is best for the client and to do no harm to the client, but I have come to the conclusion that there are few clear and definitive answers to many of the questions pertaining to ethical practice. In addition, I eventually realized that I did not have to make ethical decisions alone, and over the years I frequently have sought consultation from experts and colleagues on matters that I am teaching and writing about.

Although knowing the ethical standards of our profession is essential, this knowledge alone is not sufficient for becoming an ethical counseling professional. Making ethical decisions involves acquiring a tolerance for dealing with gray areas and ambiguity. All of us need to establish our own perspective on what it means to work ethically because our values and personal ethics come into play when we seek to make sound ethical decisions in our work. For me, the cardinal rule is doing what is in the best interests of the client rather than settling for doing the bare minimum to avoid legal and ethical actions against us. Too often risk management strategies presented in workshops in ethics and the law are designed to keep us from getting into trouble and jeapordizing our careers. Although avoiding malpractice actions is a realistic goal, I do not think this goal encompasses the essence of being an ethical person. In this chapter I describe some aspects of my 40-year journey toward becoming an ethical professional.

My Experience in Designing and Teaching Ethics Courses

The Beginnings

In the early 1980s I designed a course titled Ethical and Professional Issues in Human Services, which was an elective course for undergraduate students majoring in human services. A first step in getting the course approved was to consult with the chairperson of the Counseling Department to secure support for the proposal. However, instead of supporting the proposed course, the chair viewed the course as inappropriate "because human services majors should not have to make decisions on matters of ethics." This administrative stance reflected a firm conviction that an ethics course belonged solely in the graduate program. Despite lack of support from the Counseling Department, the university curriculum committee approved the course, and I taught this undergraduate ethics course for many years.

If I had stopped when I did not get support from the chair of the graduate program, I never would have had an opportunity to teach this course. Furthermore, the many students who enrolled in this course would have been deprived of a stimulating undergraduate elective class. Instead of being deterred, I found a way to pursue what I considered to be a worthwhile project. Sometimes we are inclined to give up when we run into a road block. Over my teaching career of almost 50 years, I have found that it is possible to work within the system and at the same time remain true to my ideals.

Current Teaching Practices

I still teach a graduate ethics course once a year in the master's in counseling program at CSUF. I greatly enjoy introducing students to the topic of ethics because I believe it is one of the most important courses in their program. It means a great deal to me to assist students in their journey of becoming ethical counselors and provide them with a context in which they can clarify their thinking and learn to work through myriad situations involving ethics. It is also gratifying to meet former students and hear about how they have been able to use their experience in the ethics course in their work settings. I find this course to be enjoyable and beneficial for both professors and students, and I am a firm believer that meaningful, stimulating, and demanding ethics courses can truly enhance good professional practice.

My colleague and friend Patrick Callanan has been volunteering to coteach this ethics course for many years. We teach using a combination of didactic and experiential approaches aimed at getting students to think critically and ethically about what it means to be an ethical practitioner. The students perform traditional tasks such as writing reflection papers each week; reading and thoroughly studying a chapter each week on various aspects of ethics; completing take-home quizzes; taking a multiple-choice final examination on the entire textbook, *Issues and Ethics in the Helping Professions* (Corey et al., 2011); and viewing and writing reactions to a CD-ROM program on ethical vignettes. *Lying on the Couch: A Novel* (Yalom, 1997) is required reading. This is a fascinating treatment of a range of ethical quandries that capture the attention of students and that lend themselves to role playing, discussion, and critical thinking. This book seems to bring to life common ethical dilemmas that counseling practitioners may confront. Another excellent book is *The Gift of Therapy* (Yalom, 2003), in which a wide range of topics are briefly discussed, including personal therapy for therapists, working in the here and now, being honest with clients, many dimensions of therapist self-disclosure, and death and the meaning of life.

Emphasis in the course is on discussion, small groups, enactment of ethical dilemmas, and examining one's values. We invite guest speakers who offer a diversity of perspectives and strive to involve the class in discussion and interactive exercises. At times, former students who are now engaged in community mental health or private practice share their perspectives on their journey toward becoming ethical counselors.

We make frequent use of brief role-playing situations and invite students to assume both the counselor's and the client's positions in a given vignette. Of course, students are not graded on this role playing, but I suspect they grade themselves harshly and allow their performance anxiety to get in their way. This is a good way for students to think about how they would deal with ethical dilemmas before they are faced with them in actual practice. Role-play scenarios typically provoke lively discussion and reinforce the idea of multiple pathways in coming to an ethical conclusion. They are a powerful way to learn how to respond to an ethical situation.

Creating an Educational Video Program on Ethics

More than 10 years ago, Marianne and I were involved in making an educational video program dealing with ethical dilemmas. Along with our colleague Robert Haynes, who produced this video, we identified a number of topics and situations involving ethics that do not have simple answers for either students or experienced practitioners. In *Ethics in Action: CD-ROM* (Corey, Corey, & Haynes, 2003), we created vignettes dealing with ethical decision making in areas such as teen pregnancy, working with countertransference, a clash of cultural values, divorce and family values, extramarital affairs, conflict of religious values, abortion, end-of-life decisions, sexual orientation, boundary issues, sexual attraction in counseling, bartering, and gift giving. We applied an ethical decision-making model that we had developed in our ethics book to each of the vignettes in the video program and worked with students by guiding their reasoning and identifying actions they could take to deal with a variety of ethical scenarios. The students had multiple opportunities for role-playing both counselor and client. Although we did not have a script, we did focus on the ethical dimensions in each of these vignettes, and the importance of including the client in the ethical decision-making process was reinforced. We asked students not to role-play good counseling skills but to enact common mistakes counselors often make, such as imposing their values or giving clients advice instead of assisting them in exploring a problem. In addition, we asked students to "give voice" to some things that counselors might be thinking but not verbalizing. By having a chance to assume the roles of both counselor and client, students gained an appreciation of the challenges faced by counselors and what it might be like to be a client.

The students in the program had expected to find concrete answers to each of the dilemmas enacted, yet they soon learned that all of the situations portrayed could have been dealt with in a multitude of ethical ways. Students were too quick to want to refer a client instead of seeking ways to work with the client. We realized the value of guiding students in thinking about a host of options besides referral. When they were encouraged to think of other options, they discovered they could come up with ethical alternatives. Time and again they saw how their personal values could influence what they might say or do in the various scenarios. This experience convinced us that referrals are not appropriate simply because we are uncomfortable with a client's value system.

I believe in teaching students the process of making ethical decisions from the very beginning of their training program. Becoming an ethical practitioner begins with students learning about the established ethics codes of the various professional organizations, but it does not end there. I do not build my course on a foundation of rule-bound ethics and principles of right and wrong. Instead, I emphasize virtue ethics as a foundation for practice, which focuses on the character traits of the counselor and nonobligatory ideals to which professionals aspire rather than on specific rules. Virtue ethics asks, "Am I doing what is best for my client?" "Am I doing the right thing for the right reasons?" and "How can my practice reflect the highest possible standards of conduct rather than the minimum necessary to stay out of trouble?" I am convinced that becoming an ethical counselor is contingent on becoming a loving, compassionate, caring, nonjudgmental, and empathic person. By developing personal characteristics such as confidence, competence, courage, and a desire to make a difference, we are better prepared to grapple with ethical and moral dilemmas. We need to be virtuous individuals if we hope to become ethical practitioners.

In all the courses I teach, I do my best to convey the message that awareness of ethics is central to effective practice in counseling. Being an ethical counselor is not merely a way to avoid a malpractice suit but is a route to counseling that makes a life-changing difference. In my group counseling practice, my policy has always been to create a climate that encourages group members to take the risks necessary to bring about the changes they desire. I too have been willing to take the risks I thought were necessary to create an optimum learning climate. For example, I frequently did workshops off campus in a residential facility, which some would say poses liability issues. Although I was not indifferent to the possibility of legal action, I did not let this concern deter me from what I was convinced was the best clinical practice. I firmly believe that creating solid relationships with clients is the best possible risk management strategy.

For me, both writing and teaching keep me abreast of recent developments and trends in this field. The writing enhances my work as an ethics educator, and the interaction with students and mental health profesionals alerts me to their concerns regarding ethical practice. I have found many ways to include a discussion of ethics in the courses I teach, and I am an advocate for integrating ethics throughout the counselor education curriculum.

My Journey Toward Becoming an Ethical Professional

I encountered many ethical dilemmas in my small part-time private practice in the early 1970s. There were few specific rules and standards in the ethics codes in those days, especially in the area of boundaries and multiple relationships. Views on ethical practice have changed quite a bit in the intervening years. In these brief examples, I share how my thinking about ethics has evolved from the early 1970s to now and raise some questions to reflect on for each case.

Case of a Depressed Client

Many years ago I saw a client for relatively long-term counseling. Ted would come to sessions weekly with nothing specific to talk about, and I assumed the burden of trying to figure out what he wanted from counseling. He did not talk much, and I asked numerous questions to get him to interact with me. Ted had few people in his life, and he often spoke of not having much to live for. Ted was depressed and did not see a great deal of hope for himself, yet he faithfully came to counseling. I was not very challenging with him, and I did not ask him often enough why he was coming to counseling and what he was doing differently in his daily life as a result of our work together. When I directed the discussion toward what he thought he was learning, he would say that he got a lot from our meetings, but he was not very specific.

At one point Ted began talking about ending his life. His depression and talk of not really wanting to go on for long was very unsettling to me. I brought this case to a supervisor who helped me to see that I was not being honest with Ted by withholding my personal reactions, nor was I being helpful by not confronting his behavior. In my own personal therapy, however, I did talk about how Ted was affecting me. With the help of my therapist, I began to see parallels between Ted and my father. Both were depressed men who often talked of dying, and with both men I felt rather helpless. Looking back on this case, I realize that Ted was not getting the best of me and that it was ethically questionable for me to continue seeing him if no demonstrable progress was being made in his therapy. My countertransference was getting in the way of confronting Ted, and this experience convinced me of the importance of becoming aware of countertransference and taking steps to manage these reactions. I learned that it is important to work through my own unfinished business when it obstructs my ability to be effective with clients who trigger some of my personal problems.

Consider what you would do if you worked with a client who mirrored some of your personal struggles. If you were Ted's counselor, would you continue the therapeutic relationship if there were no clear signs that he was profiting from this relationship? How do you imagine you would react to Ted's telling you that he does not have much to live for?

Case of a Client Accepting Child Care

A client I had been seeing for several months told me she wanted to get a part-time job to help finance her schooling. Sue was single and still living at home with her parents, but she became somewhat dependent on me and frequently asked for my advice. When she brought up the possibility of providing child care for our children, I agreed to hire her for short durations. Sue enjoyed being with our daughters, and they liked her. This seemed to be working out well for all concerned until Sue began talking in her sessions about what she missed as a child and being envious of our daughters. I had underestimated her feelings for me, especially in viewing me as a father figure. I think her transference toward me was complicated by being with our children and in our home. When it was clear that this arrangement was problematic for Sue, we mutually agreed to discontinue her providing child care. She continued her therapy with me, and we talked about what working in our home brought up for her.

If I were seeing Sue today, I would not consider having her take care of our children because of the potential problems that could arise. This is a dual relationship that has the potential to be harmful to the client and to blur the boundaries necessary for an effective counseling relationship. I did not give adequate thought to the potential benefits and risks that this could pose for my client, nor did I realize how this could have interfered with her progress in therapy. In retrospect, I learned from this mistake and saw that I was placing an unfair burden on Sue.

At the time, the ethics codes did not mention dual relationships involving mixing variables such as therapy and child care. My own need to have someone I could trust stay with our children probably overshadowed considering what was in Sue's best interests, which I did not clearly see at the time. Although Sue initiated the idea of taking care of our children in our home, she was probably not aware of the feelings this might evoke in her and how this could complicate her work with me in therapy. Knowing what I know today, I would reflect more about the potential impact of her transference.

I encourage you to reflect on this case and ask yourself whether you think it is ever ethical for a therapist to employ a client for any kind of work. What possible benefits, if any, can you see for Sue in doing this work? How could this arrangement either help or hinder Sue's therapy? If Sue were a former client, would it be ethical or wise to accept her services?

A Client Who Did Not Follow Through

There was a time when we gave a client who was in one of our groups money to purchase some exercise equipment for us. Ralph knew that we wanted some exercise equipment, and he let us know that he had a friend who was in this business. Some time after we gave Ralph the money to get this equipment, he became apologetic for not having the product to deliver to us and said there were some delays. This went on for some time until he finally admitted to having used the money that we gave him to buy drugs for himself. Ralph indicated that he had a relapse and that he would eventually make good on his promise to deliver the equipment we paid for.

Looking back on this event, it is clear how this kind of arrangement poses problems for both the client and the therapist. It was poor judgment on our part to agree to let him get this exercise equipment for us. This taught me to more carefully consider arrangements such as this in the future. It proved to be problematic for Ralph, and we were disappointed in the outcome, especially since we had a good deal of trust in Ralph. We also had to confront ourselves with the fact of his relapse and our failure to recognize this. We wondered how we could have missed this.

In reflecting on this case, what ethical dilemmas do you think are involved? Was it wise for us to give Ralph money to purchase this exercise equipment? What problems might doing so have posed for Ralph?

Accepting a Gift

Some years ago, several members from one of our weeklong residential groups surprised us with the gift of a tandem bicycle on our wedding anniversary. At that time, most ethics codes were silent on the matter of accepting a gift from a client. We were struck by the generosity of these former group members and graciously accepted the gift. Doing so did not seem to pose a problem, whereas we thought that refusing the gift could have negative repercussions because these individuals had chosen to do this for us. In retrospect I can see that there was a potential for this situation to be seen as taking advantage of the feelings these former members had toward us.

Today the ethics codes of some professional organizations provide guidelines for deciding whether or not to accept a gift from a client. Faced with this situation again, I would give more thought to the monetary value of the gift, the clinical implications of accepting or rejecting the gift, the group members' motivations for presenting us with this gift, and my own motivations for accepting or rejecting the gift. I would be likely to include the group members in an open discussion of the ethical aspects involved in this situation, and it is unlikely that I would accept such a significant gift.

If you were in this situation, what are some factors you would consider in making the determination of whether or not to accept the gift? What potential problems, if any, could you see in refusing this gift? Would it have made a difference if the gift had little or no monetary value?

Hiring a Former Client

Al, who made his living as an architect, was a member in one of our groups, and he heard Marianne and me talking about wanting to add a room to our house. He brightened up and let us know that he would be delighted to draw up some blueprints for the room addition and remodeling. Once Al was no longer in the group, we talked the matter over with Al and hired him to provide plans for the building project for a mutually agreed-upon fee. Al drew up the plans and gave them to us on time, and we were satisfied with his work. We paid his usual fee for his services, and he was pleased that he could be of assistance.

Hiring this former group member to provide these services worked out well, both for him and for us. However, in reflecting on this arrangement, I recognize there could have been some pitfalls. If Al were perfectionistic, regardless of how the plans turned out, he might have felt that he had let us and himself down as well. There are too many potential problems in hiring a former client to justify doing this as a practice. What if Al's plans had not been satisfactory to us? What if Al had failed to provide us with the plans in a timely way as he had promised? Although none of these problems materialized, the potential for possible harm was present. I cannot say that I would never consider hiring a former client; however, I would carefully consider the services offered and the characteristics of the client before agreeing to such an arrangement.

Three decades ago, the few specific ethical guidelines pertaining to maintaining professional boundaries tended to be rather general. In recent years there has been a shift in the ethical climate in which we practice, and there has been a shift in my thinking on some of these situations, but not simply because the ethics codes have become more specific. I have learned how important it is to think preventively and to seek consultation with colleagues in any cases that could pose difficulties for the therapeutic relationship. My concerns are not so much of a legal nature or even motivated primarily by practicing from a risk management perspective. Instead, I have come to appreciate the paramount importance of carefully thinking through any potentially problematic situations that could pose even a slight risk of harming the client or taking advantage of a client's vulnerability. In addition to seeking consultation from experts and having open discussions with colleagues about my practices, I have shifted toward including the client in a discussion of potential consequences prior to considering any form of boundary crossing.

Would you consider hiring a former client to perform services for you for any reason? What potential problems can you see for my former client in rendering services for me? What problems do you foresee in hiring a current client to provide services you might want?

A Developmental Approach to Ethical Reasoning and Decision Making

Even if we resolve some of the perplexing ethical issues at the initial stage of our development as a counselor, these topics can take on new dimensions as we gain experience. The definition and refinement of ethical concerns is an evolutionary process requiring an open and self-critical attitude. I often attend continuing education workshops on law and ethics, and I continue to be surprised by how much there is to learn. I have an increased appreciation for the complexity of the process of becoming an ethical practitioner. It is essential to formulate an ethical decision-making model that we can apply when we are faced with an ethical quandary. Being willing to consult with colleagues and supervisors is a sign of professionalism, and it supports the perspective that becoming an ethical professional is an ongoing process rather than a place at which we finally arrive.

In the late 1970s, the director of professional education at a mental hospital asked if I would be willing to conduct group process workshops for his staff because the main treatment modality used was group therapy. Before accepting this offer, I said I needed to think about the ramifications. When I discussed this with Marianne, she said, "Do you know what you are getting yourself into? What do you know about working with patients who are sex offenders?" Marianne's questions led me to pause and reflect on my competence to provide training in group work in this setting. I agreed that I did not have expertise with their patient population, but I had competence and experience in doing training workshops in group treatment. I thought I could assist the staff in finding better ways of facilitating their groups and in helping them to adapt certain concepts and techniques to their work setting.

When Patrick Callanan and I went to the hospital to present to the staff on facilitating groups, the director asked us to return to do some practical workshops with small groups. Eventually, Patrick Callanan, Marianne, and I conducted a number of 4-day workshops in group process for the treatment staff over several years. From the feedback we received from those who participated in these groups, our training was effective in helping them develop and refine group facilitation skills.

A significant learning for me was the value of extending myself in a new situation, even though I had limited knowledge of their patients and the overall treatment program. Had I too quickly declined this offer, my colleagues and I would not have had a basis for assessing the limits of our competence. I learned the importance of seeking consultation and engaging in honest self-reflection in sorting out the pros and cons of accepting such a consultation offer. A key ethical issue for counselors is learning how to assess our competence for a specific job.

Managing Personal and Professional Boundaries

There is a close relationship between developing appropriate boundaries in the personal and professional realms. If I have difficulty establishing and maintaining boundaries in my personal life, chances are that I will have difficulty when it comes to managing boundaries in my professional work. Establishing and maintaining consistent yet flexible boundaries is neccesary if clients are to develop a sense of safety and trust in the counseling relationship. I have found that boundary issues are a major concern of both counseling students and experienced professionals alike. A perusal of the disciplinary section of professional journals provides evidence of how widespread boundary problems are and how often they result in ethical and legal violations.

In the 1960s there was a widespread lack of professional boundaries on the part of many mental health professionals, which resulted in exploitation of clients. Perhaps as a reaction against these unethical practices, the pendulum began to swing in the other direction in the 1980s, with some professional codes issuing injunctions against any kind of boundary crossing and general prohibitions against multiple relationships. Since that time, there has been an increased recognition that some boundary crossings cannot be avoided, that some multiple relationships can be beneficial, and that the proper focus is how to manage multiple relationships as oppposed to prohibiting them.

Begin by reflecting on the quality of your personal boundaries in your family of origin and how you manage boundaries in your personal life. Take some time to answer these questions for yourself: How sensitive and respectful are you in relationship to the boundaries of others? Do you experience difficulty in establishing boundaries with family members and friends? If you struggle with having a clear sense of identity and with having others respect who you are, you may find it difficult to maintain sound boundaries in your professional life. If you are successful in establishing boundaries in various aspects of your personal life, you have a good foundation for creating sound boundaries with clients.

Establishing and maintaining effective boundaries in your professional work constitutes a major ethical issue, and counseling professionals with many years of experience often still have difficulty with this issue. One important aspect of maintaining appropriate professional boundaries is to recognize boundary crossings and prevent them from becoming boundary violations. A *boundary crossing* is a departure from a commonly accepted practice that could *potentially* benefit a client. In contrast, a *boundary violation* is a serious breach that harms the client and is therefore unethical. Flexible boundaries can be useful in the counseling process when applied ethically. Some boundary crossings pose no ethical problems and may enhance the counseling relationship. Other boundary crossings, however, may lead to a pattern of blurred professional roles and become problematic.

Bartering, or exchanging counseling services for other goods or services, is one kind of boundary crossing that can be problematic. This practice can result in misunderstandings, reduced clinical effectiveness, and potential exploitation. Current ethics codes do not universally prohibit bartering, but some guidelines are suggested before entering into a bartering arrangement. Clearly, we must avoid bartering if it is exploitive or harmful to the client, or if it is clinically contraindicated in any way. It is essential that it is the client who requests a bartering arrangement, and it is important to determine whether such arrangements are an accepted practice among professionals in your community. It is a good idea to seek consultation from a trusted colleague who can provide an objective evaluation of the proposed arrangement in terms of equity, clinical appropriateness, and the danger of potentially harmful multiple relationships. In addition, we need to consider the cultural implications of bartering and discuss relevant concerns with clients. Of course, all of these arrangements need to be documented and guided by a clear written contract.

Any crossing of boundaries should occur only when it is clear that doing so will likely benefit the client. Thus, boundary crossings need to be evaluated on a case-by-case basis by considering the potential benefits as well as the risks involved. In the case I described earlier of my client rendering child care services, steps I could have taken to prevent ethical problems included seeking consultation, discussing with the client the potential advantages and disadvantages of providing child care, or simply not entering into such an arrangement. This was clearly not beneficial to my client, and we soon agreed to terminate this arrangement.

Multiple Roles and Relationships

Establishing professional boundaries often involves learning how to ethically manage multiple roles and relationships. Multiple relationships occur when counselors are involved in one or more relationships in addition to the primary client–counselor relationship. This may involve assuming more than one professional role or blending a professional and nonprofessional relationship. Terms frequently used to describe these multiple relationships are *dual relationships* and *nonprofessional relationships*. Sexual contact between a counselor and a client is an example of a dual relationship that is always unethical, unprofessional, and, in many states, illegal. In the 1960s, most codes of ethics did not explicitly state that sexual contact in therapy was unethical. In fact, I recall attending a panel presentation at a professional conference in the late 1960s at which some panelists took the position that sex with their clients could be beneficial and could be an expression of caring. Some time later the codes of ethics of all mental health professions included a standard that prohibits sexual intimacies between the professional and a current client. Most of these codes prohibit sexual relationships even after the professional relationship has ended, at least for a specified number of years (usually 3 to 5 years). Even after this time has elapsed, the burden of proof is on the therapist to demonstrate that the former client was not harmed or exploited. An argument can *never* be made that a sexual relationship is an appropriate part of a professional relationship, even though years ago some psychotherapists claimed otherwise.

Many nonsexual multiple relationships can be quite challenging to manage as well. Examples of nonsexual multiple relationships include accepting clients who are family members or friends, combining the roles of supervisor and therapist, forming business arrangements with current or former therapy clients, or combining personal counseling with social relationships. Today none of the various codes of ethics state that nonsexual multiple relationships are unethical, and many of the codes acknowledge the complex nature of such relationships. Some multiple relationships cannot be avoided, are not harmful, and have potential benefits for clients. From my perspective, the mere existence of a multiple relationship does not, in itself, constitute unethical behavior. It is important to avoid exploiting or harming clients in any way, but prohibiting all forms of dual or multiple relationships does not seem to be the best answer to the problem of exploitation of clients. Actually, few absolute answers are available to resolve dilemmas pertaining to multiple relationships.

As a counselor and a counselor educator, I cannot always perform a single role when working with clients, nor do I think it is necessarily desirable to limit myself to one role. Many times, my work situation requires me to balance multiple roles in professional relationships, such as counselor, mentor, coach, supervisor, advocate, and teacher. Although I do not believe that engaging in multiple roles with a client or a student is necessarily unethical, doing so does call for careful monitoring on my part to ensure that exploitation does not occur. Seeking consultation from a supervisor or several colleagues is a strategy I use to reinforce my self-monitoring. I have also found it to be effective to involve the client or the student as much as possible in deliberating about ways to effectively manage multiple roles and relationships. When I function in more than one role, I carefully reflect on potential problems *before* they occur to determine whether the potential benefits outweigh the potential risks. Some of my colleagues argue that it is a good idea to avoid engaging in multiple roles with a client unless there is a sound clinical justification for doing so. They add that in such cases it is wise to take steps to safeguard clients by making use of informed consent, consultation, supervision, and documentation.

For a more detailed discussion of boundary issues and multiple roles and relationships, you may want to consult the following sources: *Dual Relationships and Psychotherapy* (Lazarus & Zur, 2002), *Boundaries in Psychotherapy: Ethical and Clinical Explorations* (Zur, 2007), and *Boundary Issues in Counseling: Multiple Roles and Responsibilities* (Herlihy & Corey, 2006b).

Our Values and Ethical Practice

Our own values influence our counseling practice and need to be examined when considering ethical practice. In teaching ethics I find that students sometimes pay more attention to ethical violations such as breaching client confidentiality, abandoning a client, engaging in sexual misconduct with clients, and practicing beyond one's competence. However, they sometimes do not pay close attention to the effect of their own values on their counseling relationships. We can impose our value on clients in a subtle manner, and some students argue that it may be appropriate for them to teach their values to clients.

Our values are core beliefs that influence how we act, in both our personal and professional lives. Our personal values will influence how we view counseling and the manner in which we conduct ourselves in our professional work. Our value system influences every facet of our counseling practice, including the way we conduct an assessment of a client, our views of the goals of counseling, the interventions we choose, the topics we select for discussion in a counseling session, how we evaluate progress, and how we interpret a client's life situation.

Respecting My Clients' Values

As a counselor, it is not my function to persuade clients to accept or adopt my value system but to help clients clarify their own values. I consider it my ethical responsibility to be aware of how my beliefs and core values affect all aspects of my work. There may be times when I do not agree with some of my clients' values, but I need to respect the values that guide their lives and their right to hold divergent values from me. This is especially true in situations involving clients who have a different cultural background from me. It is critical to understand and respect my clients' worldviews rather than convincing them that they should see the world through my eyes. My role is to provide a safe and inviting context in which clients can explore the congruence between their values and their behavior and to assist them in determining whether they may want to change some of their behaviors or modify certain values.

My students sometimes mistakenly think that they do not have a right to hold their own values and that they should be accepting of all value systems. The message I want my students to hear is that although they have a right to embrace a value system they have adopted, they also need to respect the rights of clients to live by a different value system. At the same time, I stress that they should not be attached to the outcomes or choices their clients make. Likewise, whether you are a student or a counselor, my hope is that you have examined the sources of your values, that you have questioned the values that influence how you behave, and that you have taken ownership of your values.

As long as you remain open to examining the meaning of your life and remain curious, you can and most probably will revise your way of living from time to time. In his wisdom, Socrates said that the unexamined life is not worth living. If you accept this dictum, you will most likely apply this to your own life and encourage those with whom you work to examine the source of their own values to determine how well these values are working for them.

My Role and Function as a Counselor

If a person seeks a counseling relationship with me, it is important to discover what this person is expecting from the relationship. If I try to figure out in advance how to proceed with clients, I am depriving them of the opportunity to become active partners in their own therapy. It is the client's place to decide on the goals of his or her therapy. A good question to reflect on is, "Why is this person coming in for counseling?" If I keep this focus in mind, the client's agenda, rather than my agenda, becomes supreme. I remember a student who said, "I have worked very hard on figuring out my life and as a counselor I have a desire to share what I know so my clients won't have to struggle needlessly." Even if clients express a desire for me to give them answers, I don't see it as being beneficial to them in the long term. My role as a counselor is to work with clients in ways that will empower them to make their own life decisions.

In many respects I am mentoring clients by offering hope, guidance, and encouragement, yet I am doing far more than merely giving advice and answers. I remember wanting my own therapist to provide me with advice and answers. I figured that he had enough life experience to share with me so I would not have to live in confusion and uncertainty. I was afraid of making "wrong" life choices. Remembering this tendency on my part to want others to direct my life makes it easier for me to have compassion for those who do not trust themselves to find their own way. Directing others is not what counseling is about.

Evolution of My Personal Values

In Chapter 1 I alluded to the impact that my school experiences— from elementary school to gradute school—had on the development of my values and personality. Spending most of my time in Catholic schools did not lend itself to critical examination of life and how to live. The messages I internalized were that there are right ways of living and that we should not question authority. Many of my values were rather narrow and rigid, and I was certainly not encouraged by teachers to question what I had been taught about the right way to live. If I dared to question or think for myself, I became anxious. Because I did not think I had the right to find answers within myself, I sought answers from outside authorities.

When I began my high school teaching career, I met and worked with a few teachers I greatly respected who had diverse views of the world. These colleagues seemed quite "liberal" to me, yet I envied their capacity to think "outside the box." Several of my teacher colleagues challenged some of my narrow thinking. We had many discussions about values that motivated me to begin thinking more critically, and I began an uncomfortable process of questioning what I had been taught as unquestioned truths. Over years of seeking, I encountered many interpretations of reality. I had one vision of reality, which I thought was the only way to view the world. I was not aware of my tunnel vision until I was challenged by others. My own experience with embracing a limited view of the world has alerted me to the problems involved when counselors believe they have the truth and that their job is to impose their way on their clients. Challenging my thinking has affected my view of the role of the counselor's values in the counseling relationship. My job is to assist clients in questioning, clarifying, and perhaps modifying some of their values if they so choose, but it is not my role to impart my values or to tell clients how to live.

Questions and Responses on Values in Counseling

When I speak to graduate students and new professionals, or when I meet with a small group of students to share ideas about creating a professional path, a number of ethical questions tend to surface about the role of values in the counseling process and how counselors can address possible value conflicts. Some common questions pertaining to how a counselor's personal values can influence the client–counselor relationship, along with my responses, are presented in the following pages. Perhaps you have thought about some of these issues yourself.

Question: What is the difference between imposing versus exposing your values?

Response: If you are imposing your values, you are directly attempting to influence a client to adopt your values, beliefs, attitudes, and behaviors. Most of the professional codes of ethics caution professionals against imposing their values. Sometimes I may determine that it is appropriate to reveal some of my values to a client, but at other times exposing my values could be counterproductive and could be seen as covertly influencing the client. For example, if my client has decided to get a divorce, I don't see how my values are relevant in this decision-making process. Before revealing my values, I would assess the impact my sharing is likely to have on the client. I might ask myself, "What is prompting me to reveal and discuss my values with a client? How will doing so benefit my client, or possibly get in the client's way? Will my disclosure unduly influence my client?" When I do reveal my values, I strive to do so in a way that does not communicate that my client should adopt them. In this case, my agenda would be to explore any concerns my client might have pertaining to his or her choices.

Question: Can I share my values with a client if I think this will lead a client toward a productive path?

Response: It is difficult to be completely value neutral. For example, I value physical exercise, self-care practices, and choosing one's own path in life, but I must be careful not to try to persuade clients to accept values that I deem life-affirming. If a client is neglecting taking care of himself, is it my role to urge him to begin treating himself better? If a client never exercises and complains about being lethargic, is it my place to create an exercise plan for her? If a client is allowing a significant other to determine his path, should I rally with him to strive for autonomy? I must be careful, because part of me might want to influence the person to adopt "healthier life choices." I need to remind myself that my role is not to fashion the lives of others but to ask why they are seeking counseling.

Question: What can I do if some of my values conflict with a client's values?

Response: In working with a diverse range of clients, you are likely to experience value differences pertaining to culture, sexual orientation, family life, divorce and separation, gender-role behaviors, extramarital affairs, sexual activity outside a committed relationship, religion and spirituality, abortion, and end-of-life decisions, to mention a few. Merely having different values from our clients does not mean that we cannot work effectively with them. By accepting this person's right to live by a system of values that he or she chooses we can establish an effective therapeutic relationship. It may be appropriate to seek consultation to explore what it is about us that is making it difficult to work with a person because of a value divergence. Our task is to assist people who seek our help to look at what they are doing, evaluate whether what they are doing is working for them, and decide what changes they might consider if what they are doing is not fulfilling to them. If a client tells me that she is not satisfied with the direction of her life, I can assist her in reexamining her values and seeing what options are open to her with respect to modifying some of her behaviors.

Question: Is a referral the appropriate course to take with clients when I have a value clash?

Response: Merely having different values from a client does not require a referral. Before making a referral, open a dialogue with your client and find out if he or she wants to work with you. Disclosing that we are unable to get beyond value differences with a client can be very burdensome to the client. I frequently say to my students that a referral should be considered as an option of last resort. When a referral is decided upon, *how* it is suggested is very important. If you think you cannot work with an individual because of value differences, make it clear that it is *your* problem and not the client's.

You might be counseling a client who is involved in what you consider to be an unhealthy relationship, yet he is not willing to challenge the relationship, nor does he want to terminate the relationship. If you think the client should end this relationship, ask yourself why your client must embrace your values. Before making a referral, explore your part of the difficulty through consultation. What barriers within you would prevent you from working with a person who has a different value system? Why is it necessary that there be congruence between your value system and that of your client? Merely disagreeing with a client or not particularly liking what a client is doing is not an appropriate reason for a referral. It is good to keep in mind that *it is not about you* but about your clients!

Question: Do religion and spirituality have a place in the practice of counseling?

Response: Traditionally, religion and counseling were viewed as antagonistic forces. More recently, spiritual and religious beliefs—both the counselor's and the client's—and how such beliefs might be incorporated into therapeutic relationships have become topics of increasing interest. It is important to be open to dealing with spiritual and religious themes clients present in counseling. When clients let us know that they have concerns about the spiritual path they are on, or detours they may have encountered, we can explore these paths with clients, but I hope we will not make it our agenda to prescribe ways of finding meaning or deciding for clients which path to follow.

Assessment is a process of looking at a range of factors that could be influencing a client's problem. From my perspective, exploring spiritual and religious influences is just as significant as raising questions about one's family-of-origin influences. It is essential to understand and respect the client's religious and spiritual beliefs and to include such beliefs in assessment and treatment practice, if this is important for the client. A client's spiritual beliefs can be a major source of strength as the client makes crucial life decisions, and these beliefs can be a part of the counseling experience.

Spirituality must be addressed if it is a concern of the client. There are many paths toward fulfilling spiritual needs, and it is not the counselor's task to prescribe any particular pathway. It is important to monitor yourself for subtle ways that you might be inclined to impose your values on your clients, whether directly or indirectly. The key here is to remain finely tuned to what your client wants to explore and the purpose for which he or she sought therapy.

Question: Is it appropriate for me to share my religious or spiritual beliefs if I am convinced that my beliefs and practices have provided me with a meaningful life?

Response: If a client were to inquire about my personal beliefs, I would want to explore with her the reasons she wants to know about my values and beliefs. What has worked for me is not an answer for my clients in their search for meaning in life. My spiritual path is my own, and my clients will need to discover their own spiritual paths. I need to be careful about introducing religious themes in a counseling session, for doing so might be leading the client. However, I want to be alert to talking about religious values if a client introduces them. If a client asks for my advice on a religious or spiritual problem or concern, I would be hesitant to offer such advice. I try to keep in mind that it is the client's place to determine what specific values to retain, replace, or modify. Being prescriptive about religious and spiritual practices may be appropriate in ministerial work, but it is not appropriate for professional counseling.

Many Possible Answers

I have not attempted to give you the "right" answers to these questions that are often posed to me. Instead, I wanted to share my thinking as a way for you to formulate your thoughts on these questions. You may have a very different set of responses to these questions than mine, and I encourage you to find answers within yourself.

Concluding Comments

I have found that students who are becoming counselors sometimes look for concrete answers to potential ethical dilemmas. Students in my ethics classes typically want to know the "correct ethical path," yet they continue to hear me say that there can be many appropriate paths toward gaining a fuller appreciation of an ethical dilemma. I teach students to think critically and to realize that ethical practice is very complex and defies simplistic solutions.

New counselors do not have to make ethical decisions alone. I greatly value the process of consulting with colleagues with different areas of expertise when I am searching for a way to work through an ethical concern. It has been valuable for me to consult with people who have a different perspective than I might have on certain matters. Rather than just affirming my viewpoint, a colleague with a different approach often helps me to expand my thinking. Regardless of how long I have been in practice, I am convinced that we can always profit from seeking consultation, reflecting on what we hear, and documenting the recommendations given. Ultimately, each of us then has the task of making what we deem to be the best ethical choice.

Although we may resolve some ethical concerns early in our development as counselors, we will still gain a deeper level of understanding of ethics with experience and reflection. We need not burden ourselves with the expectation that we should resolve all possible ethical problems today. The definition and refinement of ethical concerns is an evolutionary process that requires all of us to adopt an open and self-critical attitude.

For a more in-depth discussion of becoming an ethical counseling professional, I recommend reading a number of standard textbooks on ethics in counseling. A few of these are *Issues and Ethics in the Helping Professions* (Corey, Corey, & Callanan, 2011), *Ethical, Legal, and Professional Issues in Counseling* (Remley & Herlihy, 2010), *The Ethical and Professional Practice of Counseling and Psychotherapy* (Sperry, 2007), *Counseling Ethics and Decision Making* (Cottone & Tarvydas, 2007), and *Ethics in Counseling and Psychotherapy: Standards, Research, and Emerging Issues* (Welfel, 2010). For those of you interested in reviewing casebooks that will help you interpret the various ethical standards contained within ethics codes, I recommend *A Guide to the 2002 Revision of the American Psychological Association's Ethics Code* (Knapp & VandeCreek, 2003), *The Social Work Ethics Casebook: Cases and Commentary* (Reamer, 2008), and *ACA Ethical Standards Casebook* (Herlihy & Corey, 2006a). Two excellent desk reference manuals are also available: *Ethics Desk Reference for Psychologists* (Barnett & Johnson, 2008), which interprets the APA code and provides guidelines for ethical and effective practice; and *Ethics Desk Reference for Counselors* (Barnett & Johnson, 2010), which interprets the ACA code and offers recommendations for preventing ethical problems. Although these casebooks and desk reference manuals are useful for interpreting and clarifying standards, they can never replace informed judgment and ethical reasoning on the part of the individual counselor.

Chapter Seven
Choosing a Career Path

Introduction

The direction of your career path will most likely change during your professional life, and mentors can be very useful in pointing you in a specific direction. Reflect on the input from supervisors and mentors as you decide what will work best for you and what course of action you will take. Ultimately, you will chart your own path by putting into action what you have learned. As with the developmental stages of life, a variety of factors emerge or become influential at different times throughout our career decision process. You might choose a professional specialization because of your interests in a given area or because of your life experiences and personal struggles. Instead of selecting *one* occupation that will last a lifetime, it is probably wise to choose a broad field of endeavor that appeals to you and remain open to opportunities that may present themselves.

My own career path seems to be more of a process than a straight line. Over the years I have found many ways to maintain my interest in teaching by working with colleagues, by coteaching, by becoming involved in experiential approaches to the teaching/learning process, and by remaining a learner myself. My own professional evolution has involved learning about counseling in general and then narrowing my focus as I took other turns in my journey. Teaching has always been my primary area of interest, and from this general area I eventually developed specialized interests in the areas of counselor education, ethics in counseling practice, theory and practice of counseling and psychotherapy, and group work.

Personal Stories of Others Who Are Creating Meaningful Careers

Decisions about work can be part of a developmental process, and your work may change along with your interests throughout your lifetime. The personal stories you will read in this chapter illustrate how some professionals have changed careers at different phases in life. Seven individuals (Honie Abramowicz, Julie Tomlinson, Toni Wallace, Jamie Bilezjikjian, Leslie Culver, Amanda Healey, and Michelle Muratori) explain how they created their own professional paths, yet some common bonds link these personal journeys. As you read, reflect on the lessons learned that you can apply to your own career path. What are the highlights of each of these stories for you?

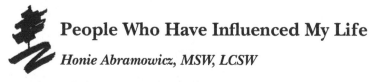 ## People Who Have Influenced My Life

Honie Abramowicz, MSW, LCSW

As I walked down the aisle at graduation to receive my master's degree in social work, my mind wandered back some 39 years. I was 10 years old, sitting in this nonempathetic hospital social worker's office, telling her that I too was going to study psychology and become a social worker or some type of counselor. What I really wanted to tell her was that I would become a better social worker than she was and that I would help people to feel understood and find hope. As they called my name out, I snapped out of my trance and accepted my diploma. In the days following my graduation, I thought a lot about the type of job I would find and my ability to help others solve their problems.

My first position in the helping field was counseling at-risk youth, which was followed by a variety of positions including administrative work, program development, advocacy, grant writing, and training. After I received my license in social work, I returned to doing counseling in a nonprofit organization, working with a variety of clients. Currently, I am a licensed clinical social worker working in private practice, primarily with adolescents and adults. I consider myself to be a holistic counselor utilizing an integration of techniques and approaches from various theories and orientations to help my clients gain insight and find their own solutions to their problems.

I can still picture myself at 10 years old, feeling frightened and all alone in some social worker's office as she asked me questions to substantiate an opinion she had already formed without knowing any facts. Her lack of empathy and understanding of what I was going through made me feel insignificant and helpless. This negative experience helped me realize how important it is for counselors to help clients gain a sense of being listened to and understood. This poignant memory of my past has played such a large role in my life. It was the impetus for me to become the type of social worker I am: someone who wants her clients to feel valued and to become empowered. I do this by listening to my clients' stories using all of my senses and by observing and understanding what they are experiencing. Through empathic listening, I can help my clients gain a more accurate understanding of themselves and their situation.

Even though my desire to be a social worker started at age 10, I did not go into the field until I was in my 40s. I guess I needed to learn a few important life lessons and gain more insight into myself before becoming a helping professional. I had a lot of self-doubt about my abilities to succeed in college, but my husband pointed out all of the things I had succeeded at since I had left college some 20 years before. When I started back, I was challenged by many things. Writing papers was my biggest challenge because I feared that others would criticize and judge my writing and think I was inept. I also feared not fitting in or being accepted by the other students because they were all so much younger.

In one of my first counseling classes, the professor asked for a volunteer to help him demonstrate how to utilize a Gestalt technique called "the empty chair." I took the risk of volunteering to be the client, and it was a turning point for me. The professor asked me what fear I wanted to address, and I chose to address my fear of completing written assignments and being judged incompetent or incapable. As I was addressing the empty chair, the professor asked me whose critical voice was coming from the empty chair, and I answered that it was my father's voice. From this experiential work, I began to discover that my feeling of not being good enough and my harsh self-criticism stemmed from my early misperceptions and irrational beliefs about interactions with my father and others. Taking the risk of volunteering in front of all my young peers and my professor helped me begin to face my fear of being seen as incapable. My classmates congratulated me on being brave enough to address my fears and opened up to me about similar experiences and feelings they had.

My experiences have helped me to realize that people often are not who you think they are. The support and encouragement from both my husband and my daughter helped me to challenge myself and to recognize abilities that I did not think I possessed. My professor helped me to see that some of my past perceptions were faulty beliefs that were keeping me from reaching a higher potential. I have incorporated these insights into my approach to therapy, helping clients to see a more accurate account of themselves, their beliefs, and their abilities.

The support, encouragement, and good modeling I have received from others has helped me to grow and overcome my challenges. Becoming a social worker has allowed me to do the same for many other people. In addition to helping clients, I have mentored social workers and counseling interns for the past 11 years. I have found this experience to be enlightening, rewarding, and fulfilling. Not only do I have an influence on their lives, but they influence my life as well.

∾

Commentary

Although Honie had a negative experience with a social worker, she decided at an early age to become a social worker. For Honie, this past memory played a key role in her life. Have you had any experiences such as this that still influence you today? How did you relate to those negative experiences with professionals?

Honie describes some of her fears and self-doubts regarding succeeding in college, especially in terms of writing papers. She had to learn how to argue with critical inner voices and learn new patterns of self-talk. Honie never would have dreamed that someday she would be a social worker occupying a range of positions such as counselor, administrator, program development coordinator, advocacy worker, grant writer, supervisor, trainer, and mentor. Her experiences in holding these positions within the general field of social work are probably not unusual, however, for the career paths of many of us evolve over the course of our careers.

Questions for Reflection

- Where do your career interests lie, and what line of work do you find most exciting?
- What would you most like to be doing 5 years from now? What are some steps you can take today that will help you realize this vision?
- Can you identify any of your negative self-talk, and if so, how do you deal with this?

- Have you faced your own fears and doubts about pursuing your academic and career path? What internal and external resources have helped you at these times?

Rekindling My Dream and Redefining My Life

Julie Tomlinson, MSW

In my mid-30s a personal crisis shook up my life such that I felt I had nothing to lose by risking a totally new direction. I had floundered through various junior colleges and had dabbled in various jobs, but I remained completely unfulfilled. So I took the opportunity to reflect and take inventory of my life, what I had and what I wanted. What I wanted was to rekindle my dream, and what I needed was to rebuild my belief in myself. There is a saying that reminds me of this time in my life: "Only deeply plowed earth can yield a bountiful harvest." Indeed, it felt as though everything in my life had been turned over.

I gathered my strength and all my various school transcripts and headed into the counselor's office at the local state university. I was encouraged to learn that with my previous transcripts I could complete a bachelor's degree in human services in just 2 years. This degree was a good foundation for applying to graduate programs. In the human services program, I was inspired and encouraged by several caring professors. I constantly pushed myself academically, and I opened myself emotionally to the experiential group classes. My academic successes helped me to regain confidence in my abilities. The self-exploration classes gave me an opportunity to gain perspective on some old wounds, begin to look at the fresher ones, and get to know myself in a deeper way. As a potential therapist, I knew it was important for me not to be afraid to go where my clients would need to go by exploring possible blind spots and hot spots I might have.

As completion of my bachelor's degree became a reality, it was time to determine what was next. Pursuing either a master's in counseling or a master's in social work seemed the most direct route to gaining a license to practice psychotherapy independently. After much debate and conflict, and after seeking the counsel of various professors and friends, I chose to pursue the master's in social work. Ultimately, this choice was based on many personal factors that I weighed and debated. One of my foremost concerns was to obtain a degree and a license that would be widely recognized and that was transferrable to other states if needed. Choosing social work also meant leaving the familiarity of my undergraduate university for a larger private university with a more competitive reputation.

Entering this master's program was just short of terrifying. It was completely unchartered territory academically, and it involved a major financial commitment. It also brought up my personal insecurities about not being good enough. As I shared these fears with friends, family, and advisers, I was continually reassured that I would be able to meet the challenges ahead. Early in the program, many logistical challenges arose, such as the need to refine my organizational techniques for handling such a large volume of information. I had to learn time management and study skills to keep up with the required reading and research, and it was quickly apparent that all extracurricular activities would fall by the wayside in my pursuit of this degree.

Thankfully, in my second year of the program, I realized that I could manage the academic workload and the demands of fieldwork and still have "a life." I began to deliberately schedule time for a hike, lunch with a friend, or a motorcycle ride down the coast. It became apparent that although the demands of life had picked up, the speed of life had not slowed down. It was important for me to learn how to integrate self-care and time with people I cared about into even my busiest weeks. I also did not want to graduate from the program and look back and see that I had not developed relationships with my classmates and future colleagues. I began to reach out more, organizing study groups and making myself generally more available to social offers. Two years and 63 units later, I graduated with a master's in social work with honors from one of the country's most revered and respected universities.

Unfortunately, my graduation coincided with a major nationwide economic downturn that paralleled a state budget crisis. This prompted unprecedented hiring freezes, furloughs, and salary cuts in many federal, state, and county agencies. In some agencies where my fellow students had been placed, their supervisors were even being laid off. This created a bleak outlook for new graduates entering the workforce. Although choosing my last year's field placement had been based in part on the likelihood of its postgraduate hiring potential, this became a moot point in the new economic climate. At the VA hospital, positions were posted as open, but no hiring authorizations were being granted. In addition, many of the positions typically filled by entry-level social workers were now attracting a greater pool of licensed social workers who had lost their jobs or were looking for more stable positions with better benefits.

Out of work for almost 2 months after graduation, my ongoing contact with former coworkers and my program manager finally paid off. An opportunity to complete a short-term contract position opened up in the clinic where I had interned my final year. I had maintained a good relationship and had a good reputation for my work, so they were able to hire me immediately. Currently, I work as a clinical triage social worker who is the first point of contact for Iraq War veterans following their enrollment process through the patient registration office. My primary duties are to provide initial screenings, crisis interventions, brief counseling, and referral services. I love the work even though it can be very draining because of the unpredictable volume of the walk-in clinic. I frequently have to remember those time management skills I developed in graduate school and close my door to get myself centered or take a walk during lunchtime.

As I mature into my career, I anticipate ongoing challenges and unexpected stressors along the way. I am still looking for a permanent full-time position, and I hope to find a clinical position so I can provide direct psychotherapy. However, I take advantage of every opportunity I have with veterans to educate them, to offer treatment options, and to open the door for possibilities they may not otherwise have considered. I realize, too, that just as I need to be creative and adaptable with my clients, I need be creative in my personal life and my career pursuits.

Finally, I am so grateful for the friendships I initiated and continue to develop with my classmates. I now count on them to provide professional advice, to be available socially, and to be understanding friends. I am grateful for the richness and support my fellow alumni add to my life. I am inspired by their strengths, and I continue to learn from them. Although I could have completed school without developing these friendships, my personal and professional experiences would have been an empty shell. When I look back over these last 4 years, I realize that I have completely transformed my life.

∽

Commentary

Like so many of the authors of these personal stories, Julie admits to being highly anxious and uncomfortable about becoming involved in unchartered territory academically. As you began your academic program, perhaps you also faced some risks. By reflecting on the outcomes of the risks you took, you may find a direction to pursue in designing your career path.

Julie's story highlights financially difficult times and bleak prospects for employment. Her story offers hope and direction for staying focused on your career goals even in times of hiring freezes, salary cuts, and dwindling employment prospects in county, state, and federal agencies. Julie networked with former coworkers to find openings in a tight job market. Although she was discouraged about her job prospects upon graduation, she did not give up. If you are encountering similar difficulties in finding a position in mental health work, you may not reach your career goals as quickly as you would like. You may find some of Julie's self-care techniques helpful in preventing discouragement from getting the best of you.

Julie eventually decided that it was possible for her to keep up with the demands of graduate school and also to have a quality personal life. She arranged for quality time with a circle of friends and found enjoyment in solitary activities as well.

Questions for Reflection

- Do you put your personal life "on hold" because of the demands of school or work? Have you been willing to put yourself in your schedule book to do what you enjoy?
- Are you able to maintain a balance between your workload and taking time to maintain friendships? What changes in this area do you most want to make?
- Julie struggled with making a choice between counseling and social work as her professional field. If you are uncertain about the direction of your professional career, what can you do to gain more clarity?

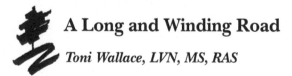

A Long and Winding Road

Toni Wallace, LVN, MS, RAS

I had never really been to college; I am a licensed vocational nurse who has worked in obstetrics for more than 40 years. My job for the past 23 years has involved working with substance-abusing pregnant women. I am part of a comprehensive program that incorporates prenatal care with drug treatment.

I wanted very much to learn more about the psychosocial lives of the women I worked with and how I might empower them to make changes in their lives and the lives of their children. To do this I needed more education, but how does a single mom in her mid-40s, with three teens, go back to school and realize her dream? That was the question on my mind when I decided to find out what it would take for me to get a degree.

Fitting in college courses with an already full plate took some organizing. I had no idea what degree would be most beneficial, so the first step was making an appointment to see a counselor at the nearby junior college. I was pleasantly surprised at how inviting this interaction was, and I learned about both general education requirements and some majors I might consider.

I started back to school taking six units, one of which was a course in human services, which was a turning point for me. My instructor encouraged her students to explore the many and diversified career paths in the helping professions. She brought in guest speakers throughout the semester to talk about their jobs and what educational avenues to take to obtain the needed education. One of the speakers was from the university I would eventually transfer to. He was a dynamic speaker who had a passion for his work, and I was sold before the end of the class.

I moved ever so slowly toward my goal, an undergraduate degree in human services. Never in my wildest dreams did I see myself going on to an advanced degree. But it became a reality with the help and encouragement of instructors, family, and friends. I was very fortunate to have the encouragement of my employer, who provided flexibility in my work schedule. Without that flexibility I would not have been able to enroll in the courses I needed to accomplish my goals.

The road was not easy. I had to begin from scratch because I had been out of high school for more than 20 years. My math skills were lacking and my study habits nonexistent. The junior college offered returning students free tutoring; I took advantage of the offer and used the math tutors. I also found a "study buddy" early on, and we not only graduated with our Associate's degrees together but transferred to the university and received our bachelor's and master's degrees together. Having this support was instrumental in my academic success.

Transferring to the university was overwhelming, and I struggled with insecurity and fear of failure. I received a scholarship, and this helped on the financial end of things. Once at the university, I began taking courses toward a bachelor's degree in human services. Throughout my undergraduate and graduate education my instructors were always approachable. With the encouragement of one of my instructors, I was introduced to a mentor who joined me on my journey of learning who I was as a person as well as learning ways to help others to explore the choices given them in life.

In the master's in counseling program, I picked up another study partner, and the three of us encouraged one another through some really tough times. Not only did we have to make time for our classes, internships, and projects, but we also had our home lives and jobs to handle. As friends we went through illnesses, deaths, marriages, and grandchildren together. Without this support, I might not have completed my journey. Often I doubted my abilities, but I was encouraged to push my boundaries, to explore different areas of counseling, and to join in conversation without feeling that what I had to say was of little interest. This open dialogue helped in all areas of my development as a counselor, and it also enabled me to be a better parent, sister, friend, and coworker.

I cannot say it was an easy road, but I can say that it was and is worth the journey. I continue on that journey as I work toward my hours as an intern in marriage and family counseling. I have found an inner strength that I did not know I had. I have developed friendships that will continue throughout my life, and I hope that I can continue to transfer some of my learning into a positive outcome for the women I work with by developing a relationship of trust. These women are learning that they, too, have a choice.

My advice for returning students is to take baby steps. I found ways to meet my commitments to family, work, education, and myself. I made sure to take time off to rest and replenish my inner self, and I continually worked to balance the many facets of my life. As the responsibilities stacked up, it was most important to take care of myself. A lesson I learned early on was that the most important factor for success was not having straight As but having a B for balance. I am delighted to report that I found that it was not too late to start on my path toward success.

~

Commentary

I find Toni's story inspirational, especially for those who may find themselves in a similar situation. She demonstrated the courage to return to pursue both undergraduate and graduate programs at a university in her mid-40s as a single parent with three teens. In her career as a nurse, she realized that she needed specialized knowledge and skills to continue to meet the challenges that were posed by her changing career path. She is living proof that it is never too late to pursue a new academic and career path. Toni's career path changed as her interests changed over the years; her career evolved toward providing counseling with a targeted population. Although she made the commitment to broaden her career aspirations, Toni acknowledges that the choices she made involved sacrifice and entailed risks. She also recognizes that it would not have been possible to pursue her dreams without a support system in the form of a close group of friends who navigated their educational paths together.

Questions for Reflection

- What lessons stand out for you in Toni's story? If you were in her situation, what challenges do you think you would need to address?
- Have you ever told yourself that it is too late to get involved in a change of career?
- In what ways can you take care of yourself as you face the demands of work, home, and school?

Overcoming Fears to a New Path

Jamie Bilezikjian, MA

The Board of Behavioral Sciences requires 3,000 hours of practicum and internship experience before applicants can take the marriage and family therapy (MFT) licensing test. When I heard this, I thought, "Wow that is a lot of hours!" I was already overwhelmed with the idea of having to first complete a master's in counseling psychology. How was I going to tell my husband that in my 40s I wanted to give up a well-paying corporate job as a pharmaceutical representative to become a marriage and family therapist? The commitment to this new career path would be huge in terms of time, energy, and financial resources. So I mulled this decision over for 3 or 4 years, choosing to focus on my fears: What if I failed in school? Who would hire an MFT intern who was nearly 50 years old? What if I turned out to be a terrible therapist? Then the thought occurred to me: What if I stayed in a job I no longer enjoyed for another 20 years because it was safe?

Well, I am now 50 years old with a master's degree and the majority of my intern hours completed. My past corporate experience helped me in graduate school in the areas of time management, paper writing, and classroom presentations. What my business experience did not prepare me for was practicum and internship. Those old fears started to crop up again: What if I did not help people but actually caused them more pain and distress? This is where supervision and mentoring came to my rescue.

For my practicum I was assigned to a homeless shelter in a large suburban area that was designed to serve families. This shelter is a private, nonprofit, transitional living program where clients can stay for up to 2 years. As a trainee, my practicum hours were focused on counseling school-age children. I was petrified: It is bad enough to worry about hurting adults, but I would be working with children! Then I met my supervisor, a clinical social worker, who encouraged me to voice my fears in our supervision sessions. In the beginning I fell into the same trap that so many new student counselors do, thinking that it is the work *I* do that will help the client. My supervisor reminded me that it is the work that *they* are willing to do that will bring clients insight and healing. When my practicum came to an end, the shelter asked if I could stay on for my intern hours, and I am now completing my hours for licensure there.

What ultimately helped me make the decision to pursue a career path in counseling was my determination to face my fears head on and to educate myself. I reminded myself of how many times in my life a major change came with the fear of failure. For me, fear always accompanies major changes like leaving home for the first time, pursuing a college degree, and interviewing for a new job. Realizing that I had overcome my fear of failure in all these circumstances helped me start this new path. I also made it my goal to educate myself about the counseling field. Through family members and friends, I contacted as many professionals in the helping field as I could find. I talked with them about their professional journey and asked for their advice.

Coming from a corporate and business background, I was initially leery about supervision. In most work environments, a meeting with your supervisor often means a review or a reprimand. Either way, you need to come across as confident and capable. The last thing I would want to do is admit that I am feeling unsure about the job I am doing. The opposite is true for counseling or social work supervision. If I could give advice to new graduate students in social work and counseling, I would stress the importance of letting yourself be open to constructive criticism during your practicum and internship. As a student intern, bring your most difficult cases for review. Some of my most valuable learning experiences have occurred during supervision sessions.

I recently had an encounter that reminded me of the importance of good supervision and mentoring. A former female client from the shelter called to express how well she was doing now. She and her teenage children had been in our program for 2 years and had just left. She was able to go back to school and get a certificate as an assistant in a health care field. She told me that she had just gotten the first job in her life that had a career path. Then she said, "You believed in me before I believed in myself." Yes, I had always believed in her ability to ultimately succeed. As I thought about what she said,

I realized that my supervisor had done the same thing for me. Indeed, supervisors often believe in us before we believe in ourselves.

∽

Commentary

Jamie is one of several individuals who have described making a career shift in their 40s. In her case, she gave up a financially secure corporate job to prepare herself for a new career in marriage and family therapy. Like many others, she had nagging thoughts about failing in graduate school, not finding employment, and not being a competent therapist. What helped Jamie combat her fears was making full use of supervision and mentoring. She realized that her fears over succeeding in graduate school and in a professional career were not unlike other fears that had accompanied major life changes.

An interesting point in Jamie's account is the challenge of adjusting to a different set of expectations between the corporate world and the counseling profession. In the former world, she would never want to admit that she was uncertain about what she was doing. In her counseling training, she learned that she could expose her vulnerabilities and bring her most difficult cases to her supervision sessions.

Questions for Reflection

- What could help you to overcome some of your fears about succeeding in your career?
- How open do you see yourself as being in your supervision sessions?
- Have you had supervisors or teachers who believed in you before you believed in yourself?
- Are you considering any shifts in pursuing a new career path?

How Hurricane Katrina Changed My Life

Leslie Culver, MS, NCC

Hurricane Katrina forced my evacuation from New Orleans. I stayed on a cotton farm owned by friends in the Mississippi Delta for 1 month and then returned to the devastation that remained in New Orleans. I also found myself suddenly unemployed for the first time in my life. However, the months that followed the storm afforded me the luxury of time for self-reflection as I did my small part to help rebuild my native city. I had spent the 4 years prior to Katrina in marketing, developing creative campaigns, coordinating events, and producing promotional print materials. Although I enjoyed working in the business world, and climbing the corporate ladder certainly had its perks, I knew there was something else of importance that I should be doing. I craved a career that was challenging and fulfilling, something that would make the best use of my unique skills and personality. I also felt a genuine desire to help others lead healthier lives. After Hurricane Katrina, more than ever, I was committed to doing this work in New Orleans.

In retrospect it makes sense that in the chaos of post-Katrina, I would be drawn to a helping field, and then to the counseling program at Loyola University New Orleans. Years earlier I had completed my undergraduate degree in English literature there. I took great comfort in their centuries-old Jesuit approach to education, which encourages critical thinking and emphasizes developing the whole person. Loyola University's master's degree in counseling was built on these same principles. The program strives to produce competent, ethical counselors through academic, experiential, and intrapersonal learning.

As the first few weeks of classes progressed, I became confident in my decision to pursue counseling as a career. I was inspired by my professors who worked in private practice and relayed their own clinical experiences to the students in class. I knew within that first semester that not only did I want to help others through counseling, but I wanted to teach others how to help as well. The most challenging part of my master's degree program was the transition from academic learning to practical application of that knowledge in a clinical setting. It was incredibly daunting to actually sit across from another human being who was most likely suffering and expecting me to help. Early in my practical experience, I came to terms with the fact that counseling skills were not something that could be instantly mastered, nor was book learning sufficient to conquer these skills. I realized that the counselor formation process was a lifelong journey that would require practice, supervision, consultation, and continuing education.

Individuals living in post-Katrina New Orleans desperately needed mental health services. I had the good fortune to work with many different populations and modalities in my practicum and internships. I worked with children (play therapy), adolescents (activity therapy), adults (traditional talk therapy), couples (both traditional and tandem therapy), and groups. The group work was particularly difficult for me. I felt anxious in the way one might feel nervous doing public speaking—I was self-conscious. But I forced myself to power through several types of groups in an effort to figure out what wasn't clicking for me. I cofacilitated a men's domestic violence group, an active parenting group, a grief support group for widows and widowers, and a self-expression group for children who had lost a parent. Even though I deeply appreciated the principles of group work and had positive encounters within these various groups, these experiences solidified for me that I would be most effective as a counselor in one-on-one sessions.

I would encourage students to work with as many different populations and modalities as possible to find the right fit for themselves and to remain open as they explore these different areas. I planned to skip an elective play therapy course because I was convinced I wanted to work exclusively with adults, but after encouragement from a field site supervisor, I decided to enroll in the course. It turned out to be an invaluable experience that equipped me with a useful skill set and led to an interest in working with children.

After graduation I accepted a part-time counselor position at the nonprofit agency where I had been interning and enrolled as a full-time student in the doctoral program in counselor education at the University of New Orleans. I needed to gain more experience with clients to develop my clinical skills and to work toward licensure, but I was adamant in my decision to continue formal studies so that I could pursue teaching and research opportunities. Just as clients will continue to fascinate and challenge me with their individual stories, research offers the same possibilities.

The first three semesters of my doctoral program have provided a period of tremendous personal and professional growth for me. Although the course work is stimulating and important, my experiences outside the classroom are critical to my professional development. The experience of coaching and supervising master's students has added a new dimension to my educational experience and counseling repertoire. Involvement in extracurricular professional activities has added another dimension. I joined the Executive Board of Alpha Eta, our university's Chi Sigma Iota chapter, which led to involvement in a number of professional workshops, service projects, and school activities. I attended the American Counseling Association's conference, which broadened my understanding of the profession and sparked new ideas for future research. In developing my research interest and skills, I was fortunate enough to find an experienced and invested professor who mentored me and guided me through my first research and grant writing process, and with whom I continue to work. I also secured a position as a graduate assistant to concentrate on my schoolwork and research endeavors. I forged relationships with other doctoral students, and we continue to provide one another with significant support, insight, and humor as we move through our journey together.

These experiences have served me well and have been the source of significant lessons for me. Here are a few suggestions I would like to share with those who are beginning graduate school. Immerse yourself in your studies, and take advantage of the opportunities offered through your program. Do the work—attend class and read the assignments. Foster relationships with professors and peers, as they will be invaluable to your growth. Find a mentor whose style and interests mirror your own. Get involved with school activities. Consider working as a graduate assistant. Join local, state, and national professional organizations. Attend professional workshops and conferences. Engage in self-reflection. Try to avoid making assumptions and remain open. Stay humble. Take care of yourself. Set appropriate boundaries, and strive for work–life balance. Remind yourself that the "starving student" phase is temporary. Enjoy the process.

Upon completion of my doctoral degree and state licensing requirements, I look forward to the combination of practicing counseling, conducting research, teaching within the field, and being an active member of the professional community. I am thrilled to have begun a lifelong study in counseling, and the prospect of giving back to the profession is equally exciting. The counseling process is a unique, powerful undertaking, and I wholeheartedly accept the challenge.

～

Commentary

Sometimes a crisis can lead to a new path, as it seems to have done for Leslie. Hurricane Katrina brought chaos, but as Leslie took steps to help rebuild her city she also rebuilt her career path. Leslie admits that she enjoyed her work in the business world, but her career in the corporate world did not satisfy her quest for a profession that could make the best use of her talents and skills.

For me, Leslie's decision to leave the business world, even though she enjoyed it and was successful in moving up the corporate ladder, was striking. As she launches her new academic and career path in counseling, she claims that her passions are in the areas of teaching and research. She also finds coaching and mentoring master's students rewarding. Leslie points to the importance of creating relationships with other doctoral students as they progress together on their journey. In her story, Leslie identifies specific lessons that

have served her well, and she offers suggestions to those who are
beginning graduate school.

Questions for Reflection

- Which of Leslie's suggestions for graduate students have the
  most personal meaning for you?
- To what extent have you created relationships with your peers
  and colleagues that you can draw on for support?

Finding a Purpose in the Work I Do

Amanda Healey, MA, LPC-MHSP, NCC

Looking back on the road that led me to decide to become a counselor
educator, I can recall many successes and failures, hardships, and
challenges. All of these experiences, even the situations that may have
seemed insurmountable and difficult, have created the path I walk
and the person I am. Today I am in the last semester of my doctoral
studies, excited about my future, and grateful for the people who have
supported me along the way. I would not have made it through some
of my more difficult moments without those friends and mentors I
recognize as family. The relationships I have built and strengthened
throughout my education have been very important in shaping who I
am and continually motivate me to be a better person. I cannot
imagine anyone making it through a graduate program in any field
without a caring and invested support system. By developing my
collegial relationships, I not only have made lifelong friends but have
nurtured a professional circle that will provide me with opportunities
for service, research, and continuing education.

I do not separate my personal and professional associations and goals
because I believe the two are integrally connected and thus influence
one another. My desire to become a counselor educator arose after
working in my community as a counselor with children in foster care
following the completion of my master's degree. To make what I
perceived to be needed change within the mental health system, I soon
understood that I would need to act from a different level. I think my
work as a clinician was individually valuable, but I felt I could make a
greater contribution as an educator, supervisor, and researcher. The
decision to move forward with my education was supported and
encouraged by faculty from my master's program, with whom I had
maintained contact and developed meaningful relationships. In an
effort to help me achieve this goal, they provided me with opportunities
to publish and present on a state and international level. They

introduced me to other professionals and discussed their perceptions of the counseling field with me to help prepare me for what was to come.

Before entering graduate school, I had a clear idea of my research interest areas and sought to accept only offers that would help me pursue those topics of interest or further my overall goal of obtaining a job as a counselor educator. Service in the community is also very important to me, so I made time to volunteer for the local Planned Parenthood and the National Gay and Lesbian Task Force's Equality Project, both of which were continuations of work I had begun prior to entering the doctoral program. Above all, I have always tried to find a valuable purpose in the work I do.

When I am working on conceptual or research articles for publication, service activities, supervision, or my dissertation, at times I can get overwhelmed with the many details of what needs to be done. At those moments, I keep in mind the reason I decided to pursue my doctorate and reflect on how the various projects I am involved with address my goals and help to create a better system. I know that nothing I do alone will have a significant impact on our profession or society, but I can influence those around me and make a positive contribution with the help of my colleagues.

Looking back on my journey so far, I know the relationships I fostered were, and continue, to be of great assistance to me. Through them and my own determination, I have been able to achieve my goals and have been honored to receive recognition from various professional counseling organizations for my work. I have paced myself and focused on producing quality work, putting as much energy and attention as possible into whatever I decide to do. Creating a clear workable plan for achieving long-term goals has been important for me. Without a balance of involvement in valuable work, time to reflect, and leisure, I would have found it difficult to pursue my goals toward becoming a counseling professional.

∼

Commentary

Amanda decided that she could make the greatest contribution by becoming a counselor educator, supervisor, and researcher. She believed that limiting herself to clinical work was not the professional path that would be fulfilling to her. At times, you may want to do it all: research, teaching, clinical work, administration, and community work. Although you may feel torn between various areas of interest, it may not be critical that you decide on any one of these career areas. For instance, if you eventually hope to secure employment as a counselor educator, you will likely have to fulfill a number of functions besides teaching to keep your position in a university. You will have to do professional writing, participate in community service, engage in some research activities, serve on committees, and advise and mentor students. You are likely to find ways to combine different roles to create a path with several different, yet related, career areas.

Questions for Reflection

- As you reflect on Amanda's story, how can you best narrow down your own career choices?
- Are there several complementary areas that you can see yourself putting your efforts toward?
- What kind of career path would you most hope to establish for yourself? How can you determine where you can make the greatest contribution?

Counseling Academically Talented Students

Michelle Muratori, PhD

Upon starting my graduate training in counselor education at The University of Iowa (UI), I accepted a graduate assistantship at a center on campus that served academically talented youth. Prior to that experience, I had worked with diverse client populations such as chronically mentally ill men living in a residential facility, pregnant teenagers from the inner city of a large urban area, and families at risk of losing their children to Child Protective Services, to name a few. All of these clinical experiences broadened my perspective on the counseling process and led me to be open-minded about populations I might serve in the future. As different as these experiences were from one another, I loved interacting with my clients and learned so much from them.

At the Belin-Blank Center UI, I quickly discovered that the students (able students who entered college a year early) assigned to me were struggling with a range of issues. After working in rather intense settings, I actually wondered if these "gifted" students would have problems that I could help resolve. I learned that, like traditional freshmen, these students dealt with conflicts with their roommates, deficits in their study skills and time management skills, high stress levels, homesickness, and a host of other adjustment issues. I developed a keen interest in their academic, social, and emotional adjustment and conducted two research studies (including my doctoral dissertation) on this topic.

Eventually, I used the salient points from this research as the premise of my first book, *Early Entrance to College: A Guide to Success* (Muratori, 2007). Because I had written a dissertation that was more than 500 pages, the prospect of writing a book didn't seem that daunting to me. After all, I felt like I had already written one! My greatest challenge was juggling all of my other responsibilities during the time period when I was under contract to write the book. I was extremely busy with work-related projects and teaching classes on a part-time basis, and adding working on my book to my schedule created additional pressures. After some ambivalence, I made a commitment to myself to do whatever was required to finish the book. I achieved my goal and felt tremendous satisfaction and relief when the book was finally published.

While I was working on my dissertation, I was recruited for a position as a senior counselor and researcher at the Johns Hopkins Center for Talented Youth to work with students who had exceptionally high mathematical or verbal reasoning abilities. As a group, these students were even more intellectually precocious than the college students I had counseled at The University of Iowa. I accepted the position, which required me to move to the east coast. Like the early entrants I had served, I was about to face my own adjustment period.

In this position, which I still have, I admittedly was humbled to know that the 12- and 13-year-old students I was providing guidance and support to could run circles around me in terms of solving math problems. In suggesting this, I am neither overestimating their ability nor underestimating my own. It is a fact. The students I serve are smarter than I am in terms of their mathematical reasoning abilities. There would have been a time when I would have been ashamed to admit that, but not today.

During my formative years, my sense of self had largely been defined by my academic accomplishments and strong work ethic. Later on, as I engaged in my own self-exploration and personal growth, I learned to define myself in other ways; however, being intelligent and accomplished never ceased to be important to me. So in taking on the professional challenge of counseling exceptionally able students, I was simultaneously challenging some of my deeper fears about being "adequate enough" or "smart enough." I can't begin to tell you how liberating it was to realize that there was no way I could compete with a 12-year-old who was excelling in calculus or, possibly, college-level math. I stopped trying to prove to myself that I was "smart enough." This was a turning point in my personal and professional development.

One measure of my growth was accepting the fact that I had something special to offer these amazing young people even though they were so brilliant. Had I not worked through my own feelings of intimidation and inadequacy, I would not have been able to get out of my own way to be fully present for them. I am glad that I did accomplish this because to be competent in my role as counselor to this underserved population I need to be able to advocate for their educational and social/emotional needs.

As a counselor, I enjoy the challenge of helping these students and their parents. I find it meaningful to develop educational programs that are tailored to each student's unique needs and circumstances. When students' educational needs are being met, they also feel better about other aspects of their lives. Along with that, I enjoy building relationships with these families and empowering them to advocate for themselves. The greatest reward for me is hearing from students and their parents who contact me from time to time just to check in and give me an update on how things are going. It feels good to know that I have made a difference in their lives and that they have felt supported by me. I also wonder how the clients and students I served long ago are doing. Even though I no longer have contact with them, I remember the lessons they have taught me, and for that I am very grateful. All my educational and professional experiences combined have broadened my understanding of the helping process. My experiences at the Center for Talented Youth have only strengthened my passion for helping *all* young people, not just the gifted, develop their talent.

~

Commentary

As is true for others who shared their stories, Michelle did not submit to her fears of not being smart enough or adequate enough for a task she wanted to pursue. Because of her courage in challenging her fears, and her willingness to follow her passions, she found a career niche in counseling the gifted. She derives a great deal of meaning from creating educational programs tailored to the unique needs of the students she is serving.

Questions for Reflection

- What stands out most for you about Michelle's story of finding a passion and pursuing it?

- Michelle found a way to combine her interests in counseling and writing. Can you incorporate your various interests and talents into your professional life?
- If writing is one of your interests, what would you most like to write about?

Some Final Thoughts

When making career choices, it is useful to get ideas from others to help narrow down your options and to find ways to achieve your aspirations. However, after getting this input, you need to make choices in light of your own circumstances. I encourage students to search for the answers within themselves when deciding on a career path. Here are a few ideas that may help you create the kind of professional path you desire.

Have the courage to pursue your passions. Let your interests be your guide. Envision what you would love to do, and then figure out how to move in that direction. If you could do anything you wanted, where would you be and what would you be doing 5 years from now? What steps can you take today to move in that direction?

Realize that you are never too old to return to a university and pursue a different academic and career path.

In following a career interest, it is extremely important to not allow your feelings of inadequacy and intimidation to get in your way. One way to develop trust in yourself is to face any feelings of inadequacy by taking risks.

Reflect on ways that you can use your personal skills and knowledge to make a difference in the lives of others and what special talents you have that you can put to the service of others. Think about the kind of career that will provide you with opportunities to make a contribution to others.

Find at least one mentor whose style and interests mirror your own. Ask about ways you can get involved in collaborative projects. Consult with your mentors periodically about matters related to your studies and your career. Talk with your favorite professors, and ask how you can get involved in projects with them. Ask them for tips for succeeding in your graduate program, for finding your professional niche, and for succeeding in your career.

Join professional organizations on the state, regional, and national levels. Read the journals of these organizations, attend the conferences they offer, and submit a proposal to present at conferences. Go to the presentations that interest you, and look for ways to network and collaborate with professionals with whom you share similar interests. Inquire about any job possibilities that may be opening up.

Establish long-term and short-term goals, and make a concrete timeline for accomplishing specific tasks. Learn time management skills, and apply these skills to your projects.

Take time to reflect on what you are doing that has worked for you in the past and is currently working for you, and then continue these patterns. Trust yourself to come up with your own plan for creating the kind of professional life you want—and then take steps to put your action plan in place. "A journey of a thousand miles begins with a single step," said a Chinese philosopher. What steps are you willing to take now to begin your journey?

I find two books very useful in providing ideas for creating a career path. One of these is *The Emerging Professional Counselor: Student Dreams to Professional Realities* (Hazler & Kottler, 2005). This book provides ideas regarding the process, opportunities, and struggles faced by new professionals and counseling students as they make educational and career transitions. In the other book, *Journeys to Professional Excellence: Lessons From Leading Counselor Educators and Practitioners* (Conyne & Bemak, 2005), 15 key people in the counseling profession share their personal and professional stories. They describe how they chose their career paths, how they dealt with challenges they faced, what factors contributed to both their successes and their failures, and how they balance their work and personal lives. In addition, they offer suggestions for those entering the profession.

Chapter Eight
On Being a Writer

Introduction

As you pursue your journey in the counseling profession, you will find it necessary to do various kinds of writing. Although you may not be thinking about writing a book or a journal article, if you are currently in a graduate program, you will engage in a number of writing projects. In addition to papers for your courses, you might have a project for your master's degree or a doctoral dissertation. If you eventually work in a community agency, you will need to write a self-evaluation at different review points. In addition, you may need to write case notes for all your clients and other written reports for your supervisors. You may be asked to write letters of recommendation or to participate in writing grants for program funding or to write reports for accreditation purposes. Chances are that you will attend professional conferences, and at some time you will likely submit a proposal to present at a conference. If you aim to become a counselor educator, to retain your position, or to qualify for promotion you will most likely be expected to publish articles in professional journals. Some of you may write chapters for books or even write your own books. Learning how to express yourself, both orally and in writing, goes with the territory of a career in the counseling professions.

In this chapter I provide some practical suggestions for a variety of writing endeavors, especially in areas such as papers for graduate school, dissertations, proposals for presentations at conferences, case notes, letters of recommendation, journal articles, and writing a book. I also talk about my own experiences in writing and relate some of the lessons I learned along the way.

Writing Papers for Graduate School Classes

Most of us are not born talented writers, as you may know from your own experience. In my undergraduate English composition course, I remember struggling and getting a fair number of C grades on essays. Sometimes my essays would be returned with numerous comments in red ink, and I would have to write multiple drafts. I am surprised that this did not destroy any desire I may have had to write materials for the classes I eventually found myself teaching! I cannot recall being allowed to write about topics in a personal manner. Most of the writing I was required to do involved abstract subjects, and there was little room to bring myself into the writing in personal ways.

From my first assignment as a high school English teacher in 1961 to the present time as a professor of counseling and human services, I have been assigning papers to students in every class I teach. Over these many years, I have required common themes in almost all of these papers: critical thinking, reflection, personalizing a topic, and creative expression. These dimensions were missing from most of the writing I had to do in high school and college, and I came to firmly believe that writing could help students reflect on certain aspects of their lives.

I want students to bring themselves into their writing, and I give them room to decide how they can make a writing assignment a personally meaningful project. For instance, in the high school English classes I taught, I asked students to think about and reflect on the direction of their lives. The title I assigned for one of their papers was, "If I Had 24 Hours to Live, I Would _____." Another assignment involved having students write a paper on "My Philosophy of Life." I am not interested in having students do summary reports or write about topics that are not connected to their life experiences in some way. I typically assign papers that give students an opportunity to develop their thoughts around key themes in the course. At the present time, in the ethics course I teach, my students write a series of essays on various ethical dilemmas they might encounter and show how they would work through these dilemmas effectively. In my group counseling course, students discuss some aspects of each of the theories of group counseling that apply to them personally, and they are also expected to write about a few concepts or techniques from each theory that they would want to incorporate in their work as a group facilitator. Over the years, I have consistently required my students to write reaction papers and position papers on a variety of subjects pertaining to the course. They also write a comprehensive paper toward the end of the semester. These papers are done outside of class time, and I give them specific guidelines for writing quality papers. I read these papers myself and try to make meaningful comments in addition to grading the papers. Here are some of the suggestions I give to students for writing personal and meaningful papers:

- Write directly and informally, yet write in standard English. Use personal examples to support your points when these examples are appropriate. Make sure your essays reflect university-level writing skills. Use complete sentences, develop your paragraphs, check your spelling, and put together a paper that reflects quality. Have someone proofread your paper.
- Create an outline, and check to see that each point in your outline pertains to your central message. Look for a central theme or message in your essay. Ask yourself, "What are the two or three main points that I want to convey?"
- State your message concisely in the opening paragraph of your essay, and have a concluding paragraph as well.
- The theme you develop should be clear, concise, and specific rather than global and generalized. Develop your thoughts fully, concretely, and logically.
- Give reasons for your views rather than making unsupported statements. When taking a position, provide the rationale for your position.
- Write a paper that reflects your own uniqueness and ideas, not one that merely summarizes the material in the book. Approach the material in an original way.
- Focus on a particular issue or a topic that you find personally significant. You will often have a choice in what to focus on, so select an aspect of a problem that will enable you to express your beliefs. Above all, do not leave yourself out of your writing.

You may have different kinds of writing assignments than the ones I have described, but you may want to consider using some of these suggestions in your writing. In many of your classes, you will be given some freedom in selecting a topic of personal interest. I have found that selecting a topic that I want to learn more about, or an idea that I am passionate about, makes writing more meaningful and easier to accomplish. For most of us, writing entails a great deal of effort and some personal pain, even when we are passionate about the topic. You may find it useful to write a draft copy of your essay and ask a classmate to read your paper and give you feedback, or take your essay to the center on your campus where you can get help in writing quality papers. Your writing career may begin in your graduate program—but I hope it will not end there.

My Experience With a Dissertation for the Doctoral Program

During my doctoral course work between 1962 and 1966, I developed a real interest in existential psychology, especially through the books on the subject by Rollo May and Viktor Frankl. I am quite certain that my existential inclinations had to do with core aspects of my personality. What initially captured my attention about existential psychology was the theme of freedom and the anxiety that comes with making choices. Perhaps this was due to my not believing I could make choices for myself and my own struggles in making life choices. As I began questioning how I was living my own life, these notions of using my freedom and accepting responsibility for my choices made sense to me. This brought about considerable anxiety, and oftentimes I wanted to allay this anxiety by relying on ready-made moral precepts. Because this philosophical approach to living resonated with me personally, I began thinking of ways to incorporate existential concepts into a framework for thinking about the counseling process and my writing.

The proposal I developed for my doctoral dissertation had to do with identifying themes from existential-humanistic writers and exploring the implications of existential propositions for the practice of counseling. The chair of my dissertation committee strongly recommended that I give up on this idea for a dissertation because it was too grand and ambitious. He told me that I could pursue this topic after getting a doctorate and suggested I find a "workable topic" more suitable for a doctoral dissertation. My adviser was right about putting my original proposal on the back burner, for such a project would have been insurmountable. After discussing an "acceptable" dissertation topic with my adviser, I changed my proposal to investigating the personal and academic effects of two contrasting instructional methods for student success in an Introductory Psychology course.

The study sparked my enthusiasm for personal learning and convinced me of the value of experiential learning and small-group work in the classroom. However, I cannot say I enjoyed the dissertation process. I was anxious most of the time because I was required to apply a research design (involving statistics) in this study. It was a Herculean task for me to get through my two statistics courses, let alone having to actually apply statistical models to my study. From the year or so that I spent on the dissertation process, I learned the value of persisting in spite of self-doubts and difficulties. Like statistics, this project was an obstacle that I had to deal with if I hoped to obtain my doctorate. I did learn the value of getting consultation and help from a research design expert, and without this kind of assistance and mentoring, I could not have successfully completed the dissertation requirement. I learned the value of asking for help rather than thinking I had to do everything by myself. Although I found value in the study of various approaches to teaching psychology, it was not the most personally meaningful topic that I could have chosen. This reinforced my thoughts about the importance of giving students room to select topics that they deem to have personal meaning and encouraging them to bring themselves into their study and writing.

My initial interest in existential psychology continued, and I read literature in the field of the existential-humanistic approach to psychotherapy and began to write about how this approach could be applied to teaching and counseling. My interest in existential psychology has persisted to this day, and this approach is the foundational theory for my integrative approach to counseling practice.

Writing Proposals for Presentations at Professional Conferences

From the time I began my counseling career, I have regularly attended professional conferences at the national, regional, and state levels, and I frequently submit proposals for educational sessions, workshops, and panel presentations. This kind of writing is very demanding and exacting, and it takes me considerable time to put together a clear and concise proposal. Typically, I find it a real challenge to figure out how to complete these proposals when they *must* be submitted online. I like to include a colleague or several colleagues in most of these presentations as a way to promote collaboration. Most of the time my proposals are accepted, but there are times when they are not. Recently, I submitted two proposals for a particular conference, and on *both* proposals I received the following e-mail:

> Thank you for your proposal for the upcoming conference. Unfortunately, your proposal was not accepted for presentation at this conference. There were a total of 900 proposals submitted for this conference, but only a total of 600 proposals were accepted. We encourage you to submit your proposal for future conferences and we wish you success.

Furthermore, I had submitted two proposals for this group's previous conference, neither of which was accepted. I attended both of these conferences, and I did not consider it earth-shaking that my proposals were not accepted, nor did I interpret this as evidence that my proposals were worthless! However, some of my colleagues do not to attend conferences when their proposals are rejected because their universities will not provide travel money unless they are presenting.

Many of you will be attending professional conferences during your career, which is a great way to network with colleagues with interests similar to your own as well as to keep current with new developments in your field. If you decide to submit a proposal for a presentation at a professional conference, which I encourage you to do, I hope you will not be deterred from participating if your idea is not accepted. In fact, I suggest that you keep on submitting program proposals until you do get accepted. In writing a proposal, it is essential that you follow the instructions carefully and submit the proposal within the time frame provided. If your proposal is not well written, it will probably be rejected. Ask at least one colleague to review and comment on your proposal *before* you finalize it and submit it for the review process. Keep in mind that there are only so many slots available for a given conference, and a committee typically makes selection decisions based on a number of specific criteria. Just because your proposal is not accepted does not mean that it is without value. The committee may simply be attempting to balance the topics offered for a given conference, or perhaps too many outstanding proposals were received.

Writing Case Notes

Another kind of writing that most of you will be required to do, regardless of the setting in which you work, is writing case notes on all of your clients. I must admit that in my part-time private practice in counseling 35 to 40 years ago, I had few record-keeping procedures. I did not record diagnosis and treatment planning, nor did my notes cover areas considered essential by present-day professional standards. I recall keeping a folder on clients that included some observations and comments on the progress of their therapy, the dates of their sessions, and a record of fees received. Certainly, the records I kept would not be adequate from an ethical or legal perspective if I were in practice today.

Because you are required to keep adequate progress notes on all your clients, it is essential that you master the skills required for this particular kind of writing. Colleagues and supervisors will be pleased to offer you help in learning how to effectively write progress notes that are part of the client's clinical record. This clinical record includes documenting matters pertaining to diagnosis, treatment plans, symptoms, prognosis, and progress. The agency where you work will have policies and procedures to guide you in keeping complete client files. Writing case notes is not merely busywork. Record keeping serves the purposes of providing the best services for your clients and of providing evidence of a level of care that is in keeping with the standards of the profession. In addition, accurate and relevant documentation is a useful risk management strategy that helps prevent successful malpractice litigation. Although maintaining adequate clinical records is essential, it is a mistake to become overly concerned about using record keeping as a self-protective strategy.

When I talk about writing case notes in my ethics course, here are a few of the suggestions I offer. Do not alter case notes after they have been entered into a client's record. In keeping records, it is useful to consider the policies of the agency where you work as well as directives from other regulatory bodies. As you write case notes, it is a good idea to consider that your client might read them. Write in a respectful manner, avoid jargon, and focus on describing specific and concrete behavior. Remember, in today's climate there are no legitimate reasons for not keeping timely records. For a more detailed discussion of this topic, I recommend *Documentation in Counseling Records: An Overview of Ethical, Legal, and Clinical Issues* (Mitchell, 2007).

Legal and medical records have become mandated in the United States under the Health Information Portability and Accountability Act (HIPAA). In other countries, like Canada, Australia, and New Zealand, to name three English-speaking countries, HIPAA rules do not apply. In these countries, narrative therapists often keep notes and records that are transformed into letters and other documents that are sent to the clients through the mail or are presented to them in ceremonies. This is an example of how therapy can extend beyond the office. This kind of written communication between counselors and clients appeals to me mainly because these therapeutic letters have the purpose of cultivating a sense of connection. There is much that can be noted, remembered, and appreciated about clients when letters are used.

Therapeutic letters tend to reflect the unique personality and point of view of the therapist who is writing them. Therapeutic letters provide a forum in which counselors can communicate with clients on a human-to-human level, without the use of professional jargon, and with an emphasis on resiliency and encouragement. These letters have the added advantage of letting clients know that the counselor is thinking about them between sessions, and perhaps clients might do well to be thinking about themselves too. I believe therapeutic practice can be enhanced through the use of letters and documents such as those developed by narrative therapists. For a further discussion of this subject, I recommend *Narrative Means to Therapeutic Ends* (White & Epston, 1990).

Writing Letters of Recommendation

It is almost a certainty that you will be requesting letters of recommendation for entrance to graduate programs or as a part of applying for a job. Chances are that you also will be asked to write such letters for others as a part of your job. Let me briefly share with you what I look for when I write letters of recommendations for students applying for graduate school, for colleagues seeking letters for tenure and promotion purposes, and for colleagues applying for an award from a professional organization. If you were to ask me to write you a letter, I would want you to assist me in writing you the best possible letter by having you do the following:

- Ask if I know you well enough to write you a letter and if I am willing to do so. If I have reservations about writing a letter on your behalf, I will do my best to tell you in a sensitive way. Once you have heard my specific concerns, you can decide if you want to seek other endorsers.
- Give me plenty of lead time, and let me know specifically what you want and to whom the letter should be directed. I will strive to complete the letter in a timely fashion, and if I am unable to do so, I will let you know.

- Provide me with the materials and information I need to complete your letter. It helps if you identify your specific goals, such as an application for graduate school or for an employment position.
- Tell me in writing some things I may not know about you that I could use in writing a stronger letter for you. Identify several highlights regarding experiences you have had that you would like me to consider including in your letter. List a few of your major strengths and some areas where you need to do further work.
- I will do my best to write an honest and accurate letter for you that puts you in the best light. However, I do not want to make exaggerated and inflated statements about your abilities and your qualifications for a position.
- Fill out your part on all the forms and provide envelopes with the complete address and stamps. Don't make me do any extra work such as filling out forms that you should have completed.

It is good practice to write your own letter of recommendation to gain some objectivity in presenting your background. You may need to do this in the form of a self-statement in which you write about your goals and philosophy. Ask someone you trust to read your self-statement paper and give you feedback.

For a discussion of writing letters of recommendation, see Chapter 9 in *Clinical Supervision in the Helping Professions: A Practical Guide* (Corey, Haynes, Moulton, & Muratori, 2010).

Writing Articles for Professional Journals

In the past 30 years, I have authored or coauthored a number of book chapters and articles for professional journals. I generally prefer working on a book to devoting time to writing articles for publication in journals. However, publishing refereed articles in well-known journals is considered an essential pathway toward promotion in many university settings. Like program proposals for a conference, articles are not always accepted as submitted and may be returned to the author with specific suggestions for revision. Sometimes an author will receive a letter stating that the article does not fit a particular journal's focus. Authors may react in a variety of ways to such news. Some are determined to keep working on the article until a journal editor accepts it. Some feel hurt, angry, and upset and decide not to try again. Some interpret this as a personal rejection and are hesitant to continue writing.

Years ago I encountered a colleague on my faculty who looked very glum. When I asked her what was wrong, she described how upset she felt because the journal article she had submitted to her professional organization had been rejected. She was extremely depressed over this event and wondered whether she should make another attempt and submit a revised version. She needed some publications for her tenure review, and this rejection represented a major setback for her. She showed me the letter with the reviewers' responses, and I suggested that she consider some of these criticisms. I thought her overall project was worthwhile, and I encouraged her to revise her article. Unfortunately, my colleague seemed to take the reviewers' feedback personally, and she told me that she might not bother revising her article and submitting it again. By allowing her discouragement to block her path, she compromised her ability to write an article that probably would have been accepted. This situation called to my mind the importance of sticking with a project even when there are roadblocks. It also reinforced my belief that as writers we need to develop a thick skin and not take criticism too personally. If we become overly defensive, we block ourselves from considering critical feedback that may improve our writing.

Although I have had invitations to write a specific piece for a professional journal or a monthly magazine or a newsletter for a professional association, most of the time I submit articles because of my interest in a topic and my desire to share these ideas with colleagues. I too have had a few articles rejected on my first attempt. One in particular that I recall being rejected was an article I coauthored with Albert Ellis on the subject of the irrational beliefs of group counselors. One of the beliefs we addressed was, "It would be terrible if I made a mistake in the groups I lead, for that would mean I'm incompetent." We did not conduct a specific study pertaining to beliefs of group leaders, nor did we cite other research done in this area. Instead, we gave many examples of faulty beliefs of group leaders and suggested strategies for disputing such beliefs. Our goal was to explore ways to encourage group leaders to actively challenge certain beliefs they hold that often interfere with their ability to function effectively in a group.

We sent our article to the editor of a professional journal and weeks later received a letter stating that our article was not accepted for publication. Five people reviewed the article, and none of them recommended accepting it as written. The feedback we received was that we had written on too simple a level for most readers, that our style was too informal, that we did not follow APA style carefully, and that it lacked a specific research base.

Albert Ellis and I collaborated on the feedback we had received, made revisions, and resubmitted the article for consideration. The result of this effort was another letter stating that our article could not be accepted for publication in its present form. We revised our article again and submitted it for a third time—and guess what? Another rejection letter arrived. Upon receiving this third letter about the fate of our article, I entertained the irrational belief that this rejection proved I had nothing of value to say. Whereas Ellis's comment was, "They have a problem!" I was challenged to apply some cognitive behavioral techniques for disputing irrational beliefs to cope with this situation. Fortunately, I did not let this experience keep me from writing other journal articles.

If you write a journal article, my hope is that you will not be devastated if it is not accepted on the initial round of reviews. Most people I know who write articles for journals typically must revise the article at least once, and sometimes several times. Most journals have a quota of how many articles they can accept for publication, which means that most submissions are never published. If you do write a journal article, consider working with a coauthor so that you can generate and exchange ideas, and also so you can revise your manuscript as many times as necessary. Ask other colleagues who have published articles in professional journals for suggestions on how to proceed. Be sure that the article you are writing fits the general criteria for the journal you are considering, and follow the article submission guidelines for this particular journal. Many journals expect a scholarly piece with some research base, and if your article does not fit in this realm, chances are it will not be accepted.

The Joys and Pains of Writing Books

In previous chapters I have described how I developed my ideas for writing textbooks, the challenges I faced in writing them, and how my teaching and writing interests are intertwined. In this section I want to briefly share with you the process of writing textbooks along with some relevant lessons I learned from these experiences.

Writing a Book With My Daughters

One book that proved to be a challenge to write was *Living and Learning* (Corey, Corey, & Corey, 1997), which was a textbook for first-year college students. This was one of the few times that an editor approached me with an idea for a book and I actually accepted the offer. I was hesitant to sign a contract for this college success book because I had not taught this course, and I wondered if I had the expertise to do the job. I approached both my daughters, Heidi and Cindy, about this offer and convinced them that they each had unique facets and experiences they could bring to this project.

Most books in this area are slanted toward study skills and topics such as using the library, taking notes, reading, managing time, taking tests, writing, and how to read better and faster. We believed there was a need for a different kind of college success textbook. We believed that when students are not successful, it was not simply due to poor study habits but often was due to personal and interpersonal problems. We did cover most of the traditional study skills topics, but we also addressed the personal dimensions of becoming a successful student. We asked students to get better acquainted with themselves and to identify strengths and resources they could draw on to achieve success in college. Some of the nontraditional topics we covered included knowing your values and goals, enhancing relationships, understanding diversity, taking care of yourself, making responsible choices, coping with stress and crisis, and discovering your passions and creating your path.

As we began to write this book, we looked back at our own educational journeys. Each of us had faced quite different challenges in becoming better learners. None of us had had an easy road, and we agreed that there had to be a better way. This guided us as we developed the ideas for our book.

Working with both of my daughters and dealing with the inevitable frustrations was challenging for all of us. We frequently met as a threesome to brainstorm ideas, and I worked in different ways with Cindy and Heidi separately. We each selected topics that were in our areas of strength. Once we had completed an initial draft of most of the chapters, we met with our developmental editor, Alan Venable. He was a joy to work with. He stayed with us for several days, and we went over every chapter. It is rare that an editor will give this amount of time to authors. Alan was a mentor to us all, and he encouraged us to write in a simple and concise style that would appeal to students with limited reading skills. With Alan's help, we were able to convey what we considered to be the most significant messages we wanted our readers to understand.

As a result of this collaboration, Cindy, Heidi, and I volunteered to coteach a college success course at CSUF, which we continued to do for several semesters. Teaching this course gave us an increased understanding of the struggles many students face that affect their academic performance and what they can do to get the most from their educational experience. We each learned a great deal about what helps students survive and thrive as learners.

Writing Books With Twenty Contributors

I teamed up with Barbara Herlihy, a professor at the University of New Orleans, to coauthor both the fifth and sixth editions of the *ACA Ethical Standards Casebook* (Herlihy & Corey, 1996, 2006a) and another book, *Boundary Issues in Counseling: Multiple Roles and Responsibilities* (Herlihy & Corey, 2006b), for the American Counseling Association. Barbara and I did the majority of the writing, but we thought it important to present the perspectives of other professionals as well. In the sixth edition of the casebook, 20 professionals in counseling and related fields contributed articles and case studies on ethical issues pertaining to client rights and informed consent, multicultural counseling, confidentiality, competence, working with multiple clients, counseling minors, multiple relationships, end-of-life decisions, supervision, and the law and ethics. One of our tasks was to develop vignettes that illustrated good ethical practice for every standard in the *ACA Code of Ethics*. We found this exercise to be quite demanding because it required us to think of practical examples that would make the ethical principles come to life. Working on the *ACA Ethical Standards Casebook* showed me how ethics codes evolve, even within a 10-year period, and how important it is to learn to apply these codes to the range of ethical quandaries we may need to address.

In writing *Boundary Issues in Counseling*, Barbara and I were principally motivated by our desire to bring a balanced perspective to matters pertaining to multiple relationships and multiple roles. When we began writing on this topic, some writers tended toward dogmatic pronouncements, and many presenters at conferences advocated avoiding multiple relationships at all costs. We did not claim that we had discovered the answers to many complex and difficult questions, but we were troubled by this rule-bound and somewhat rigid thinking on boundary issues. We invited about 20 colleagues to contribute a variety of perspectives on controversies pertaining to boundaries, multiple relationships, and ways of thinking about such concerns. The contributors brought diverse perspectives to the discussion of managing multiple relationships and boundary issues in counseling practice, and I learned that multiple relationships are realities that counselors have to face in any work setting. Among the topics addressed were transcending boundaries in psychotherapy, involving the client in making decisions about boundaries, subtle boundary issues in supervision, managing dual relationships in small communities, multicultural perspectives on multiple relationships, dual relationships from an African-centered perspective, boundary issues in substance abuse and addiction counseling, and multiple relationships with people living with HIV. This project confirmed my belief in the complexity of the boundary issues counselors face on a daily basis and convinced me to challenge models of thinking about ethics that are based on a narrow interpretation of the existing codes.

As authors we were challenged to work with 20 contributors, editing their material and communicating with them as we revised their contributions. This work had to be done in a timely fashion and coordinated so that the books had unity. I learned how difficult it is to write in this fashion but came to appreciate the value of this exchange of ideas and the diverse views we presented on specific topics. The process reconfirmed my belief in the value of collaboration with colleagues on worthwhile projects.

Working as a Team in Developing a Book for Clinical Supervisors

Bob Haynes, a colleague with whom I had worked in various capacities, approached me to join him and another colleague in writing a practical guide to clinical supervision. Bob was the director of an APA-accredited internship training site for more than 25 years and had an abundance of experience supervising doctoral-level students in a psychiatric hospital setting. He wanted to write a practical guide to helping supervisors become more effective in their work. Because of my fondness and respect for Bob and the fact that I was convinced he had a valuable and unique project, I agreed to join him and Patrice Moulton, a colleague who worked with supervisees at Northwestern State University, on this book project.

In writing the first draft, we each took primary responsibility for about three chapters, which we then sent to one another. The three of us met for a 10-day marathon writing and revision session in July of 2001 in our mountain home in Southern California. We typically worked for 9 hours a day, and we did considerable work on the entire book within the 10 days. This marathon writing retreat was collaboration at its best, and it was a unique experience for me. Sitting alone and crafting a chapter can be lonely at times. Although we grew weary during this intensive writing endeavor, I think we all saw the advantages of being in the same room and being able to talk with one another in person. After leaving this retreat, we each went home with numerous tasks and completed the final drafts of our chapters, which we sent to one another for review and commentary. Our marathon writing sessions and the follow-up work we did both individually and collectively resulted in the publication of *Clinical Supervision in the Helping Professions: A Practical Guide* (Haynes, Corey, & Moulton, 2003).

For the second edition of this book, we invited Michelle Muratori to join us as a new coauthor. For the most part, we wrote the second edition by sending chapters to one another as e-mail attachments. We did not divide up the chapters, but instead all four of us worked on all of the chapters. We recruited 25 supervisors from the field to contribute their perspectives and experiences in a *Voices From the Field* feature in this book, which added diversity to this project and resulted in a substantially different book from the first edition. Although there were no marathon writing sessions, I met with each of the coauthors several times during the revision process. Our collaborative work resulted in the publication of *Clinical Supervision in the Helping Professions: A Practical Guide* (Corey, Haynes et al., 2010).

Is There a Book Within You to Be Written?

For the past several years my colleagues and I have organized a panel presentation on the topic "Is There a Book Within You to Be Written?" for the American Counseling Association's conferences and for other professional conferences as well. The program is always well attended, and there is a great deal of interest in writing a book. I want to share with you a condensed version of the key ideas I talk about during my time on the panel. My message to you is this: If you think you would like to write a book, begin now. There may be a book within you that is waiting to be written. You do not need to look for a publisher yet, but find a way to begin expressing your thoughts.

The motivations for writing are crucial. Writers who are externally motivated—by pressure from someone else or simply to make money—write differently from those of us who are internally motivated. Many authors I know write primarily because of a desire to express ideas and to have a creative outlet. Even if we are motivated to share a message that means a great deal to us, internal barriers must be overcome. Many of us have negative thoughts and convince ourselves that we have nothing new or of value to share. Although other books may exist that explore the theme you have in mind, you have not written your own book in your own style. I believe it is important that you put your ideas on paper, even if few read your book. It takes a strong ego to withstand the criticism of our ideas or what we write, but it is unrealistic to expect to write a book that will win universal acclaim. At times I am critical of my own ideas, and unless I continue to challenge these critical inner voices, my projects will never get off the ground. Most of the time I am able to continue writing even when I have doubts. I tend not to allow self-criticism or criticism from others to deter me from projects that I believe are meaningful.

I have written books both as a solo venture and as collaborative projects, working with coauthors and other contributors. There are advantages and disadvantages to both these methods of working. If you are going to work with a coauthor or collaborate with a colleague on a writing project, it is critical that there be a good fit between you. Although you may present different perspectives on topics that you are writing about, you need to be unified when it comes to presenting the key message of your book. Mutual respect in the coauthor relationship is essential, and it will reveal itself in the actual writing. As I have shared, oftentimes my coauthors and I will sit together in the same room and talk about chapters, each adding ideas for the multiple revisions that are necessary to create a final draft. At other times, I have to work with my coauthors through e-mail, which can work well if we know each other and can schedule some time to meet in person as well. You may discover other ways to work effectively with coauthors. What is important is to find a way that works best for you.

When I write a book as the sole author, I always seek input from external reviewers while I am writing, and I send the final draft to the reviewers again for further comment on the book as a whole. I value receiving feedback from various sources. Professors who use our books provide comments on what they like and do not like and suggest topics to add or to expand upon. Student reviewers are also very helpful; after all, they will be the ones reading and studying the book. Many times I have asked former students to review a book that I am about to revise and make suggestions on how a future edition can become a better book.

A manuscript editor goes over every line of my book manuscripts, making sure the presentation is clear, effective, and concise. For many years I have worked with the same copy editor, Kay Mikel, who is not timid about suggesting deletions or making recommendations about organizational changes. The relationship between a manuscript editor and the author is extremely important. Some authors become defensive, guarding every word and making the editing process extremely painful for everyone. Find an editor you can trust and develop a good working relationship, and I assure you that you and your book will benefit from this collaboration. I have always valued the editorial skills of a talented copy editor, and I firmly believe that good editing is required to produce a book of high quality. Making a book is a team effort, and I credit all my reviewers and editors with helping me to produce a quality product. I certainly do not take full credit, for I have learned that many people are involved in the success of a book.

How Marianne and I Collaborate as Coauthors

Marianne and I have often been asked, "What is it like to write books as a couple?" and "How do you work together when writing and revising books?" I am convinced that our professional work together in cofacilitating many groups, in coteaching and cosupervising workshops on group counseling, and in copresenting at many professional conferences has provided the foundation for developing and refining our collective ideas about subjects such as group counseling, ethics in counseling practice, and the helping relationship. These shared professional experiences have prepared the soil and allowed ideas to germinate that have been developed further in our coauthored books.

Marianne and I have successfully coauthored books for more than 30 years, which has involved both a personal and a professional commitment. When we are developing themes for a new book or thinking about aspects of a book we are revising, we bounce ideas off each other. This is truly an interactive process. Our discussions take place over an extended period of time, not only in our office in our home but when we are walking on a trail or doing other things together. We are a source of inspiration for each other, and together we find that we are able to develop material with more substance than either of us would working alone.

We each bring different strengths to our writing. Marianne is especially talented at providing real-life examples from her clinical experiences and at making sure our writing has practical and realistic applications. Among her strengths are detecting subtle nuances and sticking to the main topic we are addressing. I have a tendency to get lost in details, both when speaking and when writing. Marianne is particularly adept at pruning extraneous details and ensuring that examples illustrate a key message. My strengths are bringing my teaching experiences into the writing and integrating material by conceptualizing and organizing ideas. Frequently I am able to bring a new twist to a topic that we have been exploring.

Marianne and I share a deep sense of trust and respect for each other, which enables us to challenge each other's perspective in our discussions. Although we share many values, we do not agree on all topics. For example, Marianne believes that the concept of resistance is not therapeutically useful and is often used to blame clients rather than to understand their behavior. We have frequent arguments on this subject because I think the concept of resistance has a legitimate place in the therapeutic process. I *do* see Marianne's point that clients are too often labeled as "resistant," which only cements a negative identity. However, I believe resistance is a natural phenomenon that can be understood in context and worked with therapeutically. As another example, we both agree that it is unethical and unwise for therapists to impose their values on clients. However, I think it may be useful for therapists to expose their values so clients knows where their therapist stands on certain matters. Marianne frequently challenges me, asking why it is important for therapists to share their values with clients. She is concerned that some therapists might unduly influence their clients and points out that it is the client's values that matter in the therapy relationship, and not the therapist's comfort or agreement with certain values of the client. Although we may disagree on what importance to place on certain subjects, this does not thwart our progress in writing. In fact, respectful disagreements or discussions of differing perspectives can be extremely valuable both in teaching and in writing textbooks.

Dreaming up an idea for a book and even writing the first edition is relatively easy compared to the ongoing task of revising a book over time so that the information is kept up to date and relevant. We begin the revision process by carefully reading the current edition and making copious notes in the margins. This enables us to individually identify our thoughts on what we might want to delete or add to the new edition. We then get together and concentrate on one chapter at a time, pooling our ideas and brainstorming what might be needed for a meaningful revision. I write the revised chapter, and Marianne reads this draft and suggests changes in concepts and language. We meet together and discuss each of these changes, and the refinement of the writing of a chapter continues.

We are sustained in our efforts by the positive feedback we receive from those who use our books. The two of us work well together as a team and complement each other, but we do encounter snags and setbacks at times, some of which are described in the next section.

Getting Stuck—and Unstuck

I want to talk about writer's block, mainly because some writers never complete a book, or even a chapter, because they temporarily get stuck. I have found it useful to accept being stuck at times and then do whatever it takes to get refocused when I believe the project is worth the time and effort. One book that Marianne and I coauthored did get off to a rocky start. We proposed the idea for *Becoming a Helper* (Corey & Corey, 2011) many years ago and secured a contract for a 1989 publication. Our main purpose in writing this book was to invite readers to think about the profession they were about to enter and consider what they could do to best prepare themselves for a successful career. Once we were into the actual development of the book, we both had a number of concerns about the direction we were taking. We began to doubt that we were conveying the messages we most wanted to get across, and we wondered about the audience for the book. We were somewhat discouraged and not sure that we wanted to continue with the project.

We expressed our concerns to our editor, Claire Verduin, and she encouraged us to give the book a bit more time rather than asking to be released from our contract. A number of her suggestions helped us to get back on track and decide on the main focus of the writing. With Claire's assurance that this could be a shorter book, we were able to refocus our efforts and complete this project. From our early experiences with this book, we learned to be patient while a book idea is in the developmental stages and to remain open, as the book may take a different direction from our initial conception of the project. Once we arrived at the conclusion that we were not being forced to continue with this project, we both were freed from expectations that had been blocking our progress.

My Way of Writing a Book

A question I am often asked is, "How do you manage to write and revise books?" In sharing my style of writing and explaining what works for me, my aim is to encourage you to discover your own style of writing.

We all have different schedules and different ways of working, and our work style must be tailored to fit our own unique needs and personality. There is no one best work style, and I urge you to experiment until you find the style that brings the results you want. You may not have sustained time to work on a book project due to pressing home and family obligations as well as responsibilities at work, but I urge you to begin and to work at your own pace. Give yourself ample time to finish a book, and add this to your scheduled activities. Look at a planner for an entire year, and schedule times you are able to devote to working on various stages of your book. You may need months or even a year or more simply to think about your topic and gather ideas that you will eventually write about. Allow yourself time to reflect and brainstorm about what your ideal book will look like.

I wrote books on a regular basis for about 20 years beginning in the 1970s, and I depended on summers and semester break time for most of my sustained writing. When I look back on this time, I am surprised that I accomplished as much as I did. In those early days, to revise a book I had to literally cut up an existing book and do a cut and paste operation on a sheet of paper and then type in my changes and additions. These days I use a state-of-the-art Macintosh computer, which makes revising books much easier. In 1994 I began taking a professional leave without pay each fall semester to keep up with the demands of revising at least a couple of books each year. And in the fall of 2000, I retired from full-time teaching and joined the part-time faculty. This schedule over the past 16 years has given me the freedom to sustain a major commitment to revising existing books and occasionally to writing a new book.

In all honesty, I must admit that I have an ideal situation for productive work. We moved our primary residence from the city to a mountain community more than 30 years ago, and for many years we maintained both residences. The quiet of the mountains and the scenery certainly lends itself to reading, reflecting, and writing. I have an office at home with an expansive view of mountains, trees, birds, and a lake in the distance. On a clear winter day, the Pacific Ocean can be seen 90 miles away. I credit Marianne for her part in co-creating an environment that has enabled me to sustain a focus on writing. In growing up, Marianne learned how to figure out problems connected with a house and also acquired a practical bent. I confess that I have never been handy at fixing things or interested in attending to problems of daily living. If the toilet is leaking, my response has often been, "What are *we* going to do about this?" If something is broken in the house or the yard, I typically do not notice it. If it is brought to my attention, I am likely to say, "Now who can *we* call to take care of this?"

I have a great capacity to stay focused on work for hour on hour, and when I am invested in a project, I am able to do the work necessary to complete various phases of writing in a timely manner. Throughout my career I have been able to set long-range goals, establish a schedule for getting things done, and take the steps needed to complete projects satisfactorily. We all have many interruptions in daily life, and I am fortunate in generally being able to come back to where I left off without getting unsettled. I don't have to wait for inspiration to set in, and I have learned to forge ahead. My daughter Heidi once placed an Energizer bunny figurine on my computer with these words attached: "He just keeps going, and going, and going." During filming for our early educational videos, the crew joked and called me "Dr. Duracell," saying I never seemed to run out of energy. This may represent a compulsive drive coupled with a passion for work, but it has enabled me to work on many fascinating projects over the years.

When I begin a book project, I find it useful to write a brief outline and preface, including what the book is about, who will be interested in reading it, and why I decided to write the book. When I write, I try to envision my audience. For example, when I write chapters in my theories book, I imagine that I am talking to a small group of students, and I attempt to write in a conversational and personal way. When I bring myself into my writing in a personal way, I find I am most successful in maintaining that tone.

It helps to learn to live with imperfection. If I were overly perfectionistic, I doubt that I would ever get anything down in print. Knowing that whatever I write is open for revision is helpful for me. I do not burden myself with the expectation that I must write the perfect book for the first edition. In some ways, books are like children. Conceiving them is the easy part; it is maintaining them over many years that can be taxing. Most of our books are on a 4-year revision cycle, which means that we are revising a couple of books each year. This process demands taking a critical look at an existing edition and deciding what needs to be changed. It is interesting for me to compare the first edition of some of my books with a ninth edition. The general topics may be the same, but the development of ideas shows a clear evolution over the years as the field develops and as my coauthors and I get new ideas to write about. Several times I have mentioned the value of asking colleagues to read my work and provide me with critical feedback. I value the collective wisdom of reviewers and editors, but ultimately it is up to me to decide what I will do with the feedback I receive.

The Process of Writing This Book

I have had the idea for this book, *Creating Your Professional Path: Lessons From My Journey,* for more than 5 years. I have talked with people at conferences for years about a book on mentoring in which I would share my ideas and experiences with graduate students and new professionals to help them create a unique and meaningful personal and professional path. I wanted to share what I have learned and show how some of my personal experiences have contributed to my professional work as an educator and as an author.

Sometimes I feel like a juggler, and I have been juggling many other writing tasks while writing this book. I would have liked to have carved out time to work exclusively on this book, but these other projects made it difficult to do so. I continue to overestimate how many things I can realistically accomplish in a given day. I jot down many to-do lists, and I expect that I will get them done. Yet typically I squeeze too much into a short day. I have often said that "organization is the key to success," and I am organized when it comes to writing and teaching. I tend to have a logical mind for these tasks, and I get these projects done on schedule. However, when it comes to practical matters, I am not so organized or efficient. As my German mother-in-law used to teasingly say, "When God passed out logic, Jerry, you forgot to say, 'here!'"

This book is neither an autobiography nor a memoir, but I did want to draw on my experiences as a way of mentoring others. I recruited eight people to read the chapters as I finished the first draft. After getting their feedback, I reworked each chapter with these new ideas in mind. For me, writing a book is a team endeavor. Even though this book is highly personal, I profited from the honest and constructive feedback I received from these diligent first readers.

Marianne was one of these eight people, and she played a significant role in shaping this book. Marianne and I talked about ideas for the chapters on our daily walks so much that she grew tired of this subject of conversation. She was especially helpful in suggesting themes to expand on and in identifying both personal and professional lessons. As soon as we returned home from a walk, I would go to the computer and record the essence of our discussions. Marianne was instrumental in keeping me focused on the messages I most wanted to share, and time and again she reminded me that the focus of this book should be on my professional journey and the lessons I had learned. She continually challenged me to address why I was including a given topic or why I had not addressed certain key points. Without a doubt, Marianne's collaboration added a great deal to the spirit of this book.

Creating Your Professional Path: Lessons From My Journey has been a meaningful project for me on more than one level. I wrote this book not only for my readers but for myself as well. It gave me an opportunity to reflect on my personal and professional journey and to identify lessons I had learned. At times I found myself wondering whether anybody would be interested in what I had to say, and at other times I thought it was presumptuous to devote a book to highlights of my professional career. I had to silence my negative self-talk and stop myself from engaging in such ruminations.

I have tried to accomplish some mentoring in these chapters for graduate students and new professionals by exploring the evolution of my career, which is still, and always will be, in the developmental process. My sincere hope is that in some small way you will find value in reflecting on the lessons from my journey and find ways to apply these lessons to your own unique personal and professional journey.

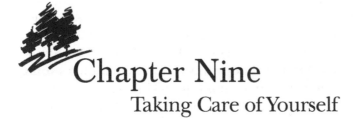

Chapter Nine
Taking Care of Yourself

Introduction

Counseling professionals tend to be compassionate people who are good at taking care of others, but often we do not treat ourselves with the same level of care. Self-care is not a luxury but an ethical mandate. If we neglect to care for ourselves, our clients will not be getting the best we have to offer. If we are drained and depleted, we will not have much to give to those who need our time and our presence. I don't see how it is possible to provide nourishment to clients if we are not nourishing ourselves.

I often hear counselors say they do not have time to take care of themselves. My usual question to them is this: "Can you afford *not* to take care of yourself?" To successfully meet the challenges of our professional work, it is essential that we take care of ourselves physically, psychologically, intellectually, socially, and spiritually. Ideally, our self-care should mirror the care we provide for others. I sometimes get busy and do not take the time to ask myself who I am becoming and whether I want to change something in my life. I believe that reflecting on who I am as a person and what kind of person I am becoming is at the foundation of self-care.

If we hope to have the vitality and stamina required to stay focused on our professional goals, we need to incorporate a wellness perspective into our daily living. Wellness encompasses more than the absence of illness; it is the result of a conscious commitment to our physical and psychological well-being. Wellness involves choosing a way of life that leads to zest, peace, vitality, and happiness. It will be difficult to maintain our vitality if we do not find ways to consistently tend to our whole being. Although most of us have knowledge about self-care, we oftentimes do not put what we know into action. This chapter looks at different aspects of self-care and its relationship to our ability to achieve the kind of personal and professional life we desire. We are challenged to find our own way of taking care of both ourselves and others.

Wellness and self-care are being given increased attention in professional journals and at professional conferences. Recently I attended a presentation on what educators and students in a counseling program can do to acquire habits leading to holistic health and a wellness lifestyle. I hope this chapter encourages you to reflect on ways that you can commit to taking care of yourself throughout your professional career. To help you begin your own reflection on self-care, I highly recommend *Leaving It at the Office: A Guide to Psychotherapist Self-Care* (Norcross & Guy, 2007).

Pathways to Developing a Healthy Lifestyle

Managing Stress

I am sometimes asked, "What can busy counselors do to avoid letting stress overwhelm them?" Achieving wellness entails learning how to recognize and manage stress in daily life. It is unrealistic to think that we can eliminate stress from our lives, but we can learn how to recognize and deal more effectively with both the internal and external sources of stress. As counselors we are especially vulnerable to stress, and many demands are placed on us in our work setting. In today's economic climate, counselors are asked to do more with fewer resources, but there are limits to what we can accomplish. We must guard against becoming preoccupied with all that we cannot do and focus instead on what we can do.

At times we may have a tendency to readily accept full responsibility for our clients and take on their stress as our own. It is important to recognize when this is happening and to develop practical strategies to cope with the stress that is adversely affecting us. Because we are responsible for contributing to our own physical and emotional exhaustion, we can take action to change this condition. We can best do this by becoming attuned to the danger signals when we are being depleted and by taking time to reflect on what we can do to become replenished.

During the early 1980s, I was both coordinating the human services program and teaching full time in this program. I was not very good at delegating tasks to other faculty members, and when I did request help on a project, I continually checked up to see what progress was being made. I would sometimes complete a job I had delegated to another person because the task was not getting done fast enough for me! I rarely did one thing at a time, and multitasking had become my normal pattern. This attitude certainly contributed to my stress level.

I have learned that I cannot live in a stress-free environment and that either stress controls me or I control stress. I struggled with learning how to let go of a sense of being completely responsible for the smooth functioning of our program. I was typically hurrying and attempting to do far too much in too short a period of time. I soon developed severe headaches and pain in my shoulders and neck. Psychologically, I was carrying the burdens of the entire department on my shoulders. One of my colleagues listened to my tales of woe and let me know that she saw me as being "stressed out" for much of the semester. My stress and tension were being converted into extremely tight muscles, especially in my neck, shoulders, and back. She recommended a Rolfing practitioner who specialized in deep tissue work to release my muscle tensions. This work is known as structural integration, and it aims at bringing the body into alignment.

When I began these sessions, I realized that stress was controlling me and that my headaches and pain were signs that I was not taking care of myself. Living a stressful existence had become my way of life, and I was not paying attention to what my body was telling me. Often I had to rush to get to my physical therapy appointment on time, which further increased my stress level. Understanding that rushing does not help me to get more accomplished but only serves to agitate me and get me uncentered was a difficult lesson for me to learn. I began incorporating structural integration sessions into my self-care program, and I continue to do so today on a regular basis.

It is rare that I have a headache these days because I have committed to preventive measures for keeping my body in good alignment. Sitting at the computer for many hours a day does take its toll on my body, and I feel the effects in tight muscles in my hands, arms, and back. It has become abundantly clear to me that I need to attend to these physical tensions. I do not view regular physical therapy as a luxury but as a route to maintaining my health and stamina. I have also learned that homework is necessary to stay physically and psychologically fit. I have learned stretching exercises, read books on taking stretch breaks, and heard lectures by my physician on the importance of stretching to keep limber. I do my stretching homework just about every day, but I don't much enjoy these exercises and sometimes aim to get them done as fast as possible. It eventually dawned on me that maintaining my health and wellness has much in common with maintaining a car's performance and longevity—it is dependent on regular maintenance. By taking care of my body and learning how to reduce the effects of stress, I am providing the maintenance needed to improve my own performance.

You will have to devise your own maintenance routine. For many, doing stretching exercises and other forms of physical exercise, or participating in a yoga class, may be realistic pathways to health. For others, jogging, tennis, going to concerts, watching a movie, reading a novel, golfing, stamp collecting, travel, knitting, cooking, fishing, and skiing, to mention just a few, may be their pathway to wellness. Health benefits are also derived from social activities such as joining a choir, playing music in a band, meeting with friends for an outing, taking an arts and crafts class, and doing fun activities with family and friends. Let's not forget the benefits of laughing with others and developing a sense of humor. I am convinced that we each need to find our own way of coping with the stress in both our personal and professional lives.

Stress affects each of us in different ways, and how stress affects us has a lot to do with our perception of reality and our interpretation of events. We can learn more constructive ways of coping effectively with the stress associated with everyday living. A good way to begin learning more about stress management techniques is by reading one of the many fine books on this subject. Two books, both by Jon Kabat-Zinn, that I have found to be most helpful are *Full Catastrophe Living* (1990) and *Wherever You Go, There You Are: Mindfulness Meditation in Everyday Life* (1994). Kabat-Zinn has achieved a reputation for teaching mindfulness meditation to medical patients to relieve chronic pain and stress.

Mindfulness

The goal of mindfulness is to keep us in the here and now, focusing on *what is* rather than on *what if*. Mindfulness is like meditation in that the aim is to achieve a clear mind and a calm body. It is a state of active attention that involves focusing on here-and-now awareness in a nonjudgmental way. I believe that being mindful is essential to being fully engaged in whatever I am doing and to being fully present when I am with another person, but I struggle in actually living mindfully. When I am able to practice the skills of mindfulness, my thinking is clearer and I am able to increase my awareness of the world around me. When I am driven by a hectic and hurried pace, I tend to become robotlike, with little real freedom. The refrain "slow down" serves as a mantra for me when I catch myself getting lost in a whirlwind of activity.

Because I live by the work ethic of accomplishing and producing, I sometimes forget the value of living in the present moment and fully experiencing what is unfolding before me. By placing so much emphasis on *doing*, I have had an ongoing struggle in recognizing the value of *being*. I find the works of Thich Nhat Hanh—poet, author, Zen master, and chairman of the Vietnamese Buddhist Peace Delegation during the war—to be most helpful in reminding me that I can get lost in *preparing* to live instead of being alive in the present moment. Nhat Hanh has helped me to recognize that living fully entails appreciating the peace and beauty that is around us and that is within each of us. The practice of mindfulness can lead to a richer life, which we can begin by simply paying attention to our breathing.

When I am not engaged in being mindful, the consequences are often costly. Not long ago I damaged the side of my car by rushing when I was turning out of a parking garage. I wasted considerable time getting estimates to repair my car, then decided I would rather live with the scrapes and dents than spend $2,000 for repairs. Whenever I see the side of my car, I remember to slow down and pay attention to what I am doing.

In hurrying and trying to do too many things at once, I have hurt myself physically as well. At an American Counseling Association (ACA) conference, I was rushing to get to a presentation I was scheduled to give for graduate students and new professionals. I was on the down escalator in the convention center when I realized that the room I was looking for was on the second floor. My mind had rushed ahead to what I would say as an opening statement, and I impetuously turned around and began running up the escalator. This proved to be a huge mistake. As I tripped, I reached out with my left arm to brace my fall and injured my shoulder and upper arm. With the help of those around me, I got up and ran to the room where my program was scheduled. In spite of being in pain, I began on time and told my audience of the "stupid thing" I had just done by running up an escalator that was going down. After the ACA conference I flew to St. Louis to attend a psychodrama conference where I was a presenter, so I did not seek medical attention until I eventually returned home. An orthopedic specialist confirmed that I had fractured a bone in my arm and also for a time had had a dislocated shoulder. He informed me that I was lucky indeed that I had not torn my rotator cuff, which he would have expected 90% of the time with the kind of fall I had experienced. This was one time that my practice of keeping physically active paid dividends. However, this one act of mindlessness and rushing cost me dearly in terms of physical pain, time, and money. I went for physical therapy as a part of the healing process for the fracture and strained ligaments, and I continue to do the exercises the physical therapist gave me for restoring the use of my arm and shoulder. This was another hard-earned lesson reminding me to live mindfully, to slow down, and to keep myself focused on where I am in the present moment. I often have to remind myself that one act of mindlessness can cost me untold hours and that hurrying does not lead to greater productivity or satisfaction.

Mindfulness is not limited to periods of formal practice. It is meant to become a way of life. For good ideas on mindfulness techniques that can be practiced in daily life, see Jon Kabat-Zinn's books mentioned previously. I have also gotten personal value from Thich Nhat Hanh's writings, including sound wisdom about mindful living from *Peace Is Every Step: The Path of Mindfulness in Everyday Life* (1991) and *Touching Peace: Practicing the Art of Mindful Living* (1992).

Meditation

Meditation is a process of directing our attention to a single focus as a way of centering. Meditation may include repetition of a word, a sound, a phrase, or a prayer. This practice sharpens our concentration and our thinking patterns with the goal of eliminating mental distractions and relaxing the body. Meditation is a tool to increase awareness, become centered, and achieve an internal focus. Meditation keeps our attention focused and anchored in the present moment. Many who practice meditation find that their attention is cleansed of distractions, which helps them to perceive reality more clearly.

During much of my waking time, I am thinking and engaging in some form of verbalization or inner dialogue. It is difficult for me to quiet my internal chatter and my busyness. Except when I am deeply engaged in a work project, I am not used to attending to one thing at a time or to fully concentrating on one action. Oftentimes I miss the present moment because I am thinking about what I did yesterday or what I will do at some time in the future. I have read many books on the subject of meditation, bought tapes on guided meditation, and listened to certain kinds of music and chanting as a route to practicing meditation. In the workshops I have attended, I have been taught that there is no right or wrong way to meditate, that there are many styles of meditation, and that each of us needs to find a meditation practice that works for us. However, my lack of patience often gets in my way of getting centered and clearing my mind of mental chatter. My mind wanders, and it is a real effort to achieve silence and to bring myself back to a place of internal quiet and centering.

I devote a short time most mornings to clearing my mind and listening to meditation music, but in all honesty, I am not a good student of meditation. When I do not make time for morning meditation, I often feel bounced around by events that happen to me throughout the day. In addition, I sometimes undo the effects of a brief meditation by rushing to get someplace or plunging into an activity. I realize that making meditation part of my daily pattern requires a concerted effort and consistent practice. I confess that I often fall short of this goal. Many writers on meditation recommend a 20-minute session in the morning, which I generally cut short because I am eager to have breakfast and get going.

Each of us can benefit from finding some way to center ourselves and to promote reflection. We can modify this recommendation to fit our situation, and we are likely to discover that devoting even a short time to centering is worth the effort. I have been told not to expect benefits from meditation until I have practiced for at least a month, but in my impatience I tend to want immediate results. Many books are available that can help you incorporate centering exercises into your daily routine. Some excellent guides to meditation are *Meditation* (Easwaran, 1991), *Going to Pieces Without Falling Apart* (Epstein, 1998), *Learn to Meditate* (Fontana, 1999), and *Wherever You Go, There You Are* (Kabat-Zinn, 1994).

Yoga

Like meditation and mindfulness, yoga is a way of life. It focuses on breathing, the body, and centering. *Yoga*, which originated in India, means "union" in Sanskrit. Yoga is often described as the union of the body, mind, and spirit. My daughter Heidi has studied yoga and practices it to maintain her flexibility and health. She teaches yoga to adults and children and has taught me some yoga poses and encouraged me to take up yoga. Heidi tells me that people who practice yoga do so for a variety of reasons, some of which are to reduce stress, enhance health, expand awareness, deepen spirituality, or achieve greater flexibility. Yoga provides numerous health benefits both in preventing and in treating physical illnesses, and it can be an excellent buffer against the effects of stress. Although I am intellectually convinced of the benefits of yoga, I have not managed to incorporate this into my self-care practices.

Developing an Exercise Program

It was not until my mid-20s that I gave much thought to exercising. Although there was no crisis that nudged me into beginning an exercise program, I eventually realized that I was somewhat lethargic and that I needed to move to increase my energy level. When I began my career in high school teaching, I decided to bicycle from our apartment to school each day. I enjoyed this and began to feel more invigorated, but I didn't realize then that bicycling would remain such a major source of enjoyment and exercise for me 50 years later. For many years I have been making the time to exercise an average of 14 hours a week. Maintaining fitness in all areas has become a priority for me.

Some of my friends tell me that I have turned my exercise routine into a compulsion. There may be some truth to this, but I enjoy walking and bicycling. Marianne and I walk on the mountain trails nearby and at times we ride bikes together, especially on level bike paths. We often go hiking or biking with friends, which is not only good physical exercise but also a good way to socialize and enjoy the scenery. Last year we spent 2 weeks at a resort town in Germany where more people ride bikes than drive cars. During our stay, I biked for more than 60 hours and covered approximately 600 miles. Marianne, several members of her family, and I took daily bike rides together, which we all enjoyed, and I spent many additional hours biking alone. I loved the gorgeous scenery and the flat bike routes. Not as much fun was getting caught in a thunderstorm and becoming drenched. On another occasion, a flat rear tire caused me to pedal furiously for miles so I would not be late for a dinner date with Marianne and her family. At times like this I become addicted to biking, which I do with a singular focus much like when I am working!

Physical activities keep me physically and psychologically fit and are enjoyable and rejuvenating. I am convinced that if I neglected this aspect of self-care I would not have the stamina I enjoy today. The Dalai Lama suggests that wellness and happiness are enhanced and supported when people spend at least 30 minutes a day in nature. I think this is especially true for me. I appreciate the Dalai Lama's outlook on life, his perspective on ethics, his view of the meaningful life, and his thoughts on wellness and happiness. Three of his books that I especially value are *Ethics for the New Millennium* (Dalai Lama,

1999), *An Open Heart: Practicing Compassion in Everyday Life* (Dalai Lama, 2001), and *The Art of Happiness: A Handbook for Living* (Dalai Lama & Cutler, 1998).

Most people are well aware of the benefits of regular exercise, yet many of us fail to make this a part of our daily living. If you are not satisfied with this aspect of your life, I encourage you to consider establishing some exercise routine that you would find enjoyable. Doing something you detest may be of little benefit, and the odds are that you won't stick with it. I urge you to find something that is suitable for your age, physical condition, and life circumstances that you want to make a part of your life. Some may prefer an exercise program in a group, some may exercise with a stationary bicycle while watching television or listening to music with a headset, and others may participate in competitive sports. There is no right path to exercising; we must devise our own plan to keep us physically active and psychologically engaged.

Establishing Healthy Nutrition and Eating Patterns

Our daily diet is one of the major factors within our control that affects our long-term health. If our primary diet is poor, it will be difficult to establish a positive self-care program. Irregular and inconsistent eating patterns influence our general level of wellness. I have observed a number of my colleagues rushing to grab a donut and a cup of coffee and not taking the time to eat well. It takes a concerted effort and consistent practice to develop better eating habits. By learning how to eat wisely and well, how to manage our weight, and how to become physically fit, we can begin a lifelong process toward wellness. By establishing healthy eating habits, we increase our ability to maintain the vitality that is necessary for us to provide quality care to our clients. Besides eating to live, we can find that eating can bring increased satisfaction to living.

When it comes to eating, I do not cut corners. Breakfast is one of my main meals, and dinner often takes well over an hour. I almost *never* miss breakfast, lunch, and dinner. Although it takes time and effort to eat well, I have made this a priority not only because it keeps me healthy but also because I enjoy eating. I try to eat balanced meals, yet I admit that I tend to pile too much on my plate. Friends are often surprised by how much I eat, and I remember my mother asking me where I put all that food! Perhaps my drive to exercise is partly responsible for maintaining my weight. I sometimes proudly say that I can still fit into my wedding suit that I wore 45 years ago. It is a shame that it is no longer in style, or I would still be wearing it today!

Finding and Maintaining Balance in Life

A central facet of my life is work, yet I have come to realize that balance is essential. Although it may sound as if I work constantly and get little sleep, such is not the case. Over the past few years, I have kept my work down to about 41 hours a week (when I am at home working and not on vacation). For me, finding balance in life entails far more than balancing my personal and professional lives. Finding balance involves taking responsibility for taking care of myself physically, emotionally, socially, mentally, and spiritually.

Religious faith or personal spirituality is a key ingredient in a balanced life and a vital part of wellness and health. Religion plays an important role in my life, and I do my best to put my religious and spiritual beliefs into practice in my daily interactions. Religion provides me with a pathway to finding meaning in my existence. I believe God is inside us all and is a reflection of creation. This belief helps me to see the Godlike qualities in others and to treat them with kindness and love.

Spiritual practices provide an inner source of strength, give meaning and a sense of purpose in life, and enhance our sense of well-being. Spirituality can serve as a compass and a guide for the life choices we make. Some people are deeply spiritual yet do not consider themselves to be religious. Whatever your spiritual journey involves, finding meaning in life will enhance your well-being.

There is no formula for balanced living; each of us must discover our own balance. In the following story, Mark Reiser, a doctoral student in counseling, describes how he is blending his love for counseling and astronomy to create a balanced life. He reminds us of the importance of making time to do the things we enjoy on a regular basis.

It Is All About Finding a Balance in Life!

Mark Reiser, MS, LPC

I am currently entering the fourth and final year of my doctoral program in counselor education. Although I have not yet decided exactly what career path I will explore upon completing my degree, I have never had serious doubts about my pursuit of my graduate degree in counseling. Thus far, graduate school has thrown plenty of challenges my way—both academically and personally—but it has also been one of the most beautiful times in my life.

If I had to describe, in just one word, the most critical piece to both my happiness and my success while in graduate school, it would be *balance*. Balancing my academic demands and responsibilities with my personal hobbies and passions has been paramount to my mental health. I have placed great importance on providing myself with a wide variety of challenges—even in fields well outside of counseling. And although I have carefully listened to and considered the advice and suggestions of my mentors, I also have listened to my own heart and learned to trust my intuition.

The fundamental balancing act for me is between academics and personal time. Basically, I have tried to live the motto "Work hard, play hard." I have always put great effort into my academic studies. As an undergraduate, I probably worked *too hard*. I studied the vast majority of every night and worked hard through most weekends too. I didn't know how to prioritize *me*.

As I have gone through graduate school, I have learned that keeping my passions alive keeps me healthy. If I do not go trout fishing, hiking, or skiing at least once a week, something is wrong. I need to make time for these activities to help me stay happy, grounded, and fulfilled. We are always going to have to deal with challenge, difficulty, and stress. We don't have a choice in this. But we *do* have a choice in how we deal with it. I have found that my problems look a little different after a day of fishing on a beautiful trout stream. My frustrations don't seem as daunting after exploring the high alpine country and finding serenity at a solitary mountain lake. And I just never feel quite as sad after a day of dancing in and out of the pine trees on the ski slopes.

Another area in which I have sought to find balance has been the variety of academic avenues that interest me. Although I am currently working on a degree in counselor education, my bachelor's degree was in a completely unrelated field—physics and astronomy. As I have pursued my counseling degree, I have been fortunate enough to be able to work as a teaching assistant in the physics and astronomy department. Astronomy is quite possibly my biggest passion in life, so being able to continue feeding this passion while I earn my counseling degree has been ideal for me. In addition, counseling routinely invites me to be more creative and artistic (utilizing my "right brain"), but I enjoy the fact that teaching astronomy allows me to nurture my analytical and logical self (utilizing my "left brain"). My identity as a counselor and counselor educator is extremely important to me, but I have a strong identity as an astronomy teacher too. Keeping both of these dimensions thriving has been a true blessing for me.

Finally, I have learned to balance the advice of others with the voice of my own heart. I have always valued the mentors in my life. I could even say that I may have put some of them on a pedestal. I deeply respect and revere my adviser in counselor education. When he makes an observation, I take it to heart—perhaps too much so. I am also very close to my previous research adviser, for whom I worked when I was a student of physics and astronomy. Both of these mentors have served as male role models for me, and I tend to treat their words like gospel, sometimes putting far too much importance on whether or not they approve of the path I have chosen.

Over the last several years, however, I have slowly learned that my own intuition is worth a lot too. In fact, I have come to realize that my own heart is the most important guide in my life. One such example came a few years ago. My mentor in counselor education suggested that I select a graduate assistantship that was more congruent with counselor education (as opposed to astronomy). Without a thought, I did just that. After about a year, I realized that I desperately missed teaching astronomy. I chose to go back to that, and I have loved being back in the astronomy classroom. I will always value and appreciate the suggestions of my mentors, but I owe it to myself to honor the feelings in my own heart.

I am already looking back on my experiences in graduate school with great sentimentality. It has been a time in which I have learned how to navigate through major challenges in my life. In the process, I have thought a great deal about the dualities that consistently shape my life. Over the last several years, keeping these dualities in a healthy state of balance has been a key to my ongoing happiness and satisfaction with graduate student life.

ᔕ

Commentary

Mark realized that his life was out of balance, and he decided to take steps to arrange his priorities so that he could get the most out of his life. I appreciate his willingness to *make* time for activities that he really enjoyed. Mark reminds us of the importance of not getting lost in work to the extent that we forget to do things we enjoy. It is too easy for me to say that I don't have time for fun or for self-care. In the long run, however, I have found that I am not able to get as much as I want from my work when I ignore this balance. I like Mark's emphasis on finding balance in life, and his story reminds me that balancing our professional life with leisure and recreation is an essential aspect of self-care.

Questions for Reflection

- If you have had a mentor, do you tend to follow his or her advice more than your own inner voice? How can you find a balance between listening to what mentors tell you and trusting your own intuition?
- What kind of balance do you want in your life? What difficulties do you experience in finding this balance?
- How does your work and academic life affect your personal life? How does your personal life influence your ability to accomplish your professional goals?
- To what extent do you make time for things you most enjoy? If you are not having as much fun as you would like, what can you do to change this?
- Make a list of the activities you enjoy doing. How many of these activities are a part of your life? What can you do to incorporate more of these things into your daily living? Are you willing to make a commitment to try one of these activities this week?

Coping With Crisis

In our work as counselors, we may work with people who are experiencing a crisis or with people who are survivors of some kind of traumatic event. Today counselors often are called upon to help people make sense of difficult life circumstances. It takes specialized knowledge and skills, as well as training, to effectively intervene with people whose lives may be severely disrupted because of unfortunate circumstances. There are many excellent books and workshops available for counselors who expect to work in the area of crisis intervention. My focus here is on how we respond to crisis events and maintain our balance. Maintaining a balance in our lives is difficult enough when things are going smoothly, but when we are experiencing a personal crisis or listening to the accounts of clients, keeping this balance often requires tapping into both internal and external resources. Reflect on these questions: How does my work with people in crisis affect me personally? How can I take care of myself when doing this demanding work? How have I experienced crisis situations in my own life, and how have I dealt with them? What have I learned from a personal crisis that I could apply in my professional work?

If your professional work involves counseling people who are suffering from the effects of a crisis or a traumatic situation, you are aware that this can drain your energy. If you are not able to prevent the suffering of others from becoming your own source of suffering, you may experience fatigue, which has been referred to as *compassion fatigue, empathy fatigue, secondary traumatic stress, vicarious traumatization,* or *burnout.*

Burnout is a stress-related syndrome that results from the cumulative drain on your capacity to care for others. In *Empathy Fatigue: Healing the Mind, Body, and Spirit of Professional Counselors,* Mark Stebnicki (2008) stated that counselors who are psychologically present for their clients often pay the price of being profoundly affected by clients' stories that are saturated with themes of daily stress, grief, loss, anxiety, depression, and traumatic stress. Counselors who experience *empathy fatigue* may be heading toward professional burnout, which is a state of physical, emotional, and mental exhaustion that results from constant or repeated emotional pressure associated with an intense, long-term involvement with people. Burnout is the result of severe, prolonged, mismanaged stress. It is characterized by feelings of helplessness and hopelessness and by a negative view of self and negative attitudes toward work, life, and other people. By increasing our awareness of the early warning signs of burnout and developing practical strategies for staving it off, we will be better able to respond effectively to what is expected of us in our work. When stresses are not coped with effectively, the end result can be burnout.

The importance of self-care for all counselors cannot be overemphasized because our ability to be fully present for our clients depends on our state of being. When we are involved in crisis intervention work, it is essential that we are able to debrief with others, to receive adequate supervision, and to have our own support group. To maintain our effectiveness when working with clients who are experiencing a crisis, such as loss and grief, we must be aware of how we have reacted to crisis in our own lives so that our personal issues do not block a client's therapy. For a discussion of counselors who work with clients experiencing loss and grief, I recommend Keren Humphrey's (2009) book *Counseling Strategies for Loss and Grief.* The final chapter focuses on counselor roles and offers suggestions for ways counselors in this field can take care of themselves.

Self-care is also essential when we are faced with our own crisis situations. If we are in a crisis state ourselves, it is unlikely that we will be able to pay attention to the pain of our clients or to effectively carry out our professional functions. At these times it is absolutely necessary for us to reach out to others who can listen to us and to find a support system that will help us get through the crisis. Religious faith or some form of personal spirituality helps many people work through a loss, grieve, and develop resiliency. Family members and friends can be a tremendous source of comfort to us when we are in pain.

Sometimes we may need to take time out from our professional endeavors because of the disruption in our own lives. If taking time away from work is not an option, we may need to ask for help in meeting our professional responsibilities. Seeking supervision, asking for assistance from colleagues, and participating in personal therapy can help us to continue to function in our work. We need to be patient with ourselves and accept that we are not impervious to the effects of a personal tragedy or crisis. Taking care of ourselves at this time will benefit our clients in the long run.

Two crisis situations have struck close to home for me. About 20 years ago, my brother's son was brutally kidnapped and murdered. As might be expected, this was a most difficult time for my brother Bob and all of the family. The four young men responsible for stoning Jeff to death were apprehended, and the lengthly court proceedings following this senseless crime were difficult for Bob and all of us. With time the pain subsided, but memories associated with this time remain with me. It was especially hard for me to be a part of my brother's and my mother's suffering. I became aware of how difficult it was for me to offer any kind of counsel to them, or to others in our family, other than to listen to them and to express my own feelings of loss.

Another time of crisis involved learning about my mother's diagnosis of cancer. Being 94 years old, my mother decided not to go through radiation treatments or chemotherapy. She had only short stays in the hospital and was able to remain at home during her relatively short illness. My family continued to visit her often, and she kept her sense of humor and courage right until the end of her life. My mother wanted to remain in her home until her dying day, and with the help of hospice she was able to do so and was lucid until a few days before her death. I found this to be a very difficult time. I was very fond of my mother, and it was hard to accept that her time was limited. I dealt with the situation largely by bracketing off my sadness and staying focused on work. In our frequent visits, I was struck that my mother accepted dying in the same way she had approached living. She kept her interest in others to the end, and she modeled for me what it means to die with dignity. Losing my mother taught me that we each find our own way of coping with personal crises and losses. There is no one right way to accept loss or to grieve.

At this point, take a few moments to reflect on how you have dealt with crisis situations in your own life. What has it been like for you to face a personal crisis? How did you deal with this crisis? What did you learn about yourself from being in a crisis? How have your personal experiences with crisis contributed to your ability to work with others who are going through a crisis situation? In the story that follows, Bridget McKinney shares how she overcame the obstacles to pursuing her doctoral program despite a series of crises in her personal life.

Pursuit of a PhD and
Personal Triumph Through the Process

Bridget McKinney, MS, NCC

As a master's student I was fortunate to have a great mentor, and my success is partly due to his influence. He was the type of person who gave straightforward advice. He once said, "Bridget, if you plan to go for your PhD, you should present at conferences, collaborate on research, and get experience in the field." A PhD was a long-term goal, but I was not 100% certain at the time that I would apply. Nonetheless, I did what my mentor suggested. I volunteered for all projects offered and sought out opportunities to build my resume. Looking back, I am thankful I took his advice.

After completing my master's program, I chose to take time to work in the field. I moved to New York from Louisiana and worked at a mental health agency for 2 years. It was the best thing for me to do at that time. It allowed me the opportunity to discover myself and what I wanted from the profession of counseling. As I worked as a mental health counselor, I found that I missed the academic world, and eventually I applied for a PhD program in counseling in my home state. I remember the moment I received the interview invitation. I ran around jumping and screaming as I told my sister the news on the telephone. I had waited for this moment for such a long time. To my utter delight, I was accepted. I was ecstatic to begin my new educational career to become a professor. In addition to the excitement of starting school again, I was moving back to my home state, which pleased me even more. Being close to friends and family and enjoying the culture is important to me. Those few months after my acceptance were the best time of my life.

The move from New York to Louisiana was typical and quite smooth. I landed a graduate assistant position in the College of Education and quickly became acclimated to my new surroundings and job responsibilities. I eagerly awaited the fall semester to begin my course work as a doctoral student. Everything seemed to be falling into place. Little did I know that I was about to hit a rough patch that could have derailed my studies as a PhD student.

Tragedy struck the small town where I lived near the end of the summer. On a typical summer day in Louisiana, a group of friends, spread out among five boats, went to a lake for some fun in the sun. We were to meet at a sandbar in the middle of the lake, but one of the boats, with six friends, never showed up. They were in an accident with another boat. The news of the accident was revealed the following morning. Five men had died, and the sixth was in critical condition. It was devastating news for all of us who had been on the water. The next week was rough as we began to realize it was not a dream and attended funeral services for our friends.

Only 5 days later, tragedy struck again. As I prepared to attend services for one of the men in the boating accident, I received a phone call. My stepfather had committed suicide. I was in shock and could hardly comprehend what was happening. I knew it was my responsibility to break the news to my mother, who was deeply in love with this man she had married 2 years earlier. I phoned my mother and convinced her to meet me for lunch. She said she knew something was wrong the minute she saw me with my father, who had come to provide support. I leaned over and said, "Your husband has taken his life." She could not comprehend this and was in disbelief until I told her of the details. Then she became hysterical; it was one of the most difficult moments of my life. I moved into my mother's house the next day and spent the next 2 weeks arranging for funeral services, providing my mother with support, and settling into my new home.

Another week passed and then hurricane season began. Our area experienced two hurricanes: Gustav and Ike. The last thing we wanted to do at that time was to leave home. We were emotionally drained, but we were forced to evacuate for our own safety.

As I began my first semester as a PhD student, I was a nervous wreck. I began to feel anxious that my emotional needs would affect my studies, and I was angry that this dream opportunity was being shadowed with so much sadness and grief. I had worked so hard to get to this point, and I felt cheated. I also felt guilty for having these feelings when those around me were dealing with much greater losses of loved ones. I began to attend therapy. It was the best decision I made during those tough times.

I could have postponed my return to school, but I am thankful I did not. Being in school gave me a positive outlet in the midst of the sadness and grief I was dealing with at home. One thing that kept me motivated throughout all the obstacles I faced was the notion that getting a PhD was where I belonged. I had begun thinking of a PhD while I was a master's student, and it was now becoming real. I could not allow the opportunity to slip away regardless of the obstacles I was facing. I feel blessed that I was able to follow the advice counselors often give one another: "You must take care of yourself to take care of others." Looking back on everything I experienced to get where I am today, I am glad that I did not allow these crisis situations to prevent me from reaching my goals. Being in school helped me heal by giving me a positive outlet and allowing me to do something I was passionate about.

～

Commentary

What strikes me most is Bridget's determination not to allow obstacles to block her from attaining her goal of pursuing her doctoral program. Although a number of crises appeared in her life in a short period of time, she reached out for help to get through these difficult times and to find her pathway to healing. She realized that if she could not take care of herself, she would not be able to help others through their crises.

Questions for Reflection

- What is one crisis situation you have experienced in your life? What would you have found most helpful at that time?
- What did you most want from others when you were faced with this crisis?
- How will you be affected personally as you counsel people who are going through a crisis? How can you take care of yourself and them at the same time?

Some Final Thoughts

Some will say that self-love and self-care are signs of selfishness. The world needs more people giving to others and thinking of others rather than more people being absorbed in their own self-interests. I do not believe it is a matter of self-care *versus* caring for others. We can be invested in both. I believe that we need to be interested in promoting a good life for others *and* that we can be instrumental as a catalyst in making the world a better place. But to be genuinely involved in social action and bettering society, we need to begin with ourselves.

If we are to spread joy and peace to others, we need to find inner joy and inner peace. If we are to help others to live a fuller existence, we must first be alive and vital ourselves. If we are to instill hope in others, it is essential that we have hope and optimism in our own lives. If we give and give but are not open to asking for help ourselves and are not willing to receive what others want to give us, chances are we will lose our spark of vitality and creativity.

It cannot be said too many times that to function optimally in our life's work we must take care of ourselves on all of the dimensions of being human. At times I imagine a room full of counselors, perhaps at a conference, and I am in awe at the collective power of their caring and compassion for those they serve. Counseling professionals must maintain a collective focus on being transformative agents for individuals, groups, society, and the world. Collectively, we can make a major impact on making the world a better place. Individually, we can make a significant difference in the lives of so many that we touch, and these people can extend this influence to others. To accomplish such a grand mission, we need to remind ourselves that we cannot give to others what we do not have ourselves. If we neglect to care for ourselves, simply becoming aware of this can be the beginning of change. If we take time to reflect on the quality of our lives, it is never too late to make personal changes.

In working with counseling students over many years, I have been struck by how many of them are attracted to the helping professions because of the opportunity to be an agent of positive change. We begin with high expectations for making a difference in the lives of others, yet this idealism often fades as we encounter disenchanted colleagues who attempt to dash our idealism. My hope is that you will find a way to retain your idealism.

Many family members, friends, and colleagues have made it possible for me to create a meaningful professional path. On a wall in St. Benedict's church in Hawaii is this saying: "Who you are is God's gift to you. Who you become is your gift to God." I believe that God has provided me with the means to attain a purposeful life and that my job is to use all of my talents and gifts to the fullest to make a difference in the lives of others. My hope is that you will accept and use all of your unique gifts to enhance your life and the lives of those whom you love, and that you will find ways to use your gifts in the service of others. Remember to take care of yourself so that you will be able to take care of others. I encourage you to pursue your dreams and to put your best effort into keeping yourself motivated. You *can* make a difference! It begins with *you*, but it does not end there.

References
and Suggested Readings

Ashby, J. S., Kottman, T., & DeGraaf, D. (2008). *Active interventions for kids and teens: Adding adventure and fun to counseling!* Alexandria, VA: American Counseling Association.

Barnett, J. E., & Johnson, W. B. (2008). *Ethics desk reference for psychologists.* Washington, DC: American Psychological Association.

Barnett, J. E., & Johnson, W. B. (2010). *Ethics desk reference for counselors.* Alexandria, VA: American Counseling Association.

Beck, J. S. (2005). *Cognitive therapy for challenging problems.* New York: Guilford Press.

Bitter, J. R. (2009). *Theory and practice of family therapy and counseling.* Belmont, CA: Brooks/Cole, Cengage Learning.

Blatner, A. (1996). *Acting-in: Practical applications of psychodramatic methods* (3rd ed.). New York: Springer.

Brown, L. S. (2010). *Feminist therapy.* Washington, DC: American Psychological Association.

Carlson, J., Watts, R. E., & Maniacci, M. (2006). *Adlerian therapy: Theory and practice.* Washington DC: American Psychological Association.

Conyne, R. K., & Bemak, F. (2005). *Journeys to professional excellence: Lessons from leading counselor educators and practitioners.* Alexandria, VA: American Counseling Association.

Conyne, R. K., Crowell, J. L., & Newmeyer, M. D. (2008). *Group techniques: How to use them more purposefully.* Upper Saddle River, NJ: Merrill/Prentice Hall.

Corey, G. (1973). *Teachers can make a difference.* Columbus, OH: Charles E. Merrill.

Corey, G. (1974). *The struggle toward realness: A manual for therapeutic groups.* Dubuque, IA: Kendall/Hunt.

Corey, G. (with Haynes, R.). (2005). *CD-ROM for integrative counseling.* Belmont, CA: Brooks/Cole, Cengage Learning.

Corey, G. (2008). *Theory and practice of group counseling* (7th ed.) and *Manual.* Belmont, CA: Brooks/Cole, Cengage Learning.

Corey, G. (2009a). *The art of integrative counseling* (2nd ed.). Belmont, CA: Brooks/Cole, Cengage Learning.

Corey, G. (2009b). *Case approach to counseling and psychotherapy* (7th ed.). Belmont, CA: Brooks/Cole, Cengage Learning.

Corey, G. (2009c). *Theory and practice of counseling and psychotherapy* (8th ed.) and *Manual.* Belmont, CA: Brooks/Cole, Cengage Learning.

Corey, G. (2009d). *Theory in practice: The case of Stan—DVD.* Belmont, CA: Brooks/Cole, Cengage Learning.

Corey, G., Corey, C., & Corey, H. (1997). *Living and learning.* Belmont, CA: Wadsworth, Cengage Learning.

Corey, G., & Corey, M. (2010). *I never knew I had a choice* (9th ed.). Belmont, CA: Brooks/Cole, Cengage Learning.

Corey, G., Corey, M., & Callanan, P. (1979). *Professional and ethical issues in counseling.* Monterey, CA: Brooks/Cole.

Corey, G., Corey, M., & Callanan, P. (2011). *Issues and ethics in the helping professions* (8th ed.). Belmont, CA: Brooks/Cole, Cengage Learning.

Corey, G., Corey, M., Callanan, P., & Russell, J. M. (2004). *Group techniques* (3rd ed.). Belmont, CA: Brooks/Cole, Cengage Learning.

Corey, G., Corey, M., & Corey, C. (2010). *Groups: Process and practice.* (8th ed.). Belmont, CA: Brooks/Cole, Cengage Learning.

Corey, G., Corey, M., & Haynes, R. (2003). *Ethics in action—CD-ROM.* Belmont, CA: Brooks/Cole, Cengage Learning.

Corey, G., Corey, M., & Haynes, R. (2006). *Groups in action: Evolution and challenges—DVD* and *Workbook.* Belmont, CA: Brooks/Cole, Cengage Learning.

Corey, G., Haynes, R., Moulton, P., & Muratori, M. (2010). *Clinical supervision in the helping professions: A practical guide* (2nd ed.). Alexandria, VA: American Counseling Association.

Corey, M., & Corey, G. (2011). *Becoming a helper* (6th ed.). Belmont, CA: Brooks/Cole, Cengage Learning.

Corsini, R. (Ed.). (1973). *Current psychotherapies.* Itasca, IL: Peacock.

Corsini, R., & Wedding, D. (Eds.). (2008). *Current psychotherapies* (8th ed.). Belmont, CA: Brooks/Cole, Cengage Learning.

Cottone, R. R., & Tarvydas, V. M. (2007). *Counseling ethics and decision making* (3rd ed.). Upper Saddle River, NJ: Merrill/Prentice Hall.

Dalai Lama. (1999). *Ethics for the new millennium.* New York: Riverhead.

Dalai Lama. (2001). *An open heart: Practicing compassion in everyday life.* Boston: Little Brown.

Dalai Lama, & Cutler, H. C. (1998). *The art of happiness: A handbook for living.* New York: Riverhead.

DeLucia-Waack, J., Bridbord, K. H., Kleiner, J. S., & Nitza, A. G. (Eds.). (2006). *Group work experts share their favorite activities: A guide to choosing, planning, conducting, and processing* (Revised ed.). Alexandria, VA: American Counseling Association.

Duncan, B. L., Miller, S. D., Wampold, B. E., & Hubble, M. A. (2010). *The heart and soul of change: Delivering what works in therapy* (2nd ed.). Washington, DC: American Psychological Association.

Easwaran, E. (1991). *Meditation.* Tomales, CA: Nilgiri Press.

Ellis, A. (2004). *Rational emotive behavior therapy: It works for me—It can work for you.* Amherst, NY: Prometheus.

Ellis, A., & MacLaren, C. (2005). *Rational emotive behavior therapy: A therapist's guide* (2nd ed.). Atascadero, CA: Impact.

Enns, C. Z. (2004). *Feminist theories and feminist psychotherapies: Origins, themes, and diversity* (2nd ed.). New York: Haworth Press.

Epstein, M. (1998). *Going to pieces without falling apart: A Buddhist perspective on wholeness.* New York: Broadway Books.

Fontana, D. (1999). *Learn to meditate: A practical guide to self-discovery and fulfillment.* San Francisco: Chronicle Books.

Foss, L. L., Green, J., Wolfe-Stiltner, K., & DeLucia-Waack, J. L. (2008). *School counselors share their favorite group activities: A guide to choosing, planning, conducting, and processing.* Alexandria, VA: American Counseling Association.

Geller, J. D., Norcross, J. C., & Orlinsky, D. E. (Eds.). (2005). *The psychotherapist's own psychotherapy: Patient and clinician perspectives.* New York: Oxford University Press.

Gladding, S. T. (2009). *Becoming a counselor: The light, the bright, and the serious* (2nd ed.). Alexandria, VA: American Counseling Association.

Haynes, R., Corey, G., & Moulton, P. (2003). *Clinical supervision in the helping professions: A practical guide.* Belmont, CA: Brooks/Cole, Cengage Learning.

Hazler, R. J., & Kottler, J. A. (2005). *The emerging professional counselor: Student dreams to professional realities* (2nd ed.). Alexandria, VA: American Counseling Association.

Herlihy, B., & Corey, G. (1996). *ACA ethical standards casebook* (5th ed.). Alexandria, VA: American Counseling Association.

Herlihy, B., & Corey, G. (2006a). *ACA ethical standards casebook* (6th ed.). Alexandria, VA: American Counseling Association.

Herlihy, B., & Corey, G. (2006b). *Boundary issues in counseling: Multiple roles and responsibilities* (2nd ed.). Alexandria, VA: American Counseling Association.

Horvatin, T., & Schreiber, E. (Eds.) (2006). *The quintessential Zerka: Writings by Zerka Toeman Moreno on psychodrama, sociometry and group psychotherapy.* New York: Routledge, Taylor & Francis.

Humphrey, K. M. (2009). *Counseling strategies for loss and grief.* Alexandria, VA: American Counseling Association.

Jacobs, E. E., Masson, R. L., & Harvill, R. L. (2009). *Group counseling: Strategies and skills* (6th ed.). Belmont, CA: Brooks/Cole, Cengage Learning.

Johnson, W. B. (2007). *On being a mentor: A guide for higher education faculty.* Mahwah, NJ: Erlbaum.

Johnson, W. B., & Ridley, C. R. (2008). *The elements of mentoring.* New York: Palgrave Macmillan.

Kabat-Zinn, J. (1990). *Full catastrophe living.* New York: Delacorte.

Kabat-Zinn, J. (1994). *Wherever you go, there you are: Mindfulness meditation in everyday life.* New York: Hyperion.

Kirschenbaum, H. (2009). *The life and work of Carl Rogers.* Alexandria, VA: American Counseling Association.

Knapp, S., & VandeCreek, L. (2003). *A guide to the 2002 revision of the American Psychological Association's ethics code.* Sarasota, FL: Professional Resource Press.

Kottler, J. A. (2010). *On being a therapist* (4th ed.). San Francisco, CA: Jossey-Bass.

Lazarus, A. A., & Zur, O. (Eds.). (2002). *Dual relationships and psychotherapy.* New York: Springer.

Linde, L. (2009). A challenge to mentor. *Counseling Today, 52*(2), 5.

Mitchell, R. W. (2007). *Documentation in counseling records: An overview of ethical, legal, and clinical issues* (3rd ed.). Alexandria, VA: American Counseling Association.

Monk, G., Winslade, J., Crocket, K., & Epston, D. (Eds.). (1997). *Narrative therapy in practice: The archaeology of hope.* San Francisco: Jossey-Bass.

Muratori, M. (2007). *Early entrance to college: A guide to success.* Waco, TX: Prufrock Press.

Neukrug, E. (2008). *Theories in action: Counseling DVD.* Belmont, CA: Brooks/Cole, Cengage Learning.

Nhat Hanh, T. (1991). *Peace is every step: The path of mindfulness in everyday life.* New York: Bantam.

Nhat Hanh, T. (1992). *Touching peace: Practicing the art of mindful living.* Berkeley, CA: Parallax Press.

Norcross, J. C. (2005). The psychotherapist's own psychotherapy: Educating and developing psychologists. *American Psychologist, 60*(8), 840–850.

Norcross, J. C., Beutler, L. E., & Levant, R. F. (2006). *Evidence-based practices in mental health: Debate and dialogue on the fundamental questions.* Washington, DC: American Psychological Association.

Norcross, J. C., & Goldfried, M. R. (Eds.). (2005). *Handbook of psychotherapy integration* (2nd ed.). New York: Oxford University Press.

Norcross, J. C., & Guy, J. D. (2007). *Leaving it at the office: A guide to psychotherapist self-care.* New York: Guilford Press.

Norcross, J. C., Hogan, T. P., & Koocher, G. P. (2008). *Clinician's guide to evidence-based practices.* New York: Oxford University Press.

Patterson, C. H. (1973). *Theories of counseling and psychotherapy.* New York: Harper & Row.

Polster, E., & Polster, M. (1973). *Gestalt therapy integrated: Contours of theory and practice.* New York: Brunner/Mazel.

Prochaska, J. O., & Norcross, J. C. (2010). *Systems of psychotherapy: A transtheoretical analysis* (7th ed.). Belmont, CA: Brooks/Cole, Cengage Learning.

Reamer, F. G. (2008). *The social work ethics casebook: Cases and commentary.* Washington, DC: NASW Press.

Remley, T. P., & Herlihy, B. (2010). *Ethical, legal, and professional issues in counseling* (3rd ed.). Upper Saddle River, NJ: Merrill, Prentice Hall.

Rogers, C. (1961). *On becoming a person.* Boston: Houghton Mifflin.

Rogers, C. (1970). *Carl Rogers on encounter groups.* New York: Harper & Row.

Rogers, C. (1980). *A way of being.* Boston: Houghton Mifflin.

Rogers, N. (1993). *The creative connection: Expressive arts as healing.* Palo Alto, CA: Science & Behavior Books.

Salazar, C. F. (Ed.). (2009). *Group work experts share their favorite multicultural activities: A guide to diversity-competent choosing, planning, conducting, and processing.* Alexandria, VA: American Counseling Association.

Sharf, R. S. (2008). *Theories of psychotherapy and counseling: Concepts and cases* (4th ed.). Belmont, CA: Brooks/Cole, Cengage Learning.

Skovholt, T. M., & Jennings, L. (2004). *Master therapists: Exploring expertise in therapy and counseling.* Boston: Pearson Education.

Sperry, L. (2007). *The ethical and professional practice of counseling and psychotherapy.* Boston: Allyn & Bacon, Pearson.

Spiegler, M. D., & Guevremont, D. C. (2010). *Contemporary behavior therapy* (5th ed.). Belmont, CA: Wadsworth, Cengage Learning.

Stebnicki, M. A. (2008). *Empathy fatigue: Healing the mind, body, and spirit of professional counselors.* New York: Springer.

Stricker, G., & Gold, J. (2006). *A casebook of psychotherapy integration.* Washington, DC: American Psychological Association.

Welfel, E. R. (2010). *Ethics in counseling and psychotherapy: Standards, research, and emerging issues* (4th ed.). Belmont, CA: Brooks/Cole, Cengage Learning.

White, M., & Epston, D. (1990). *Narrative means to therapeutic ends.* New York: Norton.

Williams-Nickelson, C. (2009). Mentoring women graduate students: A model for professional psychology. *Professional Psychology: Research and Practice, 40*(3), 284–291.

Winslade, J., & Monk, G. (2007). *Narrative counseling in schools* (2nd ed.). Thousand Oaks, CA: Corwin Press, Sage.

Woldt, A., & Toman, S. (Eds.). (2005). *Gestalt therapy: History, theory, and practice.* Thousand Oaks, CA: Sage.

Wubbolding, R. E. (2000). *Reality therapy for the 21st century.* Philadelphia, PA: Brunner-Routledge.

Yalom, I. D. (1980). *Existential psychotherapy.* New York: Basic Books.

Yalom, I. D. (1997). *Lying on the couch: A novel.* New York: Perennial.

Yalom, I. D. (2003). *The gift of therapy.* New York: Perennial.

Yalom, I. D. (with Leszcz, M.). (2005). *The theory and practice of group psychotherapy* (5th ed.). New York: Basic Books.

Zur, O. (2007). *Boundaries in psychotherapy: Ethical and clinical explorations.* Washington, DC: American Psychological Association.